Assessing and Addressing
Literacy Needs

Assessing and Addressing
Literacy Needs
Cases and Instructional Strategies

Barbara Combs
University of North Dakota

Los Angeles | London | New Delhi
Singapore | Washington DC

Los Angeles | London | New Delhi
Singapore | Washington DC

FOR INFORMATION:

SAGE Publications, Inc.
2455 Teller Road
Thousand Oaks, California 91320
E-mail: order@sagepub.com

SAGE Publications Ltd.
1 Oliver's Yard
55 City Road
London EC1Y 1SP
United Kingdom

SAGE Publications India Pvt. Ltd.
B 1/I 1 Mohan Cooperative Industrial Area
Mathura Road, New Delhi 110 044
India

SAGE Publications Asia-Pacific Pte. Ltd.
33 Pekin Street #02-01
Far East Square
Singapore 048763

Acquisitions Editor: Diane McDaniel
Editorial Assistant: Terri Accomazzo
Production Editor: Belinda Thresher
Copy Editor: Jenifer Dill
Typesetter: C&M Digitals (P) Ltd.
Permissions Editor: Adele Hutchinson
Proofreader: Scott Oney
Indexer: Michael Ferreira
Cover Designer: Candice Harman
Marketing Manager: Erica DeLuca

Copyright © 2012 by SAGE Publications, Inc.

Printed in the United States of America

Library of Congress Cataloging-in-Publication Data

Combs, Barbara.

Assessing and addressing literacy needs : case and instructional strategies / Barbara Combs.

p. cm.
Includes bibliographical references and index.

ISBN 978-1-4129-7529-2 (pbk.)

1. Reading—Remedial teaching. 2. Reading—Ability testing. 3. Reading teachers—Training of. I. Title.

LB1050.5.C62 2012
372.43—dc22
2010054557

This book is printed on acid-free paper.

11 12 13 14 15 10 9 8 7 6 5 4 3 2 1

BRIEF CONTENTS

DETAILED CONTENTS

ACKNOWLEDGMENTS

First, I want to thank those children and parents who gave permission for their stories to be shared with others. Their generosity has made this book possible. Second, I want to thank my students for allowing me to revise their work into case studies that I hope will help others build an understanding of the complex issues related to assessing and addressing the needs of struggling readers. Third, I thank Cindy Grabe for her expertise and her recommendations, which resulted in the list of technology resources noted in the book. I would like to acknowledge my husband, Jerry, for his encouragement, support, and feedback throughout the development of this text. Finally, this text has benefited from reviews by many colleagues. I wish to thank them for their carefully considered comments that have guided the revision of this manuscript.

Michael A. Martin, PhD, Eastern Kentucky University

Susan Almeida, Illinois State University

Alan Frager, Miami University

Dr. Carol B. Tanksley, Associate Professor, University of West Florida

Deborah A. Farrer, EdD, California University of Pennsylvania, California, PA

Patricia E. Calderwood, Professor of Curriculum and Instruction, Fairfield University

Dr. Tara Concannon-Gibney, Adelphi University, New York

Mary Kathleen Barnes, The Ohio State University at Lima

Christine E. Sherretz, EdD, Assistant Professor, University of Louisville

Susan M. Hall, University of the Incarnate Word

Kathy R. Fox, Watson School of Education, University of North Carolina, Wilmington

Kristen Pennycuff Trent, PhD, Tennessee Technological University

PREFACE

Purpose of the Book

The goal of *Assessing and Addressing Literacy Needs: Case Studies and Instructional Strategies* is to build your understanding of the complex issues involved in assessing and providing for the needs of striving readers. To accomplish this, the book presents 12 case studies that detail the literacy struggles of children who attended assessment and tutoring sessions tied to masters' level coursework in literacy diagnosis and instruction. I have embedded the cases within a framework that includes a review of the research related to each of six elements considered essential for literacy success as well as detailed descriptions of a number of research-based instructional interventions. This book, at its core, is a casebook. It can be an effective companion text in a course dealing with the assessment and instruction of struggling readers. Because of the depth of detail in the case reports, it may also be a valuable text to use in a professional study group of practicing teachers, reading specialists, or special educators.

It is my hope that as you read the text and cases within, you will participate in active discussions that will build the problem-solving and decision-making processes that will be required of you in real-life assessment situations. I also hope that you will be able to use the information you learn about the children in the cases to make comparisons that will guide the assessment and instruction of the children you will encounter in your own instructional settings.

Organization of the Book

Chapter 1 presents a brief discussion about the reading process and factors that influence that process as well as the elements of effective literacy assessment and instruction. This chapter also includes a description of assessments used repeatedly in the case reports. It ends with a discussion of case-based methodology designed to prepare readers to engage effectively with the 12 cases presented in the book. Because the purpose of this chapter is to provide introductory information that prepares the reader for the remaining chapters, no cases are included. Chapters 2 through 7 are organized around the following six elements considered essential in learning to read: emergent literacy, word identification, fluency, vocabulary, comprehension, and engagement.

After a brief introduction, each chapter is divided into four sections. Section I consists of a review of the literature related to the element, Section II provides descriptions of ways to assess for the element under consideration, and Section III presents a number of instructional interventions that have proved to be effective in developing learners' abilities within the targeted element. Because technology can support teaching and learning to read in new and engaging ways, I have added a subsection, titled *Intervening With Technology,* where I list and briefly describe a few resources that make use of technology tools related to the focus area of the chapter.

Section IV is at the heart of this book and consists of two detailed case reports. The information used to build the cases was drawn from the course portfolios of students who took my literacy assessment and instruction classes. The portfolios included interviews, surveys, reading inventories, audio recordings, writing samples, anecdotal notes, reflective journals, and other assessments that my students selected to learn more about the children's strengths and needs. I carefully reviewed all of the information in the portfolio before writing each case report you will read here to ensure the accuracy of assessment results.

The cases include information commonly used in the preparation of formal assessment reports (e.g., family history, school history, and detailed assessment information provided to and collected by the examiner). I purposely omitted information related to recommendations for instruction. This omission is in keeping with the nature of decision-making cases. You will take on the responsibility of the decision maker. It is up to you to consider what might be done to address each learner's literacy needs.

The children represented in the reports vary in age, grade level, gender, ethnicity, and abilities, as demonstrated in the chart that follows:

Chapter Title	Name	Age	Grade	Gender	Related Information
2. Focus on Emergent Literacy	Marnie	5	Kindergarten	F	Speech services
	Danny	9	2	M	Special education services
3. Focus on Word Identification	Chad	8	1	M	Country of origin: Russia
	Kayla	8	2	F	Special education services/Native American

Chapter Title	Name	Age	Grade	Gender	Related Information
4. Focus on Fluency	Sherry	11	5	F	None
	Dale	9	3	M	Special education services
5. Focus on Vocabulary	Darrell	9	3	M	Special education services
	Brandie	10	5	F	None
6. Focus on Comprehension	Selena	8	3	F	Biracial (Caucasian/African American)
	Kari	12	6	F	Special education services
7. Focus on Engagement	Eddie	9	3	M	Attention Deficit Hyperactivity Disorder
	Lance	11	5	M	Special education services/Central Processing Disorder

I have selected cases for each chapter that I believe provide good evidence of a difficulty in the element that is the focus of the chapter. This does not mean, however, that the readers are not having trouble in other areas as well. In fact, it might be interesting to refer to information in other chapters as you proceed through the book and to consider to what extent other elements may be involved.

Instructional Features of the Book

Each chapter begins with a series of **Guiding Questions** that are aligned with the headings within the chapter. Responding to these questions will build your understanding of the element that is the focus of the chapter. This will better prepare you to read and discuss the case reports presented in Section IV of Chapters 2 through 7.

The chapters end with **Questions for Reflection and Response**. These will help you connect what you are learning to your own experiences, consider whether the information in other chapters relates to the focus of the chapter at hand, and integrate what you are learning about assessment and instruction outside of this text.

The cases in Section IV are carefully structured to support your learning and engagement. The section begins with its own set of **Guiding Questions** that are designed to help you prepare for the case discussion. In addition, each case includes stopping points. At each of these points, you will be asked to reconsider what you have learned thus far and, in light of new information, to add to or revise your responses to the guiding questions. Finally, at the end of each case, you will find a **Case Recap** that will help deepen your thinking about the case.

Important **terms** within chapters are highlighted in bold text. As a helpful reminder, a chart that lists the terms is included at the end of each chapter. A complete glossary of all the terms is provided at the end of the book.

A complete list of **references** appears at the end of each chapter. I have elected to include the references at this point rather than at the end of the book so they may serve as a quick guide to additional readings should you wish to learn more about the element focused on in the chapter. Additional research articles related to each focus area may also be found on the SAGE website at www.sagepub.com/combsstudy.

CHAPTER 1

INTRODUCTION TO LITERACY ASSESSMENT AND INSTRUCTION

Begin at the beginning and go on till you come to the end: then stop.

—Lewis Carroll

Guiding Questions

Section I of this chapter provides introductory information that will help to frame your thinking about the reading process and general assessment and instructional guidelines. Section II provides information about case-method instruction as a tool to promote your learning. Both sections will prepare you to read subsequent chapters. As you read, consider the following questions:

- Why learn to read?
- What do we do when we read?
- What factors influence literacy development?
- What are the elements of effective literacy assessment?
- What are the elements of effective literacy instruction?
- Why use case-based instruction?
- How might you use the cases in this text?

OVERVIEW

For more than 10 years, I taught courses in reading assessment and instruction on two different college campuses. For several years, I directed a summer reading program where I worked with graduate and undergraduate students as they assessed and provided targeted instruction for 50 or more students annually. Children with whom we worked varied in age, cultural background, and socioeconomic status and came from different educational settings, but they had one thing in common: They all struggled with reading or writing. As we worked together, our collective goal was to help each child grow as a reader and writer. For us, nothing was more important.

As you move through the chapters in this text, you will meet 12 of the children with whom we worked. Each chapter, with the exception of the one you are reading now, focuses on one of six elements of reading described in the literature: emergent literacy, word identification, fluency, vocabulary, comprehension, and engagement. In the first section of each chapter, you will read a review of the literature to help build or extend your prior knowledge and inform your reading of the cases. The next two sections detail common assessments and instructional interventions related to the focus element to prepare you to better understand the cases and think about what you might do to help each child.

The case reports of struggling readers are presented next, and they form the heart of the chapter. Each case fully details the assessment of a child who attended tutoring sessions or the summer reading program. Guiding questions and stopping points are provided to help you think about the learners' literacy strengths and needs as well as what you might do to help them become proficient readers and writers.

This first chapter is designed to set the stage for what you will explore in the remainder of the text. It presents general information about literacy processes as well as elements related to assessment and instruction. Finally, it provides important information about case-study methodology and outlines a framework for reading about and responding to the case reports.

SECTION I: READING PROCESS, ASSESSMENT, AND INSTRUCTION

Why Learn to Read?

Consider the case of John Laurel:

John Laurel was a 16-year-old eighth grader reading at approximately the third grade level. At the age of 15, he was placed in a residential facility for boys after his family filed a petition in the courts citing that he had become ungovernable. He was ashamed that he read so poorly and actively avoided any situation that required him to read aloud. During a social studies class, his teacher asked him to read from the course text. He began, but his pace was so slow and his reading so labored that his peers heckled him. John stood up and shouted at the teacher, "I told you I can't read this!" threw the book, and walked out.

John was one of our students. His difficulties in learning to read and write were long-standing, and at age 16, he faced a bleak future. He had already learned that reading was a basic requirement for success in academic subjects, and his failure to read had exacerbated other problems, emotional and psychological, so much so that they severely limited his ability to complete high school. He had yet to learn that his reading disability would likely decrease his ability for gainful, steady employment (Morris, 2008); result in his living at the poverty level; and increase the chance that he would be imprisoned at least once over the course of his life (WriteExpress Corporation, 2009).

As noted by Richek, Caldwell, Jennings, and Lerner (2002), "society suffers when citizens cannot read adequately. People with low reading levels comprise many of the unemployed, high school dropouts, the poor and those convicted of crimes" (p. 3). Being able to read is no less than a survival skill in today's world. Given this, working with children like John to help them acquire the skills and strategies that effective readers employ takes on huge importance.

What Do We Do When We Read?

Children are not born reading. There is no genetic predisposition toward reading; everyone must be taught (Wolfe, 2007). As depicted in Figure 1.1, reading is a complex, interactive, developmental process that requires readers to use print-processing skills, prior knowledge and experiences, and a variety of comprehension strategies to make meaning of texts (Barr, Blachowicz, Bates, Katz, & Kaufman, 2007; Braunger & Lewis, 2001; Morris, 2008).

Definitions of reading routinely list the following elements as essential in learning to read proficiently: phonemic awareness, decoding skill, word recognition, vocabulary knowledge, fluency, comprehension, and **metacognition** (Manzo, Manzo, & Albee, 2004; National Assessment Governing Board, 2008;

Figure 1.1 The Reading Process

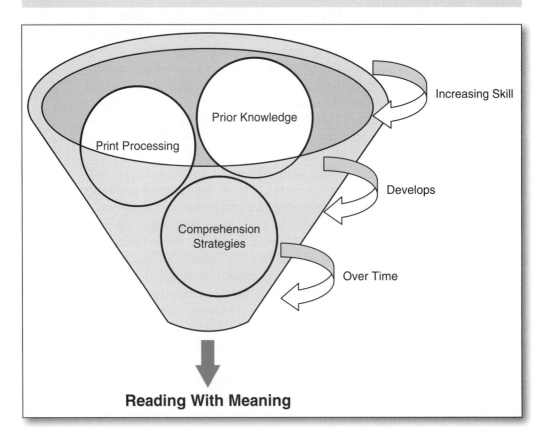

Print Processing

Prior Knowledge

Comprehension Strategies

Increasing Skill

Develops

Over Time

Reading With Meaning

National Reading Panel, 2000). Many children learn each of these elements with little difficulty and negotiate the reading process smoothly. As mature and proficient readers, they engage the following behaviors:

- They begin by forming an overview of text and then search for information to which they must pay particular attention.
- They progress through text with different levels of interaction, including interpreting and evaluating what they read.
- Based on previous reading experiences and prior knowledge, they form hypotheses about what the text will communicate and revise their initial ideas and their knowledge base as their reading continues.
- As they read, they continuously acquire new understandings and integrate these into their ongoing process of building comprehension.
- They monitor their understanding of text, recognize when text is not making sense, and employ a range of strategies to enhance their comprehension.
- They evaluate the qualities of the text.
- They use the ideas and information they acquire from text to expand their thinking about a topic, perform a specific task, draw conclusions, or make generalizations about what they have read (National Assessment Governing Board, 2008, p. 20).

About 25% of students will experience some difficulty learning to read (Morris, 2008). These children, and those described in the case reports within each chapter, need the help of knowledgeable teachers and specialists to build the skill and confidence necessary to become thoughtful, proficient readers.

What Factors Influence Literacy Development?

The development of a child's ability to read effectively and take pleasure in the act of reading is influenced by multiple factors. Manzo et al. (2004) noted three broad factors: environmental (language and sociocultural differences such as gender, socioeconomic status, ethnicity, and dialect), psychological (cognitive, attitudinal, and emotional functioning), and physiological (vision, hearing, and neurological functioning). Lipson and Wixson (2003) provided detailed information related to Manzo et al.'s (2004) broad categories in a discussion of factors that influence reading performance. These factors, summarized in Table 1.1, include elements essential for skilled reading, factors related to the learning context, factors related to the learner, and factors that are closely associated with literacy performance (correlates).

Table 1.1 Factors That Influence Reading Performance

Factors Related to the Elements of Skilled Reading	
Comprehension	• Ability to read for understanding: integrate prior knowledge; draw inferences; predict; establish purpose for reading; identify important information; and monitor and "fix up" comprehension • Ability to read to remember and learn: preview a text; make plans for reading; locate specific information; and identify the organization of the information in the text (text structures)
Vocabulary development	• Knowledge of word meanings • Ability to infer meanings of words • Ability to learn meanings of new words
Word identification and spelling	• Ability to recognize words on sight • Ability to decode unfamiliar words rapidly through **contextual analysis, morphemic analysis,** or **phonic analysis**
Fluency	• Ability to read accurately at an appropriate rate with proper expression
Contextual Factors	
Settings	• Community and culture of the learner • Classroom setting: sets of rules and routines; testing situations; ability grouping; patterns of social interaction
Instructional practices	• Instructional activities and routines • Assessment practices
Instructional resources	• Commercial reading programs • Materials: trade books; basal readers; subject area textbooks; reference materials; student writing, etc. • Use of technology
Learner Factors	
Prior knowledge and experiences	• Limited or incorrect information has a negative effect on comprehension. • Experiences that are not well-matched to school-based literacy expectations can be problematic.
Knowledge about reading and writing	• Metacognition: knowledge about and control over one's own learning, including knowing what strategy or procedure is needed at a particular time to maintain comprehension • **Phonological awareness**: ability to divide sentences into words and words into syllables and to identify common phonemes (smallest units of sound)

Attitude and motivation	• Positive attitudes and motivation toward reading can scaffold weak performance, while negative attitudes can prevent the application of strategies or the learning of new strategies.
Correlates of Reading Performance	
Social and emotional development	• Emotional problems or social difficulties have negative effects on learning.
Language development	• Delayed, underdeveloped, or different language skills, including those of English language learners, pose problems.
Physical development:	• Hearing loss • Vision problems
Cognitive development	• Perception: the ability to organize incoming sensory information • Attention: the ability to attend to school tasks, especially those that are print related • Memory: the ability to store and retrieve information effectively and efficiently

Source: Adapted from *Assessment & Instruction of Reading and Writing Difficulty: An Interactive Approach* (3rd ed., pp. 23–49), by M. Lipson and K. Wixson, 2003, Boston: Allyn & Bacon.

As you read and discuss the assessment details of each case in the chapters ahead, you may wish to revisit the table to guide your thinking and your decision-making process.

What Are the Elements of Effective Literacy Assessment?

Effective literacy assessment should address all of the factors summarized in Table 1.1. In addition, effective assessment of struggling learners should explore how students approach reading tasks and texts that are part of their grade-level instruction (Manzo et al., 2004). The student who is able to negotiate instructional-level materials successfully and willingly reads classroom materials and recreational texts is not considered to have a reading problem.

Kibby (as cited in Gunning, 2006, p. 67) identified the six essential steps (see Figure 1.2) in the assessment process that incorporate the factors outlined by Lipson and Wixson (2003).

The assessments used with the learners reported in the cases in this book were selected to reveal a solid understanding of the students' reading skills, strategies, and abilities. In addition, examiners gathered information related to the students' home and community, the classroom environment, their attitudes about reading and writing, and their levels of motivation and engagement.

Figure 1.2 Steps in the Assessment Process

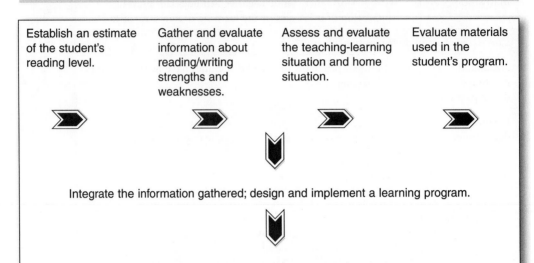

Establish an estimate of the student's reading level.

Gather and evaluate information about reading/writing strengths and weaknesses.

Assess and evaluate the teaching-learning situation and home situation.

Evaluate materials used in the student's program.

Integrate the information gathered; design and implement a learning program.

Continually assess and evaluate the learning program and make appropriate modifications.

More detailed descriptions of each of the assessment methods and tools can be found in the chapters that follow; however, a brief description of the key assessments that were used repeatedly is provided here:

• *Analytical Reading Inventory* (Woods & Moe, 1999). This is one of several informal reading inventories available today. It contains a series of graded word lists. Students' responses to the word lists guide the teacher in determining which narrative and expository passages to use for further assessment. For each passage selected, the student is asked to make a prediction based on the title and first two sentences, read the passage aloud, retell as much as she or he can remember, and answer several comprehension questions. The inventory is used to help examiners determine students' **independent,** instructional, and **frustration reading levels** and to identify strengths and weaknesses in word recognition, fluency, and comprehension. Additional information about the Analytical Reading Inventory can be found in *Analytical Reading Inventory: Comprehensive Standards-Based Assessment for All Students Including Gifted and Remedial* (Woods & Moe, 2006).

• *Developmental Reading Assessment Kit* (Beaver, 2006). The DRA is an assessment kit similar to the informal reading inventory; however, word lists are not used. Guidelines are provided for the selection of DRA texts with the caveat that the texts selected should allow students to attend more to comprehension than decoding. Two kits are available, one for use with students in Grades K through 3 and one for Grades 4 through 8. The assessments help examiners identify students' strengths and weaknesses in areas of reading accuracy, fluency, comprehension, and engagement. In addition, guidance in planning for instruction is provided. Additional information about the DRA is available from Pearson Education Inc. at www.pearson school.com.

• *An Observation Survey of Early Literacy Achievement* (Clay, 2002). The survey consists of a series of six tasks that reveal young children's understandings, skills, and strategies in the following areas: concepts about print (see Chapter 2 for more information), oral reading accuracy (through running records; see Chapter 2), letter identification, isolated word reading, writing vocabulary, and letter-sound knowledge. Information about this survey can be found at the Reading Recovery Council website at www.readingr ecovery.org.

• *Sight Word List*. The sight word list used for a majority of the cases was drawn from a graded list supplied by the Summer Reading Program and included the Dolch (1936) 220 sight words. Assessment forms for assessing sight word knowledge are readily available in online formats.

• *Burke Reading Interview* (Goodman, Watson, & Burke, 1987). This is a 10-question interview that explores the reader's perceptions about reading. Questions include the following: When you are reading and come to something you don't know, what do you do? Do you ever do anything else? Who is a good reader you know?

The complete set of interview questions, along with students' responses, is included in the individual cases in the chapters ahead.

• *Interest Surveys/Inventories*. The cases include the variety of questionnaires examiners used to gather information about the students' interests, including the sorts of activities they engaged in outside of school, their out-of-school literacy-related habits, their reading preferences, and their learning goals.

• *Elementary Reading Attitude Survey* (McKenna & Kear, 1990). This popular survey is also known as the *Garfield Reading Attitude Survey* because it uses the cartoon character Garfield the Cat in response items. Children are asked to respond to 20 items related to their attitudes toward reading. They select from among four Garfield stances, from happy to upset. The tool has been validated, and percentile ranks are available at grade levels one through six so that comparisons can be made. This survey can be found at the Professor Garfield website, http://www.professorgarfield.org/parents_teachers/printables/reading.html.

• *Writing Attitude Survey* (Kear, Coffman, McKenna, & Ambrosio, 2000). This survey also uses Garfield the Cat in response items. Children are asked to respond to 28 items related to their attitudes toward writing. They select from among four Garfield stances, from happy to upset. The tool has been validated, and percentile ranks are available at grade levels one through nine so that comparisons can be made. This survey can be found at the Professor Garfield website, http://www.professorgarfield.org/parents_teachers/printables/reading.html.

Meaningful and timely assessment will drive individualized instruction for each student.

What Are the Elements of Effective Literacy Instruction?

Effective literacy instruction derives from effective assessment. Once teachers have a good understanding of the strengths and needs of the individual learner, appropriate interventions to address those needs can be designed. Each subsequent chapter in this text focuses on one of six elements of reading and details a select number of instructional interventions that are effective. In this introductory chapter, I include several general principles of effective interventions. They are an amalgam drawn from textbooks that focus on the assessment and instruction of struggling readers and writers. As you read and discuss the details of each case in the chapters ahead, you may wish to revisit the principles to guide your thinking about the interventions you might employ. Key principles repeated in the literature include the following:

- Identify children who are having difficulty early and provide intensive, focused instruction.
- Tailor instruction to the specific needs of each learner within small group and individualized settings.
- Teach and model the strategies that effective readers and writers use.
- Provide multiple opportunities for independent reading of a wide variety of extended texts.
- Use high-quality literature that children can read with support and that is within their range of interests.
- Monitor student learning through continuous assessment.
- Build a sense of community, where children feel accepted, where taking risks and making mistakes is expected, and where children learn to believe in the power of their own efforts (Caldwell & Leslie, 2009; Gunning, 2006; McCormick, 2003; Richek et al., 2002).

One schoolwide approach that adheres to the principles listed previously is **Response to Intervention** (RTI). The International Reading Association described RTI as a "framework to help schools identify and support students before the difficulties they encounter with language and literacy become more difficult" (International Reading Association, 2010, p. 2). The RTI process involves ongoing assessment and increasingly differentiated and intensified instruction to meet learners' needs. Broad levels of differentiation have been described as *tiers* (Buffum, Mattos, & Weber, 2009; Feifer & Toffalo, 2007; Wright, 2007). Tier 1 involves the delivery of a high-quality curriculum or core program along with careful monitoring of the progress of all learners. Tier 2 engages those learners who need additional instructional time and support to meet learning expectations. Tailored interventions are provided, usually in the classroom setting—in small groups and occasionally one-on-one. Tier 3 provides intensive, individualized assessment and instruction for those learners who are still not achieving after Tier 2 interventions have been implemented. The goal of RTI is to quickly identify and provide appropriate instruction for each student as soon as she demonstrates the need for assistance (Wright, 2007). See Figure 1.3 for a graphic representation of this approach.

The students you will meet in the cases described in this book have generally been less successful in Tier 1 settings. Classroom teachers who believed additional and more targeted instruction was needed referred most of the children

Figure 1.3   Response to Intervention

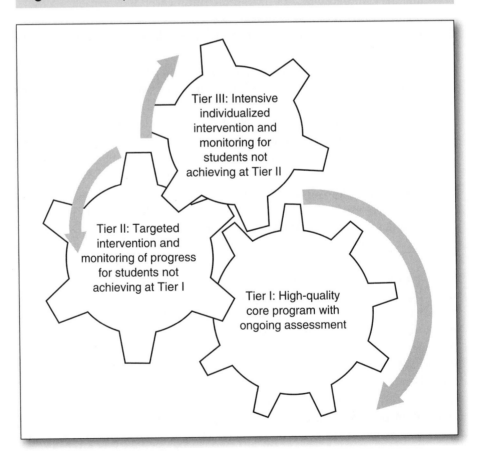

Tier III: Intensive individualized intervention and monitoring for students not achieving at Tier II

Tier II: Targeted intervention and monitoring of progress for students not achieving at Tier I

Tier I: High-quality core program with ongoing assessment

to our programs. Our goal was to assess the children using multiple tools and techniques so that we could provide highly differentiated instruction that would help them become more effective readers and writers.

SECTION II: CASE-BASED INSTRUCTION

Why Use Case-Based Instruction?

Beginning teachers, as well as those who wish to become literacy specialists, should be able to use a wide range of assessment tools and practices to support students in the complex activity that is reading (International Reading Association, 2004). In addition, teachers should be able to interpret the information collected from those varied assessments with a critical eye and make instructional decisions that support typically progressing readers as well as those who struggle (Strickland & Snow, 2002; International Reading Association, 2007). Coursework that uses case method instruction provides an opportunity for students to learn to think like a teacher. It provides an important vicarious experience through the reading and discussion of cases (Jay, 2004).

According to Manzo et al. (2004), our minds function primarily by analogy—that is, when we encounter something new, we tend to ask what or who we know that is similar. A case has the capacity to engage us in experiences that mirror real-life situations, and therefore, it offers more authentic preparation for teaching than more traditional means of instruction (Griffith & La Framboise, 1998). If we have a mental collection of cases that we have studied and discussed, when we encounter readers who struggle, our work becomes easier. Case-based instruction prepares us to respond with more knowledge and confidence when we are faced with assessing and teaching real children. We can say, "This is just like John's case; I know what I will try first."

Another important advantage of case-based instruction is its ability to engage students in the processes of analysis, critical thinking, and reflection (Merseth, 1991; Neuharth-Pritchett, Payne, & Reiff, 2004). Well-written cases can represent the messy and the complex—where neither problems nor solutions are immediately clear (Grossman, 1992). They require us to go below the surface of a situation and grapple with the multiple and nuanced issues involved in order to figure out what might be happening and what might be done (Silverman, Welty, & Lyon, 1996).

There are different types of cases, depending on the professional field in which the approach is used. The cases in this text are decision-making cases that focus on struggling readers. They are designed to guide your thinking about each child as a reader and writer, to help you become familiar with a number of assessment tools, and to hone your analysis and decision-making skills. The ultimate goal is for you to make assessment and instruction decisions that will make a difference in the lives of children for whom learning to read and write is neither easy nor enjoyable.

The 12 cases presented in this text have been placed within particular chapters because the readers' issues are strongly connected to the element that is the focus of the chapter. However, take care not to compartmentalize your thinking. You will find, as you read along, that the students often have difficulties across reading elements and that cases from one chapter can easily become part of the discussion in another chapter.

How Will You Use the Cases in This Text?

Active learning is a hallmark of case-method instruction, and it demands interaction among students in small and whole group settings (Junselman & Johnson, 2004; Neuharth-Pritchett et al., 2004). You will be challenged to apply your knowledge, air and examine alternate points of view, and reflect on your beliefs and values (Shulman & Mesa-Bains, 1993; Snyder & McWilliams, 2003). You will notice that each case has a number of stop signs that act as visual cues designed to slow you down so that you can analyze small chunks of information. Each time you come to a stop sign, you should revisit the guiding questions provided at the beginning of the section:

1. *What important facts have been revealed at this point in the case?*

2. *Based on what you know so far, what do you think might be going on? It may help to respond to the following prompt: Could it be that . . . ?*

3. *What are the learner's strengths and needs?*

4. *What further assessments or interventions might you try to confirm your ideas?*

These questions are based on the work of Omalza, Aihara, and Stephens (1997), who developed a process of hypothesis testing they labeled *HT.* It is a four-step recursive process that consists of observations, interpretations, hypothesis formation, and curricular decisions. Addressing these questions mirrors the HT process and will help you build a response that will guide and enrich your discussion of the case.

Silverman et al. (1996) offered detailed suggestions that I draw on here to help you understand and discuss the cases in this text. In preparing for the discussion of the case, follow these steps:

1. Read the case quickly to get the gist of what it is about and to identify the issues.

2. Reread the case more carefully, stopping at the stop signs to address the four guiding questions. (Be sure to incorporate information learned in the beginning sections and to revisit core textbook chapters or other course readings to help integrate the content of the text with the needs of the learner.)

3. Read the case a third time and revisit the questions, adding or revising information that you may have missed.

4. Make a list of additional questions you have about the case. What further information is needed that can be explored in the discussion?

Thoughtful reading and a well-prepared written response to a case can be very beneficial, but the importance of sustained group discussion is equally important. Such discussion will move you to deeper understandings about literacy assessment and instruction and your role in developing the reading and writing abilities of children at all levels. The instructor's role will be to facilitate the discussion, not to engage in it; therefore, your active involvement is critical. You must participate fully. At times, this means not only talking about your understandings, but also actively listening to the ideas of your discussion group. Shulman and Mesa-Bains (1994) suggested the following four ground rules for discussion:

1. Respect each member's contribution and point of view.

2. Do not interrupt! Wait for speakers to finish their statements before responding.

3. Do not let anyone monopolize the discussion.

4. Provide equal opportunity for all members to contribute. (p. 7)

Finally, it is important to remember that the goal of the discussion is not to arrive at *the* answer for each case, but rather to explore what might be happening and how you might intervene to help the learner. When you are well prepared and take your responsibility to participate seriously, the case discussions will be lively and thoroughly enjoyable learning opportunities.

CHAPTER SUMMARY

This introductory chapter provided a discussion of several concepts that will form the foundation for your exploration of the chapters ahead. First, learning to read is of paramount importance. John, and so many other readers like him, will struggle continuously unless he is helped to make real gains in his reading and writing skills. His ability to read and write is inextricably tied to his success in life. Second, the act of reading is highly complex. It is an interactive, developmental process that demands the engagement of students' minds and hearts. Third, success in reading is influenced by several factors (environmental, physiological, and psychological) that must be considered when assessing students who struggle so that appropriate interventions can be employed. Fourth, appropriate instructional interventions are those that focus on student needs while building on their strengths and encouraging their love of reading. Finally, this text incorporates a case study approach to learning that will allow you to work vicariously with children who vary in age, gender, and cultural background. As you explore their stories, you will deepen your knowledge about the assessment and instruction of struggling readers.

Terms highlighted in this chapter

metacognition 4	contextual analysis 6
morphemic analysis 6	phonic analysis 6
phonological awareness 6	independent reading level 8
frustration reading level 8	Response to Intervention (RTI) 11

FINAL QUESTIONS FOR REFLECTION AND RESPONSE

1. As you consider the short case of John, think about the children or adults you know who struggle with reading or writing. How has this struggle affected their school, work, or social lives?

2. Reflect on yourself as a reader. How did you learn to read? What do you believe you do well as a reader? When you read difficult texts, what do you do when you lose meaning? How might this self-knowledge affect how you respond to those you will teach?

3. Consider the elements of effective literacy assessment and instruction described in this chapter, along with those you have read about or experienced. How might you design and organize your classroom to identify and help those readers who are having difficulty?

Journals Online

Visit the student study site at www.sagepub.com/combsstudy to access recent, relevant, full-text journal articles from SAGE's leading research journals.

REFERENCES

Barr, R., Blachowicz, C., Bates, A., Katz, C., & Kaufman, B. (2007). *Reading diagnosis for teachers: An instructional approach* (5th ed.). Boston: Allyn & Bacon.

Beaver, J. (2006). *DRA2: Developmental reading assessment: Teacher guide.* Parsippany, NJ: Celebration Press.

Braunger, J., & Lewis, J. (2001). *Building a knowledge base in reading* (2nd ed.). Newark, DE: International Reading Association.

Buffum, A., Mattos, M., & Weber, C. (2009). *Pyramid response to intervention: RTI professional learning communities and how to respond when kids don't learn.* Bloomington, IN: Solution Tree.

Caldwell, J. S., & Leslie, L. (2009). *Intervention strategies to follow informal reading inventory assessment: So what do I do now?* Boston: Allyn & Bacon.

Clay, M. (2002). *An observation survey of early literacy achievement* (2nd ed.). Portsmouth, NH: Heinemann.

Dolch, E. W. (1936). A basic sight vocabulary. *Elementary School Journal, 36,* 456–460.

Feifer, S., & Toffalo, D. (2007). *Integrating RTI with cognitive neuropsychology.* Middletown, MD: School Neuropsych Press.

Goodman, Y., Watson, D., & Burke, C. (1987). *Reading miscue inventory: Alternative procedures.* Katonah, NY: Richard C. Owens.

Griffith, P., & La Framboise, K. (1998, February). Literature case studies: Case method and reader response come together in teacher education. *Journal of Adolescent and Adult Literacy, 41*(5), 364–376.

Grossman, P. (1992). Teaching and learning with cases: Unanswered questions. In J. Shulman (Ed.), *Case methods in teacher education* (pp. 227–239). New York: Teachers College Press.

Gunning, T. (2006). *Assessing and correcting reading and writing difficulties.* Boston: Pearson Education.

International Reading Association. (2004). *Standards for reading professionals: Revised 2003.* Newark, DE: Author. Retrieved July 7, 2008, from http://www.reading.org/down loads/resources/545standards2003/index .html

International Reading Association. (2007). *Teaching reading well: A synthesis of the international reading association's research on teacher preparation for reading instruction.* Newark, DE: Author. Retrieved July 7, 2008, from http://www.reading.org/down loads/resources/teaching_reading_well.pdf

International Reading Association. (2010). *Response to intervention: Guiding principles for educators from the international reading association.* Newark, DE: Author.

Jay, J. (2004). Variations on the use of cases in social work and teacher education. *Journal of Curriculum Studies, 36*(1), 35–52.

Junselman, J., & Johnson, K. (2004). Using the case method to facilitate learning. *College Teaching, 52*(3), 87–92.

Kear, D. J., Coffman, G. A., McKenna, M. C., & Ambrosio, A. L. (2000). Measuring attitude toward writing: A new tool for teachers. *The Reading Teacher, 54*(1), 14–24.

Lipson, M., & Wixson, K. (2003). *Assessment & instruction of reading and writing difficulty: An interactive approach* (3rd ed.). Boston: Allyn & Bacon.

Manzo, A., Manzo, U., & Albee, J. (2004). *Reading assessment for diagnostic-prescriptive teaching* (2nd ed.). Toronto, Ontario, Canada: Wadsworth/Thompson Learning.

McCormick, S. (2003). *Instructing students who have literacy problems.* Upper Saddle River, NJ: Merrill Prentice Hall.

McKenna, M., & Kear, D. J. (1990). Measuring attitude toward reading: A new tool for teachers. *The Reading Teacher, 43,* 626–639.

Merseth, K. (1991). *The case for cases.* Washington, DC: AACTE Publications.

Morris, D. (2008). *Diagnosis and correction of reading problems.* New York: Guilford Press.

National Assessment Governing Board. (2008). *Reading framework for the 2009 national assessment of educational progress.* Washington, DC: U.S. Government Printing Office. Retrieved March 13, 2010, from http://www.nagb.org/publications/frameworks/reading09.pdf

National Reading Panel. (2000). *Teaching children to read: An evidenced-based assessment of the scientific research literature on reading and its implications for reading instruction.* Washington, DC: National Institute of Child Health and Human Development.

Neuharth-Pritchett, S., Payne, B., & Reiff, J. (2004). *Perspective on elementary education: A casebook for critically analyzing issues of diversity.* Boston: Pearson Education.

Omalza, S., Aihara, K., & Stephens, D. (1997). Engaged in learning through the HT process. *Primary Voices K–6, 5*(1), 4–17.

Richek, M., Caldwell, J., Jennings, J., & Lerner, J. (2002). *Reading problems: Assessment and teaching strategies.* Boston: Allyn & Bacon.

Shulman, J., & Mesa-Bains, A. (1993). *Diversity in the classroom: A casebook for teachers and teacher educators.* Hillsdale, NJ: Lawrence Erlbaum.

Shulman, J., & Mesa-Bains, A. (1994). *Facilitator's guide to diversity in the classroom: A casebook for teachers and teacher educators.* Hillsdale, NJ: Lawrence Erlbaum.

Silverman, R., Welty, W., & Lyon, S. (1996). *Case studies for teacher problem solving* (2nd ed.). New York: McGraw-Hill.

Snyder, P., & McWilliams, P. (2003). Using case method of instruction effectively in early intervention personnel preparation. *Infants and Young Children, 16*(4), 284–295.

Strickland, D., & Snow, C. (2002). *Preparing our teachers: Opportunities for better reading instruction.* Washington, DC: Joseph Henry Press.

Wolfe, M. (2007). *Proust and the squid.* New York: HarperCollins.

Woods, M., & Moe, J. (1999). *Analytical reading inventory* (6th ed.). Upper Saddle River, NJ: Merrill.

Wright, J. (2007). *RTI Toolkit: A practical guide for schools.* Port Chester, NY: Dude Publishing.

WriteExpress Corporation. (2009). *Literacy statistics.* Retrieved March 14, 2010, from http://www.begintoread.com/research/literacystatistics.html

CHAPTER 2
FOCUS ON EMERGENT LITERACY

I'll tell you a secret—I can read words of one letter! Isn't THAT grand! However, don't be discouraged. You'll come to it in time.

—Lewis Carroll

Guiding Questions

Sections I through III of this chapter will help build your knowledge related to emergent literacy and will prepare you to read and discuss the cases. As you read the sections, consider the following questions.

- What is emergent literacy?
- What abilities develop within the emergent literacy stage?
- How can we assess emergent literacy?
- What interventions help promote emergent literacy?

INTRODUCTION

Children's brains do not come hardwired for literacy. Instead, reading and writing are complex tasks that require work and energy, as well as the help of knowledgeable others. This does not mean that children need to wait for formal schooling to begin to learn to read and write. For many children in our society, engagement with print is part of their everyday experience. However, the depth of that experience varies. Children who live in environments filled with social interactions that build oral language skills and who regularly engage in literacy-rich activities are the most likely to begin school already reading and writing in some form (Tracey, 2000). In contrast, those who have had few such opportunities will be at a disadvantage. Bursack and Damer (2007) targeted the following risk factors that, when present, make it difficult for children to learn to read:

- The children were raised in poverty.
- Their caregivers never read to them.
- They have learning disabilities.
- English is not their first language.
- They were premature babies. (p. 2)

Children who come to school with one or more (Bursack & Damer, 2007) of these factors will need additional oral-language, reading, and writing experiences that encourage their understandings about and abilities with print to emerge.

In this chapter, you will meet Marnie and Danny. Marnie has just completed kindergarten, and Danny is at the end of Grade 2. Both are experiencing delays in their early literacy development. Your challenge in readying yourself for case discussions will be to delineate those factors related to emergent literacy that you see as most important for each of them. The information provided in Sections I and II should help you do this. The interventions discussed in Section III will help you think about what approaches might be the best to promote literacy growth in each of the children.

SECTION I: WHAT DO WE KNOW ABOUT EMERGENT LITERACY?

What Is Emergent Literacy?

Emergent literacy is a term used to describe children's growing awareness of print (Barr, Blachowicz, Bates, Katz, & Kaufman, 2007). It is concerned with literacy development between birth and the period when conventional reading and writing are established (Sulzby & Teale, 1996). Teale and Yokota (2000) and Miller (2000) offered the following assumptions related to the concept of emergent literacy:

- Literacy and language develop within a framework of real-life activities.
- Reading and writing are learned together and reinforce each other.
- Oral language precedes reading and later serves as reinforcement for reading.
- Scribbling, random letters, and invented spelling are valid ways to write and spell at various stages of a child's development.
- Daily reading to children, beginning in infancy, is essential for literacy development.
- Learning to read and write effectively requires repetitive experiences over time.

As parents, caregivers, and teachers engage young children in real-life literacy-related activities, several abilities emerge. Oral language, phonological awareness, letter knowledge, and knowledge about print and story are essential for success in conventional reading and writing. The next section provides a description of each of these.

What Abilities Develop Within Emergent Literacy?

Oral Language

There is little doubt that early language development is critical to the acquisition of literacy skills. Growth in oral language is associated with the development of phonological awareness and is indirectly related to decoding ability (Foorman, Anthony, Seals, & Mouzaki, 2002). Children whose oral vocabularies are rich and varied will have an easier time because they will recognize the words they know when they encounter them in print (Snow, Burns, & Griffin, 1998). Vocabulary, or word knowledge, is also related to comprehension. The more words the child knows, the more likely it is that she or he will understand text containing those words.

Oral language develops when a child is engaged in meaningful daily experiences that require him or her to construct language in response to those experiences. Such experiences allow the child to name and describe things repeatedly in a variety of contexts (Seefeldt & Galper, 2001). Parents and caregivers are the early facilitators of children's language development since they create the social and physical interactions that allow children to explore their world. They provide multiple opportunities to use words that help children find out about themselves, others, and their physical environment (Kirkland & Patterson, 2005). Such activities require that children use words in meaningful contexts and allow them to become an established part of their **lexicon** (Seefeldt & Galper, 2001).

While most children begin school with a good deal of knowledge about language, the literacy and language practices in a given home may differ significantly from those at school. Byrnes and Wasik (2009) noted that children who do not acquire adequate levels of spoken language before beginning formal literacy instruction will not benefit from that instruction. Children whose home literacy and language experiences match poorly with those expected in school will need more time and practice to become successful achievers within the school culture (Snow et al., 1998). In addition, children whose oral language proficiency is limited will need multiple opportunities to build their oral vocabularies and understandings of the functions and forms of language.

Phonological Awareness

Phonological awareness is requisite for reading achievement (Lipson & Wixson, 2003). Children with well-developed phonological awareness understand the sound structure of English and that sentences consist of words, words consist of parts (syllables and **onsets** and **rimes**), and word parts consist of sounds and sound clusters (**phonemes**). Such awareness helps children decode unknown words. An estimated 80% to 85% of children acquire this informally as they engage with parents, caregivers, and teachers in literacy and oral language activities. The remaining 15% to 20% may need more direct and explicit activities to solidify their skills (Allington, 2002). It is important to note that phonological awareness focuses on an understanding of *spoken* and not written language. When we ask children to apply their knowledge of the sounds of language to print, phonics becomes the focus of attention (Mraz, Padak, & Rasinski, 2008).

Phonological abilities involve two kinds of processing skills: receptive and productive. According to Byrnes and Wasik (2009), **receptive abilities** include being able to note the difference between two phonemes, hear the number of syllables in words, recognize as words those words that are already in their oral vocabularies, recognize a word's onset and rime, and take notice of the prosody (rhythmic patterns, pitch, and intonation) of the language. **Productive abilities** include an ability to produce the phonemes in English; to combine phonemes into syllables, onsets, rimes, and words; and to create expressions that exhibit the prosodic characteristics of the language.

Children's phonological awareness progresses from the holistic to the segmental. That is, they move from recognizing larger to ever-smaller units of sound. They first become aware of whole words, then syllables and onsets and rimes, and finally phonemes (Byrnes & Wasik, 2009; Ehri & Nunes, 2002; Foorman et al., 2002). Initially, it is easier for children to segment sentences into words and to recognize words that rhyme and have alliteration. As awareness develops, they can count the syllables in words and separate words into their onsets and rimes (National Reading Panel, 2000; Spear-Swerling & Sternberg, 1998). When children can segment words into a sequence of phonemes, they are said to have phonemic awareness (Snow et al., 1998).

Phonemic Awareness

Phonemic awareness is a subset of phonological awareness. It is an awareness that speech is made up of a sequence of sounds (Spear-Swerling & Sternberg, 1998; Yopp, 1995). It involves the ability to focus on and manipulate spoken sounds in words (National Reading Panel, 2000). Phonemic awareness is an essential element in understanding the alphabetic principle—that the 26 letters of the alphabet represent roughly 44 different phonemes in speech (the smallest units of sound in spoken language)—and is critical to reading success (Cunningham & Cunningham, 2002; Ehri & Nunes, 2002; Teale & Yokota, 2000; Yopp, 1995). According to Yeh and Connell (2008), children who enter first grade lacking phonemic awareness are very likely to be poor readers in higher grades.

There are six tasks involved in the development of skilled phonemic awareness. These tasks, as described by Mraz et al. (2008), are listed in Table 2.1 in order of increasing challenge.

Table 2.1 Phonemic Awareness Tasks

Task	Example 1	Example 2
Phoneme isolation: recognize the individual sounds in words.	When asked, "Tell me the first sound in *bad*," the child answers /b/*.	When asked, "Tell me the final sound in *lap*," the child answers /p/*.
Phoneme identity: recognize the common sound in different words.	When asked, "Tell me the sound that is the same at the beginning of *cat, cape, cane*," the child answers /c/.	When asked, "Tell me the sound that is the same at the end of *cat, pat, mat*," the child answers /t/.
Phoneme categorization: recognize the word with the odd sound in a sequence of three or four words.	When asked, "Tell me which word does not belong in the following group: *pup, pan, race, pack*," the child answers *race*.	When asked, "Tell me which word does not belong in the following group: *sit, sat, Sam, pat*" the child answers *Sam*.
Phoneme blending: listen to a sequence of separate spoken sounds and combine those sounds to form a recognizable word.	When asked, "If you put the sounds /m/ /a/ /t/ together, what word do they make?" the child answers *mat*.	When asked, "If you put the sounds /r/ /a/ /t/ together, what word do they make?" the child answers *rat*.
Phoneme segmentation: break a word into its sounds by tapping out, counting sounds, moving a marker, or pronouncing sounds to indicate each individual sound.	When asked, "How many sounds are there in the word *cap*?" the child answers three.	When asked, "How many sounds are there in the word *shop*?" the child answers three.
Phoneme manipulation: delete, add, or substitute phonemes in words.	When asked, "What is the word *stop* without the /s/?" the child answers *top*. Or when asked, "What is the word *top* with /s/ at the beginning?" the child answers *stop*.	When asked, "What does the word *top* become with /t/ at the end?" the child answers *tot*.

*All letters within slashes / / are represented by letter sounds, not names.

Source: The tasks in column 1 are adapted from *Evidence-Based Instruction in Reading: A Professional Development Guide to Phonemic Awareness* (p. 7), by M. Mraz, N. Padak, and T. Rasinski, 2008, Boston: Pearson.

Phonemic awareness does not develop naturally. When we speak, phonemes overlap. There are no breaks to signal when one phoneme ends and the next begins (Spear-Swerling & Sternberg, 1998). Isolating and manipulating them is a challenging task that develops gradually over time as children engage in language play and early reading and writing experiences. According to Mraz et al. (2008), instruction that helps children develop this skill, whether they are beginning readers or struggling readers (at least through Grade 6), will help to improve their reading achievement.

Letter Knowledge

Studies have shown that phonemic awareness and letter knowledge are the two best predictors of children's early reading success (Adams, 1992; National Reading Panel, 2000; Neal & Ehlert, 2007). Solid familiarity with the names and visual shapes of individual letters, while not sufficient for learning to read, is a prerequisite (Adams, 1992; Bradley & Jones, 2007).

Letter knowledge is a critical predictor of early reading success.

Such knowledge indicates an ability to attend to features in print and raises children's interest in letter sounds (Adams, 1992; Elliott & Olliff, 2008). Because many of the sounds are embedded in letter names, when children know those names, they can better connect the printed characters to the sounds they hear (Foorman et al., 2002; Seefeldt & Galper, 2001).

There is no single correct sequence for learning the letters of the alphabet, but because children tend to learn things that are meaningful to them more easily, they usually learn the letters of their names first (Miller, 2000). Although children can demonstrate knowledge of the alphabet by naming the letters or the sounds they represent, Bradley and Jones (2007) noted that full understanding requires knowledge of the following four components:

- Letter shape: the ability to distinguish one letter from another whether upper- or lowercase and in various font sizes and styles
- Letter name: the understanding that a letter is a symbol, and that each letter has a name and actually represents two symbols—upper- and lowercase (Aa, Bb, Cc, etc.)
- Letter sound: the understanding that a letter's name often provides a clue to the sound that the letter represents
- Letter writing: the ability to print the letters (This ability will also demonstrate a child's understanding of letter-sound relationships and of the concept of a word versus a letter.) (p. 453)

Fluent knowledge of the alphabet facilitates children's ability to read, and so instruction that fully develops all components of letter knowledge is an essential element of emergent literacy instruction.

Concepts About Print and Story

Young children's knowledge about print, including letter knowledge, develops over time as parents, caregivers, and teachers provide them with multiple print-rich experiences. Frequent, positive encounters with picture books, newspapers, magazines, messages, and environmental print help children attend to written language and build concepts that are essential for learning to read. These concepts include the following:

- Print is different from pictures.
- A letter is different from a word.
- White spaces separate words.

- Punctuation separates sentences.
- Print goes from left to right and top to bottom.
- A book is read from the front to the end, proceeding page-by-page and reading the words from left to right and top to bottom (Foorman et al., 2002; Miller, 2000; Spear-Swerling & Sternberg, 1998).

One essential activity—storybook reading—not only builds concepts about print but also develops children's story or book knowledge, which is also essential for success in reading and writing. Children who are read to from birth through preschool develop a book language: That is, they learn to "talk like a book" (Snow, Tabors, Nicholson, & Kurland, 1995, as quoted in Neuman & Bredekamp, 2000). This ability contributes to success in learning to read (Spear-Swerling & Sternberg, 1998). As children engage with parents, teachers, and caregivers in storybook reading, they become aware that the text communicates meaning. They learn that stories have a structure with characters and plots. They begin to "pretend read" texts that others have read to them frequently. Initially, they depend on the pictures to tell the story, but over time, they will begin to attend to the print itself (Snow et al., 1998).

SECTION II: HOW CAN WE ASSESS EMERGENT LITERACY?

Children who come to school from literacy-rich environments have gained many of the abilities described previously that are necessary for reading development. Indeed, many will likely enter school already reading. Children with more limited experiences will have inadequate knowledge about the forms and functions of print and will be more likely to experience reading difficulties as they proceed through the elementary grades (Justice, Kaderavak, Fan, Sofka, & Hunt, 2009). Early and ongoing assessment of children's emerging literacy abilities is important for both of these populations so that appropriate and timely instructional interventions can be provided. Many formal and informal assessment tools are readily available, such as anecdotal records, checklists, running records, retellings, interviews, and analyses of writing samples. Also available are screening instruments that target concepts about print, phonological awareness, letter knowledge, and high-frequency word recognition. Two formal assessments that provide important information about a child's emerging literacy abilities are described in this section. They are the Observation Survey of Early Literacy Achievement (Clay, 2000c) and the Yopp-Singer Test of Phoneme Segmentation (Yopp, 1995).

Observation Survey of Early Literacy Achievement

Marie Clay's *Observation Survey of Early Literacy Achievement,* first published in 1993, consists of a series of systematic observations designed to provide a variety of information related to young children's emerging literacy. The tasks reveal how the learner works with and searches for information in printed text. They also provide the teacher with early evidence of reading difficulty. There are six tasks within the Observation Survey. Each will be described briefly. More detailed information, including the instruments and scoring guides, can be found in Clay's book *An Observation Survey of Early Literacy Achievement* (2000c).

Running Record. The **running record** is an assessment of a child's reading behaviors as he or she is engaged with an authentic text—that is, a book that a child might ordinarily read rather than a passage prepared especially for the assessment task. Clay (2000c) suggested obtaining running records at three levels of difficulty, using an easy text (95%–100% of the words read correctly), an instructional text (90%–94% of the words read correctly), and a hard text (80%–89% of the words read correctly). It is important to observe what the child does effectively while reading as well as what the child does when she or he encounters difficulties.

In general, the purpose of the running record is to record everything a child does and says while reading a text that is 100 to 200 words in length. The behaviors that are coded in a traditional running record include words read correctly (using checkmarks), substitutions, multiple tries, self-corrections, omissions, insertions, words told, appeals for help, multiple errors that result in directing the child to try an entire line or sentence again, repetitions, and errors in directionality. Of these behaviors, substitutions, omissions, insertions, words told, and appeals for help are coded as errors when scoring the running record.

After the running record is complete, the examiner calculates the error rate to determine whether the text is at the child's easy, instructional, or frustration level and then analyzes the child's errors and self-corrections to determine her reading skills and weaknesses. Analyzing the extent to which a child uses meaning (**semantics**), structure (**syntactics**), visual information, or word memory (whole-word recall) will reveal all the ways a child works with print (Clay, 2000c) and will lead to providing appropriate instruction targeted to the child's needs. It is important to add here that running records are not only used to assess young readers. They can and are used with learners of all ages to document reading strengths and weaknesses.

Letter Identification. This task provides detailed information about what letters the child can identify by name or sound. The examiner provides the child with a sheet of upper- and lowercase letters distributed randomly on the page. The child is asked to identify each letter by responding to the general question, "What is this one?" If the child hesitates, the examiner may ask one of three questions:

- "Do you know its name?"
- "What sound does it make?"
- "Do you know a word that starts like this?" (Clay, 2000c, p. 43).

Appropriate responses to any of these questions are scored as correct and coded so that the examiner can determine the child's preferred means of identifying letters (A = alphabetical, S = sound, W = word beginning), the letters he or she is confused about, and any letters that are unknown. In addition, a table listing **stanine** scores using a sample of urban first graders is provided in Appendix 2 of the book.

Concepts About Print. The **Concepts About Print** task is designed to reveal what the child knows about the way print is put together in meaningful text. Children are asked to point to certain features in one of the books especially designed for this task: *Sand* (Clay, 1972), *Stones* (Clay, 1979), *No Shoes* (Clay, 2000b), or *Follow Me Moon* (Clay, 2000a). Clay (2000c) provides a detailed script and scoring guide that consists of 24 items. As the child advances through the book, her or his responses reveal understandings about print (e.g., that text is read from left to right and top to bottom; that print, not pictures, carry the message; that different punctuation marks [comma, period, quotation marks] mean different things). As with the letter identification task, a table listing stanine scores is provided in Appendix 2 of Clay's (2000c) book.

Word Tests. The Ohio Word Test uses high-frequency words from the Dolch (1936) Word List. It assesses the extent to which the child is developing a sight word vocabulary that is matched to the most frequently used words found in texts that young children are likely to encounter in school. The child is asked to read from List A or B or C. Help may be given with the practice word but not for others. All incorrect responses are recorded and analyzed. Administration and score sheets are provided in Appendix 1. A table listing stanine scores is provided in Appendix 2.

Writing Samples and Vocabulary. Clay (2000c) suggested completing two tasks related to a child's writing. The first involves collecting three samples of the child's attempt to write stories over a period of three weeks. Using the rubrics provided in Clay's (2000c) book, these are rated for language level, message quality, and directionality. This analysis provides information related to the child's writing stage by addressing the following questions: To what extent does he or she use single letters, words, phrases, sentences, or paragraphs to deliver a message? What is the quality and completeness of the message conveyed? What does the manner in which the writing is displayed on the page reveal about the child's understanding of directionality and spacing of text?

The second task involves giving the child a blank piece of paper and a pencil and asking him or her to write as many words as possible. This is a 10-minute timed task. If the child stops before the 10 minutes is up, it is appropriate to suggest words that she might know. Each correctly spelled word written from left to right is given one point. A table listing stanine scores related to this task is provided in Appendix 2 of Clay's (2000c) book.

Hearing and Recording Sounds in Words. This is the final task in Clay's (2000c) survey. This dictation task is designed to determine the extent to which children can represent the sounds (phonemes) in words with their letters (graphemes). The examiner selects one of five possible sentences, each of which contains 37 phonemes, and first reads it at a normal pace and then dictates the sentence word by word as the child writes. If the child has trouble, the examiner may ask the child to repeat the word slowly and write what she or he hears or may tell the child to leave the word and go on. After the child is finished, the examiner writes the words in the text below the child's version and scores one point for each phoneme the child has recorded. Additional scoring conventions regarding substitutions and reversals are provided in Clay's (2000c) book. A careful analysis of the results of all the survey tasks will reveal quite a lot about the strategies the young child displays when dealing with letters and sounds, words, and texts.

Yopp-Singer Test of Phoneme Segmentation (Yopp, 1995)

The Yopp-Singer assessment is a quick measure of phonemic awareness. It is a valid and reliable tool that was originally designed for use with English-speaking kindergartners (Yopp, 1995). It can be used as a general screening device at the beginning of kindergarten or first grade or as a diagnostic tool to assess struggling readers' phonemic awareness. The instrument consists of 22 words that are likely to be familiar to children. After stating a word, the child is asked to break it apart into its constituent sounds (see Figure 2.1). Feedback is provided as the child progresses through the test. The final score is

Figure 2.1 Yopp-Singer Test of Phoneme Segmentation

Source: Test from "A Test for Assessing Phonemic Awareness in Young Children," by H. K. Yopp, 1995, *The Reading Teacher, 49*(1), 20–29. Reprinted with permission of the International Reading Association.

Yopp-Singer Test of Phoneme Segmentation

Student's name _____   Date _____

Score (number correct) _____

Directions: Today we're going to play a word game. I'm going to say a word and I want you to break the word apart. You are going to tell me each sound in the word in order. For example, if I say "old," you should say "/o/-/l/-/d/." (*Administrator: Be sure to say the sounds, not the letters, in the word.*) Let's try a few together.

Practice items: (*Assist the child in segmenting these items as necessary.*) ride, go, man

Test items: (*Circle those items that the student correctly segments; incorrect responses may be recorded on the blank line following the item.*)

1. dog _____
2. keep _____
3. fine _____
4. no _____
5. she _____
6. wave _____
7. grew _____
8. that _____
9. red _____
10. me _____
11. sat _____
12. lay _____
13. race _____
14. zoo _____
15. three _____
16. job _____
17. in _____
18. ice _____
19. at _____
20. top _____
21. by _____
22. do _____

the number of words correctly segmented; no partial credit is given. According to Yopp (1995), children who segment all or nearly all of the words may be considered phonemically aware, while those who can segment only a few or none lack phonemic awareness. The second group of children is at risk and will likely have difficulty with reading and spelling.

SECTION III: WHAT INTERVENTIONS MIGHT PROMOTE EMERGENT LITERACY?

Section III of this chapter details activities that promote the development of literacy skills and knowledge. As you read, think about how one or more of these interventions might be used with children you know to move them toward conventional reading and writing.

Storybook Reading

One overarching activity that builds all of the emergent skills and concepts is the read aloud. Daily reading and rereading of favorite books, poems, and nursery rhymes is essential for children's later reading success (International Reading Association, 1998). Daily storybook reading and interactive discussion build children's oral vocabularies and their concepts of story. Asking open-ended questions and engaging children in retellings helps them develop a sense of story: that "stories have settings, characters, problems, events, and resolutions" (Neuman & Bredekamp, 2000, p. 30).

In addition, reading with a **"print referencing style"** (Justice et al., 2009, p. 68) helps children gain print concept knowledge and alphabet knowledge. Reading with a print referencing style means that teachers use verbal and nonverbal techniques to focus children's attention on the print within the storybook. This includes asking questions about the print ("Do you see a letter that is in your name?"), making comments about the print ("This is the word *the*; it is used all the time in books."), and tracking print with one's finger ("Let's point to each word as I read the page."). Adding questions that heighten children's interest in print during the interactive read aloud is an easy and enjoyable way to build emergent skills.

While daily interactive read alouds with children are essential, children may also enjoy visiting electronic sites that provide read-aloud experiences. *RIF Reading Planet* (www.rif.org) has a number of read-along stories and songs. *Storyline Online* features videos of well-known actors reading popular picture books (www.storylineonline.net). Electronic books (e-books) are available

Reading to and with children daily will build their vocabularies and concepts about print.

from a variety of online vendors and publishers and can be downloaded to e-reader devices such as the Kindle™, iPod-Touch, and iPad. Books with accompanying CDs can be purchased so that children can read along with the narrator. It is important to note that interactive discussion, which is so necessary to promote emergent literacy skills, is missing when children are engaged in this sort of individualized reading. A steady diet of interactive read alouds followed by experiences with e-books will help build children's storybook knowledge, vocabulary, and concepts about print.

Letter Identification. Letter identification is an essential, though insufficient, skill for learning to read (Strickland, 2005). There are a variety of ways to help children learn letter shapes and names. Strickland (2005) suggested beginning with the names of family and friends and exploring them by counting the letters in the names, discussing each letter, tracing the letters using different materials such as shaving cream, and searching for the letters in environmental print and favorite storybooks.

There are a number of online sites that provide playful activities for letter learning. In Letter of the Day (http://pbskids.org/sesame/games/cookie

LetterOfDay.html), children choose cookies for Cookie Monster to eat. Each cookie represents an object, and Cookie Monster can only eat those that begin with the letter of the day. The site www.internet4classrooms.com offers a variety of alphabet resources from which to choose. Not all activities are equally useful, so it is necessary to review each one before selecting some to use.

Karen Bromley (2000) suggested creating alphabet books with children, wherein the teacher provides each child with a piece of paper with one letter written on it and the child draws or cuts and pastes objects that begin with the same letter. The collection of pages is put together into a class book that becomes part of the reading library.

Frequent reading of alphabet books is another way for parents and teachers to help children learn the letters of the alphabet. Reading the books alone does not guarantee that children will memorize the letters. Parents and teachers must engage the children in talking about the text (Bradley & Jones, 2007). In addition, Bradley and Jones (2007) offered the following guidelines for choosing alphabet books that lend themselves to teaching the alphabet:

- The beginning sound of the picture should clearly represent the letter on the page (/k/ is for kite).
- Alphabet books with clearly visible letters that have not been graphically altered are most useful for teaching the alphabet.
- Pictures that provide teachers with an opportunity to discuss the varied sounds of letters can be helpful (for example, E = eel, egg, elephant).
- Books that contain both lower- and uppercase letters can be useful. (pp. 457–459)

Phonological Awareness Activities. The goal of instruction in phonological awareness should be to create activities that engage children in explorations of sounds in meaningful ways rather than to involve them in isolated skill-and-drill (Teale & Yokota, 2000). In addition, activities must be developmentally appropriate, playful, engaging, socially interactive, and intentionally designed (Yopp & Yopp, 2000). Since children appear to be able to gain control over larger units of sound first, Yopp and Yopp (2000) suggested a developmental instructional sequence that begins with attention to rhyme and ends with a focus on phonemes. An activity for each stage in the sequence will be described—with the exception of phonemes, which will be discussed in more detail later. It is important to note that Yopp and Yopp (2000) cautioned against using a lockstep, rigid approach with this suggested sequence; rather, teachers should assess children's progress and respond flexibly to their needs.

• *A focus on rhyme.* Engaging children with poetry, nursery rhymes, and chants provides them with the practice needed to hear and recognize the sounds in language (Seefeldt & Galper, 2001). Repeating songs and poems daily while helping children to attend to the rhyming words within delights children and provides critical instruction. One activity described by Valerie Ellery (2009) is called Draw a Rhyme. First, the teacher selects a rhyming poem and reads it aloud to the children. Next, the teacher rereads the poem and omits the ending rhyming words, instead directing the children to "draw what rhymes with _____." The children can use paper or whiteboards to illustrate their rhyming words. Students share their drawings with each other while the teacher asks a question or two that helps them think about their choice. For example, "How did you know what to draw?" (Ellery, 2009, pp. 38–39).

• *A focus on syllable units.* Activities that focus on syllables within words help children build sensitivity to the sound structure of the English language (Foorman et al., 2002; Yopp & Yopp, 2000). Asking children to clap the number of syllables they hear in a spoken word is a common game that requires them to use auditory cues to attend to units of sound. Yopp and Yopp (2000) suggested using the nursery rhyme "Humpty Dumpty" to introduce a syllable blending activity. Each child is given four to five blocks that snap together. After reciting the nursery rhyme, the teacher explains that, just like Humpty Dumpty, she has some words that are broken, and the children can help to put them together again. The teacher then says the syllables within a selected word, and the children repeat the syllables and pick up a cube for each unit of sound they say. In the word *pocket,* for example, children would pick up two cubes. They snap the cubes together as they say each part and then finally say the entire word (pp. 138–139).

• *A focus on onset and rime.* The onset of a word is the initial consonant sound or sounds, and the rime is the remainder of the word chunk (Bear, Invernizzi, & Templeton, 2004). For example, in the word *clap,* /cl/ is the onset and /ap/ is the rime. Children who can hear and voice the break between the first part of a word and the rest of the word can use this skill to work out words they encounter later in print. Just as in syllable manipulation activities that allow them to clap, onset and rime is an easy activity to call children's attention to these word parts. Strickland (2005) suggested using rhyming books, such as the Dr. Seuss books, to build this skill. After reading and attending to the story, the teacher introduces a rime pattern from the story, for example the /ay/ in *play.* The children are then encouraged to think of more words they heard in the story or that they know that end with the same sound (*day, say, may,* etc.). This can be done orally, or, as Strickland suggested, the teacher can write the pattern on an index card and place it in a pocket chart. As the children provide new words, the teacher can write the onset on an index card and place it at the beginning of the rime in the chart (pp. 37–38).

Phonemic Awareness Activities. Mraz et al. (2008) cautioned that phonemic awareness instruction is a means, not an end, and that it should be included as part of a total literacy program. They listed the following general guidelines offered by Opitz (2000) to enhance children's development of phonemic awareness:

- Embed phonemic awareness activities into everyday reading and writing experiences.
- Provide time for **invented spelling** (children's own unique spellings of words, which reveal their understandings of the conventions of English, including spelling, punctuation, and capitalization).
- Conduct read alouds that focus on language features like rhyme, alliteration, phoneme substitution, and segmentation.
- Use fun, engaging oral-language activities, not skill and drill.
- Assess for student needs, and don't teach what they already know.
- Involve families. (Mraz et al., 2008, p. 30)

The Elkonin Boxes Strategy, first described by D. B. Elkonin in 1973, is useful for children who are experiencing difficulty learning with phonemic segmentation (Miller, 2000). The strategy uses pictures and blank markers and blocks or boxes to make the abstract skill of segmenting more concrete. The teacher begins with pictures or drawings of short single-syllable words. The child is given the number of markers corresponding to the sounds in the word. For a picture of a cat, for example, the child would have three markers because *cat* has three phonemes. The strategy proceeds as follows:

- Give the child three markers, three blocks, or a strip of paper on which three boxes are drawn and the target picture. Be sure to place markers in a row above the blocks or strip of paper.
- Ask the child to say the word that names the picture and to stretch the word out so she can hear each sound (or pronounce it with the child, but do not stretch the sound such that it becomes distorted).
- As the child says each sound, she should move a marker in each block or box.
- Tell the child how many separate sounds there are.
- Ask the child to tell you how many separate sounds there are.

Target word:	/c/	/a/	/t/
3 markers	–	–	–
	↓	↓	↓
3 blocks	□	□	□

As the child's ability to hear the separate phonemes improves, the teacher can use words rather than pictures and the students can draw boxes around the phonemes they hear (Miller, 2000), as in this example:

c	l	a	p

Daily writing that encourages inventive spelling is also a powerful way for children to accurately record phonemes in words. Very young children combine drawings and single letters that represent the sounds they hear as they write stories and letters, label objects, or respond to read alouds. As they grow in their abilities, they move to using strings of letters and finally words to record the sounds they hear (Au, 2000). Multiple opportunities to write for authentic purposes help children learn about the nature of alphabetic writing and the structure of spoken and written words (Bromley, 2000).

Intervening With Technology. There are a multiplicity of technology tools and resources related to emergent literacy. A number have already been described. A few more are described here:

• *Reading Rockets (www.readingrockets.org).* A good teacher resource that details instructional strategies related to the development of literacy. For each strategy, instructions, templates, examples, related children's books, information for differentiating the activity, and supporting research are provided.

• *Free Reading (http://freereading.net).* As listed online, this site is an open-source reading intervention program with written descriptions of literacy activities, lesson ideas, and activities. Audio and video resources are included.

• *Get Ready to Read (www.getreadytoread.org).* This site includes an early learning screening tool developed by Pearson Inc., descriptions of activities teachers and caregivers can do with children, and a few interactive online activities that children can complete.

- *iPad/iPod Applications.* Schools that can put hardware such as Apple's iPod or iPad in the hands of students can access a variety of applications that provide independent practice in engaging and entertaining ways. Many of these are free or available at a low cost. Super Why, which is also available online at http://pbskids .org/superwhy, is one such application. This application (or *app*) provides a number of interactive games and activities related to alphabet recognition and letter-sound recognition that children can complete and is downloadable for a small fee.

- *Digital cameras, recorders, Flip cameras.* It is possible to create activities to promote the development of emergent literacy using these devices. For example, instead of creating hardcopy alphabet books, children can take pictures of objects beginning with letters of the alphabet, and the teacher can use these to create a movie. Because the children get to choose the objects, they are likely to be very engaged in the activity and enjoy viewing their alphabet movie again and again.

SECTION IV: THE CASES

The two assessment case reports that follow will help you explore issues related to emergent literacy. At the time of the assessments, Marnie was at the end of her first year in kindergarten and Danny had just completed second grade. As you read, consider each child's developmental level and abilities. Think about what interventions might help them move to conventional reading and writing.

Guiding Questions

Section IV of the chapter will help you apply your understandings about emergent literacy to two particular cases. Read each case quickly to get the gist of what it is about and to identify the issues. Read each case a second time, and when you come to a stop sign in the case, jot down your answers to the following questions:

- What important facts have been revealed at this point in the case?

- Based on what you know so far, what do you think might be going on? It may help to respond to the following prompt: Could it be that . . . ?

- What are the learner's strengths and needs?

- What further assessments or interventions might you try to confirm your ideas?

CASE 1: ASSESSMENT REPORT FOR MARNIE F.

Background Information

Child's name: Marnie F.
Current age: 5 years, 6 months
Current grade level: End of kindergarten

Referral

Marnie's kindergarten teacher requested that she be assessed. Parental permission was granted.

Family and Medical History

Marnie is five years old. She appears to be a happy child who displays age-appropriate social and emotional behaviors. She lives with her mother, father, and two older sisters in a small city surrounded by farmland. English is spoken in the home.

Marnie's vision and hearing are within the normal range. She is, however, very small for her age and often looks tired. She has asthma and uses an inhaler as needed. Marnie's mother completed the survey *My Child as a Learner.* Family activities include "walks, rides in the car, and visiting parks." The mother noted that Marnie regularly reads aloud the books she brings home in her book bag. Her mother also noted that Marnie is shy, needs praise, and "likes to be a good girl." See Figure 2.2 for the complete response to the survey.

School History

Marnie has just completed kindergarten in a small public school within the city limits. Based on her teacher's referral, Marnie was assessed by the speech pathologist early in the school year. Results of the assessment revealed that Marnie has a one-year delay in expressive communication. She demonstrates difficulty in answering questions logically, using correct grammatical structures (especially irregular plurals and past tense), following complex directions, and completing analogies. In addition, she tends to respond quickly to questions and does not always think her answers through. Throughout the school year, Marnie attended individual and small group sessions with the speech pathologist three times per week, 30 minutes per session.

Figure 2.2 Parent Survey for Marnie F.: My Child as Learner

1. How does your child seem to feel about going to school?
   Sometimes she doesn't want to go.

2. What are your goals for your child this year?
   Learn how to read.

3. What are your child's interests?
   TV & books

4. What types of activities do you do together as a family?
   Walks, parks, rides in car.

5. Do you have a time you read together regularly? If so, when and how often?
   When Marnie come home she reads to me her books in her book bag.

6. Does your child discuss or retell stories you have read aloud?
   Yes

7. What types of writing does your child do at home?
   She doodles with her name.

8. What are your observations about how your child learns?
   No Response

9. What are some other things you would like me to know about your child?
   Marnie is shy and she needs to be praised when she does something good. She likes to be a good girl.

Source: Original form can be found in *Practical Aspects of Authentic Assessment: Putting the Pieces Together* (pp. 206–207), by B. Hill and C. Ruptic, 1994, Norwood, MA: Christopher-Gordon.

An end-of-year report indicated that "minimal to some progress" had been made in the areas listed previously.

Marnie's teacher reported that, as of the end of the year, she exhibited the following literacy-related behaviors:

- Some letter identification
- Some phonemic awareness
- Some sound/letter recognition

- Left to right directionality
- Some attention to print
- Ability to follow repetitive text

The teacher described the classroom literacy instruction as child-centered and developmentally appropriate. Hands-on activities focused on letter identification and letter/sound correspondence. (See full survey response in Figure 2.3.)

Figure 2.3 Classroom Teacher Survey for Marnie F.

---

1. Describe the learner's literacy development.

   Is developing letter identification, phonemic awareness reading strategies, left to right direction in reading, attending to print letter (sound & letter), word identification.

2. Describe the learner's strengths and needs as related to reading and writing.

   Is able to follow a repetitive text, enjoys being read to, participates in small and large group activities, and is developing strategies to develop letter identification and reading strategies.

3. Describe the instruction you are providing in your classroom for the learner.

   During this time, we focus on activities that encourage letter identification and letter/sound and letter/word identification. These activities are done through hands-on, child-centered, developmentally appropriate activities that encourage optimal learning.

Detailed Assessment Information

Session 1

Interest Survey. Marnie and the examiner worked together to complete the interest survey. She enjoys playing with friends, playing on the computer, and playing outside. At home, she writes letters to people and reads books about Charlie Brown and Snoopy and Cookie Monster. Math is her favorite school subject, and her goal for the next school year is to learn to read books. (See the full survey response in Figure 2.4.)

Attitudes About Reading. The examiner asked Marnie to complete the Garfield Reading Survey (McKenna & Kear, 1990) and read each item to her. She seemed deliberate and thoughtful in her responses and provided reasons for some of her

Figure 2.4 Interest Survey for Marnie F.

1. What kinds of things do you like to do outside of school?
   Play with my toys, share toys with friends, play outside, play on computer

2. What organized activities do you do outside of school?
   None

3. What do you write about at home?
   Spell words, write about my dad, write letters to lots of people

4. What kinds of things do you like to read at home?
   Books, look at magazines

5. What do you like to read about?
   Books about Charlie Brown and Snoopy, Cookie Monster Books

6. What do you want to be when you grow up?
   A grownup so I can teach everyone stuff.

7. What are your parents' jobs? What kinds of things do they do at work?
   Dad works at McDonalds. Makes food. Mom stays at home with new baby sister.

8. What is your favorite subject at school? Why?
   I like everything but math is my favorite because I like counting things and play with the toys (math manipulatives).

9. What would you really like to learn about next year? Why?
   Learn to read books because I want to write words on pictures.

10. Have you ever travelled? Where?
    No

11. What else would you like me to know about you?
    I like to learn stuff to read and write.

Source: Original form can be found in *Practical Aspects of Authentic Assessment: Putting the Pieces Together* (pp. 174–175), by B. Hill and C. Ruptic, 1994, Norwood, MA: Christopher-Gordon.

responses. For example, in response to prompt number 2: *How do you feel when you read a book in school during free time,* she said that she would rather play on the computer than read a book. Her full-scale percentile rank was 34. The percentile rank for recreational reading was 26 and for academic reading, 44.

In general, she circled either the very happy Garfield (4 points) or the very upset one (1 point) and made few selections in the middle of the scale.

Informal Read Alouds. Based on information gathered from the classroom teacher, the examiner decided to end the first assessment session by asking Marnie to read from simple repetitive texts that focused on the concept of color. She read two books, one about the color pink and one about blue. She relied heavily on picture clues and provided limited evidence of attending to print to identify the words. Examiner notes related to Marnie's reading of each of the texts can be found in Figure 2.5.

Figure 2.5   Informal Read Alouds, Assessment Session 1 for Marnie F.

Title of Text: *The Pink Book*	
Text Words	Examiner Notes
The pink bow.	Marnie said: *The pink bone.*
The pink yarn.	Marnie paused on the word *yarn,* looked at the picture, and then said it correctly.
The pink crayon.	Marnie said: *The pink marker.* She self-corrected after looking at the picture.

Title of Text: *The Blue Book*	
Text Words	Examiner Notes
The blue water.	Marnie said: *The blue whale.*
The blue crayon.	Marnie said: *The blue cookie.* I covered the picture and Marnie hesitated on the word "crayon." I asked her to look at the first letter, figure out what sound the letter makes, and make a guess that starts with that sound. She knew the letter was *c* and was able to produce the appropriate sound and then guessed *cookie.* I asked her to look at the end of the word. She then guessed *coat.* I showed her the picture and she reread the sentence correctly.
The blue rocket.	Marnie said: *The blue rocket ship.*
The blue house.	Marnie said: *The blue hammer.* I covered the picture and Marnie paused when she came to the word house. When I prompted her to look at the first letter she guessed *hammer.* I showed her the picture and she reread the sentence correctly.

Session 2

Reading and Writing Self-Evaluation. At the beginning of Session 2, Marnie and the examiner worked together to complete two self-evaluation forms, one related to reading and one to writing. Marnie defined a good reader as someone who *reads fast and can read many books.* She does not feel she is a good reader because she only looks at the pictures. She defines a good writer as someone who is *doing the right things* and *can write a lot of words fast.* She does not see herself as a good writer because she is "only a little kid." Marnie said that she enjoys both reading and writing activities. She likes looking at pictures in books and writing words and letters to people.

Informal Assessment of Phonological Awareness. The examiner administered an informal assessment to determine Marnie's phonological awareness. The assessment tool consisted of 72 items grouped in sets of six, and it was designed to assess the following abilities: rhyme recognition, differentiation of initial sounds in words, oral blending, oral segmentation, and phonemic manipulation. The results of Marnie's performance are shown in Figure 2.6. She had little or no concept of rhyme production, oral blending, or phonemic segmentation, but she was able to produce rhymes and demonstrated knowledge of beginning and end sounds based on picture clues.

Clay Observation Survey: Running Records. The examiner prepared for the first task in the survey (Clay, 2000c) by asking Marnie's classroom teacher the reading level of the books Marnie was currently reading during guided instruction. The teacher said that Marnie was independent or instructional at Reading Recovery Level 1, depending on the texts, and reached frustration at Level 2. The examiner began the assessment using a Level 1 text consisting of two words per page. These words were labels of the pictures being displayed. Marnie read the 13-word text with 92% accuracy, making one error and one self-correction. She appeared to be looking at the pictures but not the print. Her self-correction, however, indicated that she might be looking at the print occasionally. For example, one line of text read *The grass.* At first Marnie said, "The green grass," but she stopped and corrected her error.

Next, the examiner gave Marnie a longer Level 1 text to read. This proved to be at her instructional level and was in keeping with information that the classroom teacher had provided. She read the 24-word text with two errors, resulting in 91% accuracy. She substituted the word *hopping* for *running* (in the picture, "Mom" was running) and inserted the word *book* (in the picture "Mom" was reading) at the end of a sentence. The final text that Marnie read was at Reading Recovery Level 2. She made 23 errors through either omissions

Figure 2.6   Results of Phonemic Awareness Assessment for Marnie F.

Task	Description	Marnie's Score
Rhyme recognition	The child is asked whether or not pairs of words rhyme.	5/6
Rhyme production	The examiner says two rhyming words and the child is asked to provide a third word that rhymes with the first two.	1/6
Initial sound picture cards	The child is shown a set of three picture cards. Two of the words depicted begin with the same sound. The child is asked to select the picture of the word that begins with a different sound.	5/6
End sound picture cards	The child is shown a set of three picture cards. Two of the words depicted end with the same sound. The child is asked to select the picture of the word that ends with a different sound.	4/6
Oral Blending 1	The examiner says the first sound in a single syllable word (the onset) and then the rest of the word (the rime), and the child is asked to say the word.	0/6
Oral Blending 2	The examiner says each sound in a single syllable word and the child is asked to say the word.	0/6
Oral Segmentation 1	The examiner says a word ranging from one to three syllables. The child is asked to clap the number of syllables she hears.	6/6
Oral Segmentation 2	The examiner says a one- to two-syllable word. The child is asked to say the sound she hears at the beginning of the word.	5/6
Oral Segmentation 3	The examiner says a one-syllable word. The child is asked to say the sound she hears at the end of the word.	5/6
Oral Segmentation 4	The examiner says a one-syllable word. The child is asked to say the sound she hears at the end of the word.	0/6
Phonemic Manipulation 1	The examiner says a one-syllable word. The child is asked to say the word without the first sound.	0/6
Phonemic Manipulation 2	The examiner says a one-syllable word. The child is asked to replace the first sound with an alternate sound, creating a new word. (In this task the /s/ sound is used.)	0/6

or substitutions in this 32-word repetitive text, yielding a 28% accuracy rate. She did not attend to the print in this text; instead, she invented text based on the pictures. See Figure 2.7 for a running record of the text.

Figure 2.7 Running Record Level 2 Text for Marnie F.

Page	Record of Reading	M	S	V
2	---- -- *door* Here is √ gate.	N	N	N
4	---- -- *stair* Here is √ path.	N	N	N
6	---- -- Here is √ √	N	N	N
8	---- -- Here is √ √	N	N	N
10	---- -- Here is √ √	N	N	N
12	*Up top down the top.* Here is a chimney.	N	N	N
14	---- -- -- Here is a √	N	N	N
16	*Flowers_____* Here is a garden.	N	N	N

Accuracy: 9/32 = 28% Accuracy
Notes: No attention to the print. Marnie told the story using the pictures on the left-hand side of the text pages.

Session 3

Clay Observation Survey Tasks. During Session 3, Marnie completed the following survey tasks: *Letter Identification, Concepts About Print,* and *Word Tests.* Results are summarized in the paragraphs that follow, and raw scores and Ohio Stanine Scores are drawn from a table in Clay (2000c, p. 88). Because Marnie had completed kindergarten but had not yet entered Grade 1, the autumn stanine group seemed to be the most appropriate.

- *Letter Identification.* Marnie received a raw score of 41/54 and a stanine score of 2, placing her below average for this task. She responded with letter names only and did not attempt any letter sounds or offer words beginning with the same letter. Figure 2.8 displays the letters she incorrectly identified.
- *Concepts About Print.* The examiner used the text *Follow Me Moon* (Clay, 2000a) for this assessment. Marnie received a raw score of 13/24 and stanine score of 4, placing her in the average category for this task. Figure 2.9 details Marnie's results related to this task.
- *Word Test.* List A of the Ohio Word Test (Clay, 2000c, Appendix 1) was used to assess Marnie's knowledge of high-frequency words. Of the 20 words, she was able to identify only *the* and *and*. This resulted in a stanine score of 3, placing her in the below-average range for this task.

Figure 2.8   Marnie's Errors in Letter Identification

Uppercase Letters		Lowercase Letters	
Letter	Marnie's Response	Letter	Marnie's Response
H	T	b	p
J	F	j	k
U	N	u	v
Y	P	c	s
I	L	y	k
		q	p
		d	p
		g	q

Session 4

Clay Observation Survey Tasks. The remaining two tasks, *Writing Vocabulary* and the *Dictation Task (Hearing and Recording Sounds in Words),* were completed during this session. The results are summarized in the paragraphs that follow.

- *Writing Vocabulary.* Marnie initially responded to the examiner's request to write all the words she knew by recording a series of random letters

Figure 2.9 Concepts of Print Assessment for Marnie F.

CONCEPTS ABOUT PRINT SCORE SHEET

Name: Marnie F.*   Age: 5.6 yrs

Date: _____

TEST SCORE: | 13 /24

Recorder: _____   Date of Birth: _____   STANINE GROUP: | ____

*Used the text, Moon

PAGE	SCORE	ITEM	COMMENT
Cover	1	1. Front of book	
2/3	1	2. Print contains message	
4/5	1	3. Where to start	Swept finger left-to-right but not word-by-word.
4/5	1	4. Which way to go	
4/5	1	5. Return sweep to left	
4/5	0	6. Word-by-word matching	
6	1	7. First and last concept	Noticed upside down picture on pg.7 Pointed 1st word 1st line & 1st word 2nd line.
7	1	8. Bottom of picture	Said, "It's upside down."
8/9	0	9. Begins 'The' (*Sand*) or 'I' (*Stones*) bottom line, top OR turns book	Pointed to the beginning of 1st line swept left to write but did not notice the inversion of text
10/11	1	10. Line order altered	Said, "It's all messed up. It's all wrong all this stuff. We have to fix it. Let's not do this page.
12/13	1	11. Left page before right	He comments related to the pictures only.
12/13	0	12. One change in word order	
12/13	0	13. One change in letter order	
14/15	0	14. One change in letter order	In response to my prompt, she answered the questions on page 14. For 15 she said, "A question mark."
14/15	0	15. Meaning of a question mark	
16/17	1	16. Meaning of full stop (period)	For 17 she said, "A period." For 18 she said, "I don't know. Question marks?" Located the lower case p but not the m.
16/17	0	17. Meaning of comma	
16/17	0	18. Meaning of quotation marks	
16/17	0	19. Locate m h (*Sand*) OR m i (*Moon*) OR t b (*Stones*)	
18/19	0	20. Reversible words *was, no*	
20	1	21. One letter: two letters	
20	0	22. One word: two words	
20	0	23. First and last letter of word	Said, "That's a lot of words."
20	1	24. Capital letter	

Source: Reprinted with permission from *An Observation Survey of Early Literacy Achievement*, by M. Clay, 2000, Portsmouth, NH: Heinemann. Copyright © 2000 by Marie Clay. All rights reserved.

(*a, c, b,* and *g*). Even with some specific prompting, Marnie continued to record a string of letters. Still, by the end of the 10-minute assessment time, she was able to record the following six words: *it, he, mom, and, the,* and her name. She used capital letters most of the time but did use lowercase for *i, e, h,* and *g.* She reversed the capital *n* in the word *and.* Her stanine score was 4, placing her in the average range for this task.

- *Dictation Task.* The examiner selected Form A: *I have a big dog at home. Today I am going to take him to school* (Clay, 2000c, p. 67). This task was difficult for Marnie. She was able to record the sounds in words *I, a,* and *at,* the initial sound of *t,* and the final sound of *m.* She did not record any of the middle sounds and wrote random letters for the words *have, home, going, today* (with the exception of the initial sound /*t*/), and *school.* She did not write the second *I* in the sentence because she said she had already written that letter. The examiner credited her for knowing the sound although it was not represented on her response sheet. Her raw score was 12/37, and her stanine score was 3, placing her in the below-average range for this task (see Figure 2.10).

Figure 2.10   Dictation Task for Marnie F.

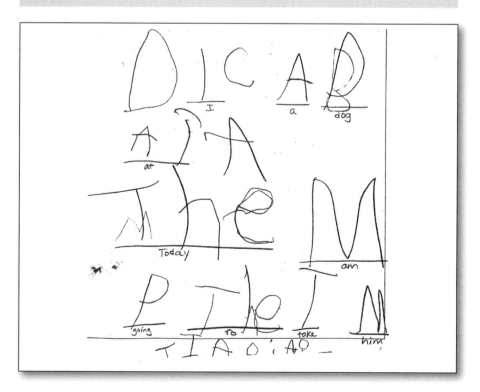

In addition to the observation tasks, the examiner analyzed three writing samples for language level, message quality, and directional principles (Clay, 2000c). Two samples were collected from Marnie's daily independent journal writing. The third sample was Marnie's response to a picture prompt, an outdoor scene that included a monkey and a lion. The examiner worked with Marnie on this task. After Marnie provided her own sentences, the examiner repeated the words slowly. Marnie wrote and then drew a picture (see Figure 2.11). Table 2.2 displays the results of an analysis of Marnie's writing samples using Clay's rubric (2000c, p. 57).

Figure 2.11 Writing Sample for Marnie F.

Monkeys climb in trees. The lion bites.

Table 2.2 Analysis of Marnie's Writing Samples

Language Level	Message Quality	Directional Principles
While most of the writing was a string of capital letters, Marnie wrote the words *the, my,* and *Mom,* putting her at Level 2 of 6.	Pictures and writing provided evidence that Marnie was delivering a simple message, putting her at Level 2 of 6.	All writing samples began at the top of the page and moved left to right to the bottom of the page, putting Marnie at Level 4 of 6.

Case Recap:

1. Review the case and the notes you have taken in response to the guiding questions one final time, and add or revise any information you may have missed.

2. Make a list of additional questions you have about the case. What further information do you need that might be explored in the case discussion?

3. Think about the factors that influence reading performance, beyond emergent literacy, which were discussed in Chapter 1. Which might be problem areas for Marnie? Which might be strengths?

CASE 2: ASSESSMENT REPORT FOR DANNY G.

Background Information

Child's name: Danny G.
Current age: 9 years
Current grade level: End of Grade 2

Referral

Danny's teacher requested that he be assessed. Parental permission was granted.

Family and Medical History

Danny is nine years old. He lives with his parents and two siblings, a younger sister and an older brother. He has a seizure disorder and is on medication to prevent seizures. The level of medication is monitored and changed as needed. His mother reported that it takes about a week for him to adjust to changes and that, during that time, Danny may be more tired, distractible, and easily frustrated than usual.

Mrs. F. completed a survey providing information about her son as a learner. She listed a series of free-time interests that Danny enjoys—most of them outdoor activities. She indicated that he dislikes writing but enjoys reading—even though he gets frustrated. Mrs. F. also wrote that Danny is a visual leaner who will do much better if his interest can be piqued. See Figure 2.12 for the complete results.

Figure 2.12 Parent Survey for Danny G.: Child as Learner

1. What are your child's free-time interests?

   plays baseball, computer games, rides bike, rollerblades

2. What types of books does your child enjoy?

   dinosaurs, truck, fire trucks, insects, snakes

3. What types of writing does your child do at home?

   doesn't like to do much writing

4. What are your observations about how your child learns?

   visually. If he is interested it makes a huge difference.

5. What are some other things you would like us to know about your child?

   Danny tries very hard to read & enjoys reading. He does get frustrated sometimes but is easily redirectable.

6. In what way do you think we can best help your child?

   Be patient—let him read books he is interested in.

Source: Form adapted from *Practical Aspects of Authentic Assessment: Putting the Pieces Together* (pp. 205–207), by B. Hill and C. Ruptic, 1994, Norwood, MA: Christopher-Gordon.

School History

Danny recently completed second grade in a small neighborhood school located near a university. His classroom teacher completed a referral form providing responses to the following four items: the nature of his reading and writing abilities, instructional strategies that have been successful, his attitude toward reading, and whether he is receiving any special services. In general, she reported that Danny is an emerging reader who "loses his train of thought" easily. He likes to be read to and will reread familiar books independently or look at the pictures in more challenging ones. She wrote the he receives additional reading-related services in the school's resource room. For the full survey response, see Figure 2.13.

Figure 2.13 Teacher Referral Form for Danny G.

1. Please describe the nature of the child's reading and writing.

   Danny displays behaviors at the emergent level on our school's reading and writing continuums. If given background information prior to reading, he can successfully decode and make meaning of very simple pattern books. His success with sight vocabulary doesn't seem constant. Writing is successful when guided by the teacher reminding him to write a letter for each sound. He will lose his train of thought with or without interruption.

2. Please describe any strategies, materials, and/or activities that have been used successfully with this child.

   The EdMark reading computer program is used with Danny in the resource room. Then hard copies of the same books are reread in the classroom.

3. What is the child's attitude toward reading and school in general?

   Danny likes to be read to when positively focused. He will sit & read to himself with a familiar book or enjoy the pictures of a challenging book. He enjoys both fiction & non-fiction.

4. Is this child receiving special services of any kind not detailed in Question 2?
   Resource room

Danny's mother provided the examiner with a copy of the school's *Special Education Integrated Assessment Report.* This report summarized test results in the areas of speech and cognitive abilities. As noted in the report, Danny's receptive and expressive language skills are below those of his peers. In addition, he appears to have a delay in processing information. His cognitive functioning falls in the "mildly impaired" range, and he is academically low in all areas, including reading and writing. It was also reported that he has difficulty with "attention and behavior management" but is taking medication to address these difficulties.

Detailed Assessment Information

Session 1

Interest Survey. During the first meeting, the examiner gave Danny an interest survey to complete. She read the questions and asked him to write the answers independently. After observing his first three responses, she stopped the activity. For Question 1, he wrote a series of random letters (Ionon—he—n—ononah), and for the next two questions, he combined letter-like formations with squiggly lines. The examiner suggested they go for a walk, and Danny was eager to go. As they walked, the examiner asked the survey questions and wrote Danny's answers. In sum, he said that he enjoys baseball, hockey, camping, and lighting fireworks. He likes reading about bulldozers and animals and wants to be in the army when he grows up. Initially, he said that his favorite subject was math but then changed his mind, saying that he did not like math because it was hard. He said that his mom worked at the university and that he did not know where his dad worked, but that "he was a hard worker." He volunteered that he had two dogs and two cats.

Attitudes About Reading. After returning from their walk, the examiner asked Danny to complete the Garfield Reading Survey (McKenna & Kear, 1990) and read each item aloud to him. Danny wrote his name and grade at the top of the form. His name was spelled correctly, but the sizes of the letters differed greatly. For example, the capital *D* and lowercase *a* were the same height. All of the letters were written above the guideline. He wrote the reverse of the numeral 2 for his grade level. Danny's overall percentile rank on this survey was 5. For recreational reading, it was 15, and for academic reading, 1. Results suggested a slightly more positive attitude toward reading for fun than for school-related purposes; however, this was offset by his extremely negative attitude toward reading in general.

Session 2

Developmental Spelling Test. At the beginning of Session 2, the examiner administered the Developmental Spelling Test (Gentry & Wallace, 1993). Danny completed it with little or no frustration. Results showed that he is in the precommunicative spelling stage. (See Chapter 3 for a complete description of this assessment.) Letters were used for writing words, but they were strung together randomly and seldom corresponded to the sounds in the words. He repeatedly wrote the letters *n*, *o*, and *u* in the strings. He was able to represent the *m* as the initial letter in *monster* (Item 1), and he may have heard the sounds of *s* in *dress* (Item 2), *n* in *human* (Item 6), *l* in *closed* (Item 8), and *t* in *type* (Item 10) (see Figure 2.14).

Figure 2.14 Developmental Spelling Test for Danny G.

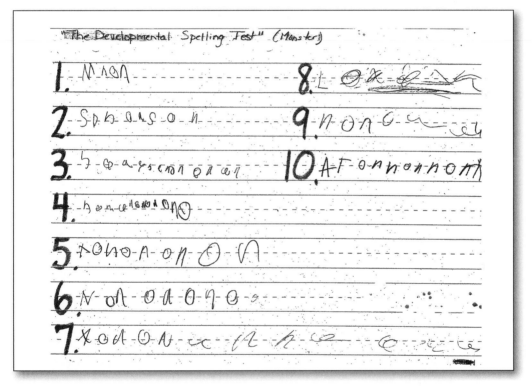

Yopp-Singer Test of Phonemic Segmentation. Because Danny seemed comfortable and attentive during the previous assessment, the examiner decided to proceed with the Yopp-Singer (Yopp, 1995) test after a short break. The examiner began by reading the directions as written on the test and providing the test example. Danny then was given the first practice item, *ride*. Rather than provide the sound /r/, Danny gave the letter name. He could not sound out or spell the remainder of the word. The examiner reviewed the directions with him and gave him the second practice word, *go*. Again, Danny gave the first letter rather than the sound. The examiner attempted to give Danny a visual cue by moving her hands and arms to stretch out the word *go*, but he did not seem to understand what was being asked of him. By the time the examiner gave him the third practice word (*man*), Danny was extremely frustrated. He put his head down on the table and began to cry, saying that he "didn't want to be in reading anymore" and wanted to call his mom. The examiner called Mrs. F. and she came to pick him up shortly thereafter.

Session 3

Danny arrived for the third session much calmer than he had been at the close of Session 2. The examiner decided to limit the amount of time Danny was engaged in the completion of assessments to reduce his frustration level. For Session 3, Danny completed an informal letter identification exercise and the pre-primer level of the high-frequency word list.

Letter Identification. The examiner used a large alphabet wall chart and a pointer to complete this task. The chart listed capital letters only. As she pointed at random to a letter, she asked Danny to identify its name. He was able to identify correctly all of the letters with the exception of the letter *V*, which he said was an *I*. The examiner began to ask Danny the sounds of the letters but stopped the assessment after the fifth letter since he was able to identify only two of the five consonant sounds, /b/ and /p/.

High-Frequency Word List. After the examiner and Danny had returned from a walk, she asked him to read from a list of high-frequency words. This particular list, used in the University Reading Center for almost two decades, was subdivided into grade ranges from pre-primer through seventh grade. She asked Danny to identify words in the pre-primer list from flash cards that she had prepared in advance, so that he would not be overwhelmed with the entire list. In addition, the examiner stopped after the first 19 words to give Danny a break and to reduce his growing frustration. He read 75% of the pre-primer list correctly. He recognized 68% of those words automatically (within one second) and made one self-correction (*Jake* for *jump*). Danny made the following errors:

said *can* for *come*

said *hi* for *help*

said *hi* for *here*

said *tie* for *it*

said *manas* for *make*

said *me* for *my*

said *see* for *said*

said *will* for *we*

Session 4

Developmental Reading Assessment (Beaver, 2001). Based on the information gained from the initial assessments, the examiner selected DRA texts at Levels 1 and 2. These texts were in the kindergarten range and the equivalent of Guided Reading Levels A and B (Fountas & Pinnell, 1996). The examiner gave Danny the Level 1 text, *Things That Go* (DeLapp & Hullinger, 1997). He provided a satisfactory prediction based on a picture walk and made only one error in the 16-word repetitive text. This he self-corrected saying, "The *pilot,* no, the *plane* (correct word) can go." As directed, he pointed to the words while reading, making a consistent one-to-one match and moving appropriately from left to right.

After a brief break, the examiner continued with the Level 2 text, *Bath Time* (DeLapp & Lyon, 2002). This was a simple decodable text consisting of 34 words with one line of print on the left page and a supporting picture on the right. He made 16 errors, resulting in a 53% error rate. He consistently missed *can,* the second word in each line, and skipped an entire page of text. Although he moved from left to right on the line of text, he did not have a consistent one-to-one match when pointing to words. He seemed to rely on the pictures more than the text. (Figure 2.15 provides a detailed summary of the results of this assessment.)

Once Danny completed the reading, the examiner opened the text to page 8 and asked Danny to find a word that began with the letter *g*. His first response was *goat*. The examiner responded, "Yes, goat starts with the letter *g*, but what word on *this* page starts with the letter *g*?" Danny responded with the correct word; *green*. The examiner then turned to page 12 and asked Danny to find a word that ended with the letter *p*. His first response was *pink*.

Figure 2.15 Summary DRA Assessment for Danny G.

Text: *Bath Time* (DeLapp & Lyon, 2002): *Level 2* (Grade Level Equivalent K, Guided Reading Level B)

Previewing and Predicting: Danny correctly labeled each item pictured on the page until he reached the last page. Rather than a single item, this page showed a girl in a bathtub with a rubber duck, a rubber frog, bubbles, and a towel hanging on the rack in back of her. When he got to this picture, he studied it but did not say anything.

Oral Reading Miscues			
Page	Text Words	Words Said	Error Type
4	can	——	Omission
4	blue	yellow	Self-correction
6	can	——	Omission
8	I can see a yellow duck	——	Omission
10	can	——	Omission
12	can	——	Omission
12	——	a	Insertion
12	pink	blue	Substitution
12	toy	soap	Self-correction
12	Line of text: I can see pink soap. Danny's reading: I see a blue toy, soap.		
14	and	——	Omission
14	can	——	Omission
14	——	a	Insertion
14	blue	——	Insertion
14	bubbles	towels	Substitution
12	Line of text: and I can see bubbles. Danny's reading: I see a blue towels, bubbles.		

Total Errors: 16

Accuracy: 53%

Total Self-Corrections: 2

> Phrasing and fluency: Danny read word by word with no intonation.
>
> Directionality: Danny moved from left to right on one line of text.
>
> One-to-one matching: Danny was inconsistent in one-to-one matching when pointing to words.
>
> Concept of letters and words: Danny was able to locate letters and words.
>
> Use of cue sources: Danny read using the pictures as cues.

Source: Form adapted from *DRA Observation Guide*, by J. Beaver, 2002, Parsippany, NJ: Celebration Press.

The examiner said, "Pink *starts* with the letter *p*; what word ends with the letter *p*?" Danny responded with the correct word: *soap*.

Examiner Anecdotal Notes

After Session 4. During the assessment, Danny was extremely distractible. Before and during the reading he had to be reminded to stay on task. He seemed fascinated with his Gatorade bottle. He is easily distracted and it is hard for him to focus on something for more than five minutes at a time.

Case Recap:

1. Review the case and the notes you have taken in response to the guiding questions one final time, and add or revise any information you may have missed.

2. Make a list of additional questions you have about the case. What further information do you need that might be explored in the case discussion?

3. Think about the factors that influence reading performance, beyond emergent literacy, which were discussed in Chapter 1. Which might be problem areas for Danny? Which might be strengths?

CHAPTER SUMMARY

This chapter focused on emergent literacy and its importance in guiding children toward conventional reading and writing. In order for literacy skills and abilities to emerge, children must acquire rich oral vocabularies, phonological and phonemic awareness, letter knowledge, and concepts about print and story. As noted at the beginning of the chapter, these competencies do not develop naturally. Young children and older learners who struggle need responsive adults who talk with them, read to them, and help them play with language intentionally so that they may gain the skills necessary to become successful readers. The next chapter focuses on word identification, a second critical element in learning to read.

Terms highlighted in this chapter

emergent literacy   21

onset   22

phonemes   22

productive abilities   23

running record   28

syntactics   28

Concepts About Print   29

invented spelling   36

lexicon   22

rime   22

receptive abilities   23

phonemic awareness   23

semantics   28

stanine   29

"print referencing style"   32

FINAL QUESTIONS FOR REFLECTION AND RESPONSE

1. Think about a young child that you know or have worked with recently. Using the information about emergent literacy presented in Section I, describe his or her developing literacy.

2. Imagine preparing for a conversation with Marnie's or Danny's parents. What would you tell them about the literacy development of their child, and what might you ask them to do to help promote his or her literacy development?

3. Imagine that you are a reading specialist working with Danny and Marnie at the same time. Select an authentic text and design a storybook interactive reading session that addresses their needs as emergent learners.

Journals Online

Visit the student study site at www.sagepub.com/combsstudy to access recent, relevant, full-text journal articles from SAGE's leading research journals.

REFERENCES

Adams, M. (1992). *Beginning to read: Thinking and learning about print.* Cambridge, MA: MIT Press.

Allington, R. (2002). Research on reading/learning ability disability interventions. In A. Farstrup & J. Samuels (Eds.), *What research has to say about reading instruction* (pp. 261–290). Newark, DE: International Reading Association.

Au, K. (2000). Literacy instruction for young children of diverse backgrounds. In D. Strickland & L. Mandel-Morrow (Eds.), *Beginning reading and writing* (pp. 35–45). New York: Teachers College Press.

Barr, R., Blachowicz, C., Bates, A., Katz, C., & Kaufman, B. (2007). *Reading diagnosis for teachers: An instructional approach* (5th ed.). Boston: Allyn & Bacon.

Bear, D., Invernizzi, S., & Templeton, F. (2004). *Words their way* (3rd ed.). Upper Saddle River, NJ: Merrill Prentice Hall.

Beaver, J. (2001). *Developmental reading assessment: K–3 teacher resource guide: Revised.* Parsippany, NJ: Celebration Press.

Beaver, J. (2002). *DRA observation guide: Bath time: Level 2.* Parsippany, NJ: Celebration Press.

Bradley, B., & Jones, J. (2007). Sharing alphabet books in early childhood classrooms. *The Reading Teacher, 60*(5), 452–462.

Bromley, K. (2000). Teaching young children to write. In D. Strickland & L. Mandel-Morrow (Eds.), *Beginning reading and writing* (pp. 111–120). New York: Teachers College Press.

Bursack, W., & Damer, M. (2007). *Reading instruction for students who are at risk or have disabilities.* Boston: Pearson Education.

Byrnes, J., & Wasik, B. (2009). *Language and literacy development.* New York: Guilford Press.

Clay, M. (1972). *Sand.* Auckland, New Zealand: Heinemann.

Clay, M. (1979). *Stones.* Auckland, New Zealand: Heinemann.

Clay, M. (2000a). *Follow me moon.* Portsmouth, NH: Heinemann Education.

Clay, M. (2000b). *No shoes.* Portsmouth, NH: Heinemann.

Clay, M. (2000c). *An observation survey of early literacy achievement.* Portsmouth, NH: Heinemann.

Cunningham, P., & Cunningham, J. (2002). What we know about how to teach phonics. In A. Farstrup & S. Samuels (Eds.), *What research has to say about reading instruction* (pp. 87–109). Newark, DE: International Reading Association.

DeLapp, P., & Hullinger, C. (1997). *Things that go.* Parsippany, NJ: Celebration Press.

DeLapp, P., & Lyon, T. (2002). *Bath time.* Parsippany, NJ: Celebration Press.

Dolch, E. W. (1936). A basic sight vocabulary. *Elementary School Journal, 36,* 456–460.

Ehri, L., & Nunes, S. (2002). The role of phonemic awareness in learning to read. In A. Farstrup & S. Samuels (Eds.), *What research has to say about reading instruction* (3rd ed., pp. 110–139). Newark, DE: International Reading Association.

Ellery, V. (2009). *Creating strategic readers: Techniques for developing competency in phonemic awareness, phonics, fluency, vocabulary, and comprehension.* Newark, DE: International Reading Association.

Elliott, E., & Olliff, C. (2008). Developmentally appropriate emergent literacy activities for young children: Adapting the early literacy and learning model. *Early Childhood Education Journal, 35,* 551–556.

Foorman, B., Anthony, J., Seals, L., & Mouzaki, A. (2002). *Language development and emergent literacy in preschool.* Retrieved September 3, 2009, from http://www.sciencedirect.com/

Fountas, I., & Pinnell, G. (1996). *Guided reading: Good first teaching for all children.* Portsmouth, NH: Heinemann.

Gentry, J., & Wallace, J. (1993). *Teaching kids to spell.* Portsmouth, NH: Heinemann.

Hill, B., & Ruptic, C. (1994). *Practical aspects of authentic assessment: Putting the pieces together.* Norwood, MA: Christopher-Gordon.

International Reading Association. (1998). *Learning to read and write: Developmentally appropriate practices for young children.* Newark, DE: Author.

Justice, L., Kaderavak, J., Fan, X., Sofka, A., & Hunt, T. (2009). Accelerating preschoolers' early literacy development through classroom-based teacher-child storybook reading and explicit print referencing. *Language, Speech, and Hearing Services in Schools, 40,* 67–85.

Kirkland, L., & Patterson, J. (2005). Developing oral language in primary classrooms. *Early Childhood Education Journal, 32*(6), 391–395.

Lipson, M., & Wixson, K. (2003). *Assessment & instruction of reading and writing difficulty: An interactive approach* (3rd ed.). Boston: Allyn & Bacon.

McKenna, M., & Kear, D. J. (1990). Measuring attitude toward reading: A new tool for teachers. *The Reading Teacher, 43,* 626–639.

Miller, W. (2000). *Strategies for developing emergent literacy.* Boston: McGraw-Hill.

Mraz, M., Padak, N., & Rasinski, T. (2008). *Evidence-based instruction in reading: A professional development guide to phonemic awareness.* Boston: Pearson.

National Reading Panel. (2000). *Teaching children to read: An evidence-based assessment of the scientific research literature on reading and its implications for reading instruction.* Washington, DC: National Institute of Child Health and Human Development.

Neal, J., & Ehlert, D. (2007). Alphabet recognition made simple. *Intervention in School and Clinic, 42*(4), 243–247.

Neuman, S., & Bredekamp, S. (2000). Becoming a reader: A developmentally appropriate approach. In D. Strickland & L. Mandel-Morrow (Eds.), *Beginning reading and writing* (pp. 22–34). New York: Teachers College Press.

Opitz, M. (2000). *Rhymes and reasons: Literature and language play for phonological awareness.* Portsmouth, NH: Heinemann.

Seefeldt, C., & Galper, A. (2001). *Active experiences for active children: Literacy emerges.* Upper Saddle River, NJ: Merrill Prentice Hall.

Snow, C., Burns, S., & Griffin, P. (Eds.). (1998). *Preventing reading difficulties in young children.* Washington, DC: National Academy Press.

Spear-Swerling, L., & Sternberg, J. (1998). *Off track: When poor readers become learning disabled.* Boulder, CO: Westview Press.

Strickland, K. (2005). *What's after assessment? Follow-up instruction for phonics, fluency and comprehension.* Portsmouth, NH: Heinemann.

Sulzby, E., & Teale, W. (1996). Emergent literacy. In R. Barr, M. Kamil, P. Mosenthal, & P. Pearson (Eds.), *Handbook of reading research* (pp. 727–757). Mahwah, NJ: Lawrence Erlbaum.

Teale, W., & Yokota, J. (2000). Beginning reading and writing: Perspectives on instruction. In D. Strickland & L. Mandel-Morrow (Eds.), *Beginning Reading and Writing* (pp. 3–21). New York: Teachers College Press.

Tracey, D. (2000). Enhancing literacy growth through home-school connections. In D. M.-M. Strickland, *Beginning Reading and Writing* (pp. 46–57). New York: Teachers College Press.

Yeh, S., & Connell, D. (2008). Effects of rhyming, vocabulary and phonemic awareness instruction on phoneme awareness. *Journal of Research in Reading, 31*(2), 243–256.

Yopp, H. (1995). A test for assessing phonemic awareness in young children. *The Reading Teacher, 49*(1), 20–29.

Yopp, H., & Yopp, R. (2000). Supporting phonemic awareness development in the classroom. *The Reading Teacher, 54*(2), 130–143.

CHAPTER 3
FOCUS ON WORD IDENTIFICATION

There was a book lying near Alice on the table, and while she sat watching the White King . . . , she turned over the leaves, to find some part that she could read, "—for it's all in some language I don't know," she said to herself.

—Lewis Carroll

Guiding Questions

Sections I through III of this chapter will help build your knowledge related to word identification and will prepare you to read and discuss the cases in Section IV. As you read the
sections, consider the following questions.

- What are the ways we identify words?

- What are the phases of word identification?

- How do we assess word identification skills?

- What are the elements of effective word recognition instruction?

- What particular interventions help to develop word identification skills?

INTRODUCTION

While word identification is only one of several factors that influence comprehension, it is impossible to construct meaning without first being able to identify
words (Clark, 2004; Pikulski, 1997). Skilled readers, having reached the level of
automatic word recognition, sail through text and only rarely slow down to
navigate an unknown word. Even then, they quickly use their print skills to make
out the word or replace it with a synonym, or perhaps skip it entirely. As long as
their actions maintain the meaning of the text, skilled readers are off once more.
The story is quite different for readers whose word identification skills are limited. They sputter through text, pulling apart words letter-sound by letter-sound.
Or they substitute words with abandon, using the initial or end sounds as clues,
often settling on a word totally disconnected from the actual one in the text. Like
skilled readers, they may skip a word entirely, but for a very different reason.
They simply have no idea how to go about figuring it out.

In this chapter, you will meet Chad and Kayla. Chad had just completed first
grade at the time of his assessment. At the age of three, he was adopted from
an orphanage in Russia. Kayla had just completed second grade. When
younger, she lived with her grandmother on an American Indian reservation
located in the northern part of the state. The information provided in Sections I
and II and the interventions discussed in Section III should help you make sense
of their cases and guide you toward understanding their abilities and their
needs related to word identification.

Section I: What Do We Know About Word Identification?

What Are the Ways We Identify Words?

Word identification is the process of determining the pronunciation and some meaning of a word encountered in print (Gentry, 2006; Harris & Hodges, 1995). Readers employ a variety of strategies to accomplish this. Ehri (2004, 2005) identified four of them: **decoding, analogizing, predicting,** and recognizing whole words by sight. Each of these will be described briefly.

Decoding is the ability to pronounce the words as the reader encounters them in the text (Samuels, 2002). Typically advancing readers are able to employ a variety of strategies to decode unknown words. Beginning readers may break the words apart, sound by sound, and then blend the sounds together. They may also divide a whole word or a part of a word into its **onset**—the consonants that precede the vowel in a word or syllable—and **rime**—the vowel and consonants that follow it in a syllable (Harris & Hodges, 1995)—and then blend these parts into a recognizable word. Older readers, those beyond the second grade, may use their increasing knowledge about **word structure** (roots, prefixes, suffixes, and syllables) to identify the word.

The ability to decode correctly and consistently requires a working knowledge of the **alphabetic principle**: the concept that there are systematic and predictable relationships between the spoken sounds of our language and the written letters or combinations of letters in our alphabet (Morrow & Morgan, 2006). Indeed, children who do not gain an understanding of this principle in early grades (K–2) are at risk of falling farther and farther behind their peers as the reading demands posed by ever more difficult texts increase (Zimmerman, Padak, & Rasinski, 2008).

Analogizing involves using known words or word parts as an aid for identifying unknown words—if I know the *b* sound in *ball,* and I know the word *cake,* I can identify a new word: *bake* (Barone, Hardman, & Taylor, 2006). Requisite skills for analogizing, or decoding by analogy, as noted by White (2005) and Zimmerman et al. (2008), include the following:

- An understanding of the alphabetic principal
- An understanding of the ways words can rhyme
- An ability to identify initial phonemes (sounds)
- An ability to separate words into onsets and rimes

Ehri and McCormick (2004) added that a store of easily recognized words is essential to reading words by analogy. As a reader's skill increases, the brain, which is essentially a pattern detector, can make easy use of this information to figure out unfamiliar words (Cunningham, 1999).

Predicting involves using letter clues, the surrounding context, and knowledge about syntax to guess what a word might be (Mesmer & Griffith, 2005). For example, consider the sentence, "The old man needed to use his _____ to keep from falling down." The structure of the sentence (syntax) indicates that the missing word is most likely a noun. The entire sentence suggests that the unknown word might be something that helps support the old man. If the initial letter is *c*, this provides an additional hint that the word may be *cane* or *crutches*. Surrounding words, sentences, or pictures may also help narrow the reader's guess.

Predicting from context is important for readers in figuring out the meaning of a word, but it is not always a reliable tool for figuring out the exact word (Snow, Burns, & Griffin, 1998). To do that, it is necessary to combine context with the other clues noted previously (Pikulski, 1997). Less skilled readers tend to over-rely on context, producing errors that alter meaning. Imagine, for example, that the reader of the sentence provided in the previous paragraph said *nurse* or *bed* because she looked at an accompanying picture showing the man in a hospital room and ignored word-level cues.

Recognizing words by *sight* is the process of identifying words from memory without analysis. Ehri (2005) noted that educators often use the term ***sight word*** to describe high-frequency words, words most frequently encountered in print, or irregularly spelled words (those that are phonetically irregular and therefore not easily decoded). In reality, any word that is immediately recognized as a whole is a sight word. Cunningham (1999) emphasized that such instant recognition should be the goal for all readers since this is what allows them to move through text quickly, efficiently, and fluently.

Even skilled readers with large sight word vocabularies will eventually encounter unfamiliar words as they engage with increasingly difficult text. Their ability to use different combinations of the word identification strategies described, without over-relying on any one strategy, sets them apart from their less skilled peers (Pikulski, 1997).

What Are the Phases of Word Identification?

The brain is not prewired to read words. Children must be taught how to find the patterns in print that will lead them to automatic word recognition

(Gentry, 2006). Ehri and McCormick (2004) described the development of word learning as occurring in five phases. In Table 3.1, each phase is briefly outlined in relation to the behaviors children exhibit.

Ehri and McCormick (2004) noted that these phases may overlap and that complete mastery in one phase may not be a prerequisite for a subsequent phase. Still, once the predominant phase has been identified, instruction can be designed to move a reader to the next phase.

Table 3.1 Ehri's Phases of Word Learning (Ehri & McCormick, 2004)

Pre-alphabetic phase	• Little working knowledge of the alphabetic principle (that is, no understanding that letters in words map to sounds) • Focus on nonalphabetical graphic features (reads *stop* upon seeing a stop sign) • Limited to reading words from memory and guessing based on context
Partial-alphabetic phase	• Develops a rudimentary knowledge of the alphabetic principle • Uses letters (usually initial letters) and context to guess unfamiliar words • Knows the consonant sounds whose letter names contain those sounds (b, d, m, p, etc.) • Not yet able to use analogizing as a tool since the sight-word store is not large enough • May not have acquired a strong left to right orientation (reads *was* for *saw*)
Full-alphabetic phase	• Develops good working knowledge of the major sound-symbol correspondences and uses that knowledge to decode unfamiliar words • Can read words by analogy because sight-word store has developed sufficiently • Reading is initially slow and laborious, but speed and facility with words grow as sight-word vocabulary increases and as familiarity with the ways sounds are typically blended to create words increases
Consolidated-alphabetic phase	• Develops solid working knowledge of recurring spelling patterns and commonly occurring suffixes • Easily stores longer words in memory because of ability to recognize word parts in chunks • Develops knowledge about more complex sound-symbol correspondences (e.g., silent e)
Automatic-alphabetic phase	• Recognizes most words in text automatically by sight • Skilled in applying various strategies to attack unfamiliar words

SECTION II: HOW DO WE ASSESS WORD IDENTIFICATION SKILLS?

Ongoing assessment of a student's ability to recognize familiar words and to figure out unknown words is necessary in order to design targeted intervention tied to the student's specific needs. Many tools and processes are available to assess and monitor student progress. Three commonly used assessments are word lists, running records with miscue analysis, and spelling analysis. All of these assessments, when used together, will yield a great deal of information about a student's strengths and weaknesses in identifying words.

Word lists can provide information about a reader's store of sight words, as well as what skills they use quickly and easily to identify unfamiliar words in isolation. A number of **informal reading inventories** containing graded word lists are available commercially (e.g., *Analytical Reading Inventory* [Woods & Moe, 1999]; *Qualitative Reading Inventory* [Leslie & Caldwell, 2000]). Lists of high-frequency words, including the Dolch Word List (Dolch, 1936) and the Fry Instant Sight Word List (Fry, 2001), can be found in many teacher resource guides and can be downloaded from the Internet.

In most cases, the student should begin by reading the lowest graded list, usually the Primer Level, or the words of highest frequency on the selected word list. The examiner should keep track of two scores as the child reads: the percentage of words read correctly within one second and the total number of words read correctly. Those words read correctly in one second have been retrieved automatically from memory, while words that are identified after a longer period of time signal that the reader is using decoding strategies (Caldwell & Leslie, 2009). The examiner should also record unknown words and those pronounced incorrectly, even if the reader self-corrects, making note of what the reader said for later analysis. When using graded word lists from reading inventories, the examiner should stop the student after she or he makes five errors in any graded list. When using high-frequency word lists, Manzo, Manzo, and Albee (2004) suggested, the examiner should stop after the student has missed three out of any four words and ask the child to look down the list to see whether she or he knows any other words.

Next, the examiner should analyze the student's responses. Lipson and Wixson (2003) proposed six questions to consider during analysis:

1. Does there appear to be any consistent pattern of errors?

2. Is the pattern of these errors comparable at each level, or does it change with increasing difficulty?

3. Does the student substitute initial consonants or final consonants?

4. Does the student attend to medial portions of words?

5. Does the student reverse letters or words?

6. What is the student's overall mastery of sight words in isolation? (p. 352)

Careful analysis will reveal the student's ability to decode, analogize, and predict words in isolation. It will also allow the examiner to determine which word-learning phase is predominant for the student.

*Running records with **miscue analysis*** provide additional, rich information about how students identify familiar words and figure out unknown ones when reading extended text. A running record, as originally described by Marie Clay (1993), may be conducted with any text, including those found in reading inventories, since the method for coding miscues in all texts is similar. When using a reading inventory, the student should start reading the graded passage that matches the highest graded word lists in which no errors were made (Woods & Moe, 1999). Reading more difficult passages should continue until the student reads a passage with less than 95% oral reading accuracy or 75% comprehension (generally described as the instructional level) (Barr, Blachowicz, Bates, Katz, & Kaufman, 2007). When using classroom basals or leveled books, the teacher should select several texts representing multiple levels of difficulty.

As the student reads, the examiner should code all miscues, including substitutions, omissions, insertions, self-corrections, repetitions, and teacher-aided words. Following this, the examiner should analyze each miscue to determine which cueing system(s) the child uses—semantic (predicting), syntactic (predicting), or **graphophonic** (decoding/analogizing)—in attempting to identify the word. Lyon and Moore (2003) offered the following principles for analyzing students' errors:

- Analyze errors by considering the difference between what the student said and what was written in the text. For example, if the student read *bit* for *bite*, he or she may not yet recognize the VCe (vowel-consonant-silent e) pattern.
- Look for patterns of error that provide evidence of the predominant phase in which the student is operating (see phases of word identification described previously).
- Look for errors that reveal particular gaps in understanding from an earlier phase.
- Ignore errors that are typically learned in a more advanced phase.

Frequent assessment of children's spelling can reveal what they know about how words work.

Analysis of children's spelling is an excellent way to assess a child's knowledge and use of word identification skills. In order to spell an unknown word, a child must think about its sound and how to represent it using letters and letter combinations (Zimmerman et al., 2008). Children's unaided writing samples and spelling inventories will provide information about a student's knowledge of how words work (Bear, Invernizzi, & Templeton, 2004).

The *Developmental Spelling Test,* created by Richard Gentry for use with students in Grades K through 2 (Gentry & Wallace, 1993), is an easy-to-use tool that provides a snapshot of a child's stage of spelling development. Gentry (2006) also aligned these spelling stages with Ehri's (2005) phases of word recognition (see Table 3.2), making it possible to target appropriate instruction.

Table 3.2 Alignment of Ehri's Phases of Word Learning With Gentry's Spelling Stages

Ehri's Phase Theory for Word Learning (Ehri & McCormick, 2004, pp. 370–384)	Gentry's Levels of Spelling Development (Gentry & Wallace, 1993, pp. 26–35)
Pre-alphabetic: • Little working knowledge of the alphabetic principle (that is, no understanding that letters in words map to sounds) • Focus on nonalphabetical graphic features (reads *stop* upon seeing a stop sign) • Limited to reading words from memory and guessing based on context	Level 1 Precommunicative: • Uses strings of letters without awareness of what the letters represent • No use of letter-sound correspondence
Partial alphabetic: • Develops a rudimentary knowledge of the alphabetic principle • Uses letters (usually initial letters) and context to guess unfamiliar words • Knows the consonant sounds whose letter names contain those sounds (b, d, m, p, etc.)	Level 2 Semiphonetic: • First use of letters to correspond to sounds • Words usually contain correct beginning and ending consonants but are greatly abbreviated

Ehri's Phase Theory for Word Learning (Ehri & McCormick, 2004, pp. 370–384)	Gentry's Levels of Spelling Development (Gentry & Wallace, 1993, pp. 26–35)
• Not yet able to use analogizing as a tool since sight-word store is not large enough • May not have acquired a strong left to right orientation (reads *was* for *saw*)	
Full alphabetic: • Develops good working knowledge of the major sound-symbol correspondences and uses that knowledge to decode unfamiliar words • Can read words by analogy because sight-word store has developed sufficiently • Reading is initially slow and laborious, but speed and facility with words grow as sight-word vocabulary increases and as familiarity with the ways sounds are typically blended to create words increases	Level 3 Phonetic: • Supplies a letter for each sound in a word • Selects letters based on sound only, without attention to conventions of English orthography
Consolidated alphabetic: • Develops solid working knowledge of recurring spelling patterns and commonly occurring suffixes • Easily stores longer words in memory because of ability to recognize word parts in chunks • Develops knowledge about more complex sound-symbol correspondences (e.g., silent e)	Level 4 Transitional: • Uses a chunking system to write—spells mono- and polysyllabic words in parts rather than one letter for each sound • Chunks may represent the sounds in a word, but correct spelling patterns may not yet be present
Automatic alphabetic: • Recognizes most words in text automatically by sight • Skilled in applying various strategies to attack unfamiliar words	Level 5 Conventional: • Most words are spelled correctly, including those with inflectional endings, contractions, compound words, and homonyms • Can think of alternative spellings and knows when words "don't look right" • Has accumulated a large sight word vocabulary

Steps for administering the *Developmental Spelling Test* (Gentry & Wallace, 1993) are as follows:

1. Tell the child that the words may be too difficult for most kindergartners and first graders to spell, so you want her to invent the spelling or use her best guess as to what the spelling might be.

2. Explain that the activity will not be graded as right or wrong, but that you want to see how she thinks certain words should be spelled.

3. Be encouraging and make the activity challenging, playful, and fun.

4. Call out each of the 10 words listed in the chart that follows, read the accompanying sentence, and call out the word again. (pp. 42–43)

Dictated Word	Dictated Sentence
monster	The boy was eaten by a monster.
united	You live in the United States.
dress	The girl wore a new dress.
bottom	A big fish lives at the bottom of the lake.
hiked	We hiked to the top of the mountain.
human	Miss Piggy is not a human.
eagle	An eagle is a powerful bird.
closed	The little girl closed the door.
bumped	The car bumped into the bus.
type	Type the letter on the typewriter.

There are three steps involved in analyzing the results. First, look for features that are prevalent at each of the following spelling stages:

1. **Precommunicative spelling:** Letters may be used for writing words, but they are strung together randomly and do not correspond to sound.

2. **Semiphonetic spelling:** Sounds are represented with letters in a type of telegraphic writing; they are often abbreviated, representing initial or final sounds.

3. **Phonetic spelling:** Words are spelled as they sound; all phonemes are represented in a word, though the spelling may be unconventional.

4. **Transitional spelling:** A visual memory of the spelling pattern is present; conventions of English orthography (the way letters appear sequentially

to create words) are apparent. The word is not just spelled as it sounds—its spelling approximates the visual representation of the word.

5. **Conventional spelling**: Common words that would be written by the typically achieving fourth grade child are spelled correctly.

Second, find the error type that is most closely matched with the error provided in Table 3.3 and write the appropriate developmental stage beside each of the child's spellings.

Table 3.3   Possible Responses to the Developmental Spelling Test

Word	Precommunicative Stage	Semiphonetic Stage	Phonetic Stage	Transitional Stage	Conventional Stage
1. monster	Random letters	mtr	mostr	monstur	monster
2. united	Random letters	u	unitd	younighted	united
3. dress	Random letters	jrs	jras	dres	dress
4. bottom	Random letters	bt	bodm	bottum	bottom
5. hiked	Random letters	h	hikt	hicked	hiked
6. human	Random letters	um	humm	humum	human
7. eagle	Random letters	el	egl	egul	eagle
8. closed	Random letters	kd	klosd	clossed	closed
9. bumped	Random letters	b	bopt	bumpped	bumped
10. type	Random letters	tp	tip	tipe	type

Source: "You Can Analyze Developmental Spelling—and Here's How to Do It" by J. Richard Gentry, 1985, *Teaching K–8*, pp. 44–45. Reprinted by permission of Highlights for Children, Inc. Copyrighted material.

Third, determine the child's developmental level—that is, the level within which most of the child's spellings occur. As an additional check, observe the invented spellings in the child's free writing. It is important to remember that this assessment has been designed to be used with young learners or those new to English and may not be appropriate for older learners who struggle with spelling.

SECTION III: WHAT INSTRUCTIONAL INTERVENTIONS HELP TO DEVELOP WORD IDENTIFICATION SKILLS?

What Are the Elements of Effective Word Recognition Instruction?

Most researchers agree that, to be effective, instruction must be systematic and explicit and must match the child's developmental level. Systematic instruction involves the teaching of a carefully planned sequence of word elements, moving from simple to more complex concepts (Barone et al., 2006; National Reading Panel, 2000; White, 2005). According to Lyon and Moore (2003), "by systematically drawing students' attention to letters, sounds, and words we are providing them with opportunities to do what the human brain does best—look for patterns" (p. 5).

There are a number of ways children learn sound-symbol relationships in instructional settings; no significant differences in their effectiveness have been found (Stahl, 1998). Four of the most common approaches are synthetic phonics, analytic phonics, analogy-based phonics, and multi-strategy instruction. A **synthetic phonics** approach first teaches children the individual sounds represented by letters and letter combinations and how to blend those sounds to pronounce words. Then, the relationships or phonics generalizations that apply are identified (Harris & Hodges, 1995). For example, after the child learns the sounds of the letters /b/, short /a/, and /t/, they can be asked to blend the sounds /b/, /a/, and /t/ to produce the word *bat*.

An **analytic phonics** approach teaches children a store of sight words and relevant generalizations, and then students are asked to apply these to decode unknown words (Barone et al., 2006). For example, after teaching students the words *bat, bus,* and *big,* they can be asked to find the common letter and sound in each word, in this case /b/. An **analogy-based** instructional approach engages students in a study of word families or word parts. They are taught to use parts of words they already know to identify new words (Morrow & Morgan, 2006). For example, children who already know the words *bat, cat,* and *mat* can be asked to use their knowledge of the /at/ sound to identify the words *fat, rat,* and *sat.*

A multi-strategy approach to instruction is based on the concept that good readers use multiple cues to identify words (Strickland, 2005). In this approach, children are taught to use all available clues, including how the word is used in the sentence (**syntactic cues**), what makes sense (**semantic cues**), and how the word looks (graphic cues), to identify a word. Regardless of the approach selected, children must have authentic experiences in reading and writing words in order to apply their newly learned skills (Barone et al., 2006). Phonics instruction is a means to an end and should never be the dominant element in any balanced reading program (National Reading Panel, 2000).

Explicit instruction requires that teachers clearly state the word identification skill to be taught and model the use of that skill to figure out unknown words (Caldwell & Leslie, 2009; White, 2005). It is possible to begin instruction with an exploration of words, so that the student has an opportunity to figure out or find a pattern on his or her own (e.g., word sorts or making words). However, to be truly explicit, the targeted concept or generalization being studied must be stated to the student at the conclusion of the activity (Mesmer & Griffith, 2005).

As described in the first part of this chapter, understandings about sound-symbol relationships and the ways written words work occur over time. Word learning is developmental, and effective instruction will closely match the child's phase of development (Mesmer & Griffith, 2005). This is especially true of struggling readers. It makes little sense to target word identification instruction that requires capabilities students have not yet acquired. However, once a child's predominant developmental phase is identified, instruction can capitalize on what she or he can do by providing activities that will move her or him from one phase to the next (Ehri & McCormick, 2004).

What Particular Interventions Help to Develop Word Identification Skills?

There are scores of activities that support the development of word identification, and these can be found in texts and online. The general instructional interventions described in the final section of this chapter are appropriate for those students in three of Ehri's (2004) developmental phases. These are the areas beyond the emergent literacy stage (discussed in Chapter 2), and they can help struggling readers who are likely to require explicit and systematic instruction. The content of a particular intervention will need to be modified to match the learner, but the instructional procedures remain the same. For example, the word sort activity described later for students in the pre-alphabetic phase may target beginning sounds or a pre-primer or primer list of sight words, whereas learners in the consolidated phase may be asked to complete sorts that focus on common syllables.

Word Banks and Personal Readers. Individual word banks are flexible and powerful tools that help children build a sight vocabulary, learn high-frequency words, and learn about word patterns (Lipson & Wixson, 2003; Strickland, 2005).

A word bank is a collection of words that a child builds over time by selecting words that she or he can remember well enough to read in isolation (Bear et al., 2004). Each word is written on a small card, and these are stored together, often in a file box or notebook. Regular review that encourages the student to interact with the words, looking carefully at individual letters and sounds, sorting for patterns, and using them purposefully in writing, will help move the student toward automaticity with those words.

Bear et al. (2004) suggested combining the building of word banks with the creation of personal readers. Tying the word bank words to meaningful, familiar texts increases the likelihood that students will thoroughly learn the words. Personal readers are student copies of **language experience charts** built by the class, personal stories that students have dictated to the teacher, and simple texts, poems, or teacher-selected passages. Each personal reader is numbered, and the date it is given to the student is recorded. The student then underlines the words she knows best, and the teacher transfers these to cards that are stored in the student's word bank. Each card is marked with the same number as the personal reader from which it came, allowing the student to match the word bank word to its corresponding item in the reader.

Students add to their individual word banks slowly, but there will come a time when the banks become so large that they lose their usefulness. Bear et al. (2004) offered the following three signs that indicate it is time to discontinue using word banks:

1. The student is at the end of the alphabetic phase.

2. The student's word bank contains at least 200 words.

3. It is possible to create word sort activities in which students recognize nearly all of the words easily. (p. 152)

Sorting. The brain is a pattern seeker (Cunningham, 1999), and sorting helps the brain discover similarities and differences within and across words. Sorting activities are a match for what the brain does naturally. Using picture sorts with learners in the pre-alphabetic and partial alphabetic phases reinforces their knowledge of letter-sound correspondences (Gunning, 2001). As children grow in their understandings about letters, sounds, and words, the teacher replaces pictures with whole words during sorting activities.

Sorting words is an engaging and enjoyable experience that allows learners to analyze and categorize words in a variety of ways. There are two types of sorts: In a **closed sort**, the teacher tells the students what feature to look for in a group of words. In an **open sort,** the students categorize the words according to features and are challenged to discover the pattern (Pinnell & Fountas, 1998). A few examples of categories for sorting are listed in the chart that follows.

Prefix/suffix	Beginning/ending sound
Number of syllables	Long vowel sounds/short vowels sounds
Rhymes	Parts of speech
Onset/rimes	Word roots
Homophones/homonyms	Synonyms/antonyms

Bear et al. (2004) suggested the following four steps when conducting closed or teacher-directed sorts:

1. Demonstrate: Introduce the words by pronouncing, defining, and using each in a sentence. Display key words or pattern cues as column headers; shuffle the cards and explicitly state the category by which students will be asked to sort the words. For example, "Today we are going to listen for the sounds of /an/ and /at/ at the end of these words." Model sorting several words. For example, "This is the word *can*. It has the /an/ sound at the end, so I will put it under the *an* column. This word is *bat*. It has the /at/ sound at the end, so I will put it under the *at* column." Allow students to complete the sort and correct errors immediately.

2. Sort and Check: This part of the activity can be done by students individually or in pairs. Students should reshuffle the cards; select an individual card; name the word aloud; and place it under the correct pattern cue in the column heading. Students may put aside any words that they cannot read. Ask students to rename the words in each column to check for accuracy. For misplaced cards, tell students how many words have been misplaced and in which column, so they can attempt to find them.

3. Declare, Compare, and Contrast: After the second sort is completed, ask students, "What do you notice about the words in each column." The goal is to help students declare their knowledge about the sound, pattern or meaning being explored in their own words.

4. Extend: Students can continue to sort the words a number of times, hunt for similar words, and add the word to their word-study books or word banks. These extensions and others solidify their understandings. (pp. 74–76)

Kathleen Strickland (2005) offered the following five steps for open or student-directed sorts:

1. Provide children with word bags or, alternatively, ask them to use their word banks and lay their words out on their desks or on the floor.

2. Ask them to sort their words into as many different categories as they can.

3. After allowing time to sort words, ask one child to read words from one category.

4. Other students then guess what criteria the child used for sorting.

5. There is no one correct way for open sorts; allow children to come up with their own categories. (p. 67)

Interactive Writing. Pinnell and Fountas (1998) described **interactive writing** as a "teacher guided group activity designed to teach children about the writing process and about how written language works" (p. 191). Interactive writing links word study to writing supporting children's spelling development as well as word knowledge.

During an interactive writing lesson, the teacher guides the students in the creation of a text that might be a classroom message, a story, or a shared experience. Children take turns writing as the text is built collectively. The goal is a product that is error-free, so the teacher spends a good deal of time engaging children in guided discussions of the ways words look and sound as well as the conventions of language. Interactive writing can be used productively across grade levels (Wall, 2008) and should be part of a balanced program that includes ample time for students to write their own texts (Pinnell & Fountas, 1998).

Cloze. As noted earlier in the chapter, one of the ways we come to identify words is through predicting—that is, using graphophonic, syntactic, and semantic cues to help recognize a given word. Bean and Bouffler (1997) suggested that requiring students to complete cloze passages provides them with opportunities to use these three cueing systems of our language. By controlling for the types of deletions, students may be compelled to focus more heavily on one of the systems. Cloze activities can be done individually or with small or large groups.

Written Cloze. Bean and Bouffler (1997) outlined a four-step process in the *written cloze* activity. First, select a short passage that is within the students' instructional level. Second, leave the first sentence intact and delete words in the remaining sentences at regular intervals (every five or every ten words). When using a controlled cloze procedure, delete graphophonic, or syntactic, or semantic elements only. Third, have the students complete the passage cooperatively or independently. Following this, discuss each of the missing words and allow the students to compare their responses to the original. Any meaningful word that addresses the element selected for study should be accepted.

Making Words. This activity is hands-on and allows children to explore sound-letter relationships, to look for word patterns, and to realize that changing one letter or a sequence of letters can change an entire word. According to Cunningham and Cunningham (1992), the steps in planning and implementing a making-words activity are as follows:

- Planning for the activity
  - Select a final word, the secret word, for study, considering the letter-sound relationships that can be made and the students' background and interests.
  - Make a list of shorter words, and from these select 12 to 15 words that
    - have a pattern;
    - constitute a mix of both little and big words;
    - use the same letters but can be ordered differently, so that children are reminded that order matters;
    - include a proper name or two requiring capitalization; and
    - are in the students' listening vocabularies.
  - Write the words on index cards, and order them from longest to shortest.
  - Order each of the two-letter, three-letter, and so on, words together, so that patterns and differences can be emphasized.
  - Store cards in an envelope and write the words and the patterns you wish to sort for at the end of the lesson on the envelope.

- Conducting the activity
  - Use a pocket chart that holds each of the large letter cards or large magnetic letters and a magnetic whiteboard. Also, prepare several bags, each with all the letters of the secret word, so that every student has the opportunity to make words.
  - Hold up and name each of the letters (not in order, so as not to give away the secret word), and ask the students to hold up their matching letter cards and then place them in front of them (at their desks or on the floor).
  - Begin with the shortest words. Write the numeral signaling the number of letters in the word on the board and ask students to choose from their letters to make the first word. State the word and use it in a sentence. Check the students' words for accuracy, and ask one child who

has made the correct word to come to the pocket chart and make the same word using the big letters. Ask students to check and correct their word if they made a mistake.

○ Continue through the list of words in this manner, each time letting the students know how many letters are in the word and cueing them as to whether they are to change one letter, move letters around, start with a capital letter, or take all their letters away to begin again from scratch. Each time, state the word and use it in a sentence.

○ When all the words but the final one have been made, ask whether anyone has figured out the secret word. If the word is known, ask one of the students who guessed correctly to make the word in the pocket chart. If the word is not known, say it and use it in a sentence. Then, tell students to use all their letters to make the secret word.

○ Display all of the word cards one at a time in the pocket chart, asking the students to say and spell the words as you do so. Sort these words for the patterns you selected in the planning phase. To do this, hold up one word that contains the pattern, explicitly state what it is, and ask the students to find other words with the same pattern. Line these up so that the pattern is visible.

○ End the activity by asking the children to spell a few new words that contain the patterns you have been exploring with them.

Intervening With Technology. Software and online resources designed to provide multiple encounters with letter-sound correspondences, onset-rime relationships, and sight words can have a powerful effect on the development of children's word identification skills (Sherman, Kleimand, & Peterson, 2004). A few are listed here.

- *Microsoft PowerPoint.* Teachers can teach a variety of word identification skills using Microsoft PowerPoint slides. Images, sounds, and animations easily capture children's attention. Parette, Blum, Boeckmann, and Watts (2009) offered a detailed description of how to prepare and use PowerPoint slides to teach word recognition.

- *Zoodles.com (www.zoodles.com).* A website that contains multiple activities in areas of math, reading, science, and social studies. After registering the child or children on the site, content can be selected matched to the child's age and interests. This website draws content from other sites such as Starfall, PBS Kids, and Between the Lions. The basic membership is free.

Educational software and online resources, if carefully chosen, can support word identification instruction in engaging ways.

- *iPad or iPod applications.* Students can access a variety of applications that provide independent practice in engaging and entertaining ways. One such app is *K–3 Sight Words.* Children can practice Dolch sight words using this application. Words are categorized by grade level, K through 3. Each word appears as a flash card, and the child can click on the listen button to hear it pronounced.

Section IV: The Cases

The two assessment case reports that follow will help you explore the issues related to word identification. As you read, consider the word-learning phase that is predominant for each child, the word identification skills of each, and which interventions might be used to help develop their skills further.

CASE 1: ASSESSMENT REPORT FOR CHAD B.

Background Information

Child's name: Chad B.
Current age: 8
Current grade level: End of Grade 1

Referral

Chad's first grade teacher referred him to the Reading Center to be assessed. She is concerned that his reading and writing abilities are weak and that he will not be successful in second grade.

Family and Medical History

Chad, an eight-year-old boy, lives on a small farm outside a rural village. His father works at a retail outlet in town, and his mother is a stay-at-home mom. He and his two younger sisters were adopted from Russia when Chad was three years old. His first language was Russian. He continued to speak Russian for the first four months after being adopted; however, English was and is the primary language spoken in his new home.

Chad's adoptive parents report that he and his sisters were placed in a Russian orphanage when Chad was two, due to neglect from their biological mother. The orphanage followed a rigid schedule, and Chad spent much of his time in large playpens where he was able to interact with other children. At the time of his adoption, he spoke Russian very well for his age. Chad's early medical and developmental history is unknown. He now seems to be in good general health.

Chad's adoptive mother completed a parent survey (see Figure 3.1) indicating that his working memory is weak and that he has recall difficulties. He is able to memorize sight words from flash card drills, but he does not recognize the words if they are presented in a different format. Chad's mother noted that he is generally happy, likes reading, and works well with teachers.

Figure 3.1   Reading Center Parent Survey for Chad B.: Child as Learner

1. What are your child's free-time interests?

   Chad loves art projects, hockey, T-ball, going on adventures in our backwoods.

2. What types of books does your child enjoy?

   He likes to be read any book. He enjoys reading books that he knows he is capable of reading without difficulty.

3. What types of writing does your child do at home?

   We have done letter practicing to improve his penmanship with great results.

4. What are your observations about how your child learns?

   He learns better one-on-one and with repetition. With his learning disabilities, we know he suffers from short working memory. If he gets frustrated and you can get him through that calmly he can continue on.

5. What are some other things you would like us to know about your child?

   We adopted our son and his two siblings from Russia. He spoke Russian very well for his age. He is generally a happy kid and willingly works with all his teachers, paraprofessionals. Very Honest.

6. In what ways do you think we can best help your child?

   Chad has difficulty even remembering the basic sight words. He can know them on flash cards but if they are put onto a piece of paper or printed on another flashcard in a different color he struggles many times with knowing that word. He loves math and does good at adding, subtracting, even fractions. Trouble with counting money and telling time on a clock. We are tutoring him with his current teacher to help him get a grasp of things preparing him for second grade.

Source: Form adapted from *Practical Aspects of Authentic Assessment: Putting the Pieces Together* (pp. 205–207), by B. Hill and C. Ruptic, 1994, Norwood, MA: Christopher-Gordon.

School History

Chad has just completed first grade in a K through sixth school located in a rural, upper Midwest community. During the school year, he received an additional 30 minutes of reading instruction per day. His classroom teacher reported that he loves to listen to stories, has a keen sense of empathy, and has even memorized the texts of stories he has heard repeatedly. However, he has not mastered all letter-sound relationships and his fluency fluctuates daily. While he has many ideas for writing, written expression is a challenge. During reading time, he receives individual support in phonics and currently reads from a pre-primer level text. The 45-minute daily writing workshop provides him with individualized support. (See Figure 3.2 for the complete response.)

Figure 3.2 Classroom Teacher Referral Form for Chad B.

1. Please describe the nature of the child's reading and writing. What does this child do well, and in what areas do you perceive weakness?

   Chad loves to listen to stories. He has a keen sense of empathy. He notices emotional parts of a story and is touched by them, much more than his peers. He remembers stories he has heard to the point where he has memorized the text. Chad has not mastered all letter-sound relationships, which causes him great stress in reading and writing. It sometimes appears as if looking at these symbols is painful for him.

   He has great ideas to write about, but to get them on paper so anyone else understands is a challenge. He was once writing facts about the Snowy Owl. He wrote this: "The Snowy Owl flies softly so the mice do not hear him." That is pretty awesome for a first grader, but only the teacher that helped him could have deciphered it, and Chad can't always remember it. Chad loves to draw and his illustrations match his written ideas.

2. Instructional strategies, activities, etc., used with this child.

   In the classroom, we work individually with Chad to reinforce, review, and encourage his learning of letter-sound relationships and phonic skills. Many visual cues and songs are used for association. He is currently reading from the 1.1 pre-primer book. (Chad's fluency really fluctuates with the day, but he joins the rest of the class to listen/join in on the literature they are reading.) We have writing workshop for 45 minutes. He receives lots of individual support and encouragement here as well.

The Title I instructor reported that, after a lot of repetition, Chad is able to memorize sight words. Sounding out words is difficult for him, and he spends a lot of time decoding, so his fluency is often compromised. He can, however, read through familiar books very quickly and accurately on some days.

Comprehension is good if stories have been read to him first. (See the full report in Figure 3.3.)

Chad's IEP (Individualized Educational Plan), completed in May, was given to the Reading Center examiner. The report stated that Chad's working memory is below that of his age-equivalent peers and that his expressive vocabulary skills are below average. He makes occasional errors in letter sounds and has particular difficulty pronouncing multisyllabic words. Still, according the assessment results, his articulation and phonological awareness skills are typical of those of an end of first grader.

Figure 3.3   Title I Teacher Referral Form for Chad B.

1. Please describe the nature of the child's reading and writing.

   Chad has memorized sight words with a lot of repetition. Sounding out can be difficult as he has a tough time associating sounds with some of the letters. Since he spends a lot of time decoding words, his reading can be choppy. Chad can read through books he knows very quickly and accurately on some days, some days he needs more time. Comprehension is good, especially after stories have been read to Chad first.

2. Please describe any strategies, materials, or activities that have been used with this child.

   In addition to classroom word-attack strategies, it has been recommended for Chad to use flashcards with the word and a picture, then to cut the picture off once he has the word down. Chad's parents practice reading with him at home, and he is also receiving reading instruction from the resource room teacher.

3. What is the child's attitude toward reading and school in general?

   When Chad becomes frustrated with school or reading, in general, it shows as he becomes angry, or we say "crabby." When teachers talk to him about "attitude," his mood changes or improves.

4. Is this child receiving special services of any kind?

   Title I Reading 30 min./day

Any comments or suggestions?

Chad would benefit from additional practice over the summer to retain the skills he has learned. He would benefit from more exposure to sight words as he needs repetition to memorize them.

Detailed Assessment Information

Session 1

Interest Survey. The examiner asked Chad the questions on the interest survey (Hill & Ruptic, 1994, pp. 175–176) and wrote down the following answers as he spoke:

- Chad is an active child who enjoys playing basketball, T-ball, and hockey and wants to be an explorer when he grows up.
- His favorite subject is reading because he likes "learning about stuff." However, he doesn't like reading when it is hard.
- When asked about his reading goals, he said he wants to learn more words so that he can become a better reader.

Chad answered the interest interview questions very quickly. Sometimes his answers didn't make sense, and so the examiner reworded the questions to be sure she understood what Chad meant.

Attitudes About Reading and Writing. The examiner read the Garfield Writing Attitude Survey (Kear, Coffman, McKenna, & Ambrosio, 2000) to Chad first and, after a brief snack break, followed up with the Garfield Elementary Reading Survey (McKenna & Kear, 1990). Chad's percentile rank on the Writing Attitude Survey was 63. On the Reading Survey, his full scale percentile rank was 46, with a clear preference in recreational reading (65th percentile) over academic reading (34th percentile). For both surveys, Chad circled many of the responses before the examiner had completed the statements. Also, he interrupted several times to ask the examiner unrelated questions.

Session 2

Burke Reading Interview (Goodman, Watson, & Burke, 1987, pp. 219–220). The examiner recorded Chad's answers to the 10 questions on the interview (see Figure 3.4). It was clear that Chad felt that he had only one strategy as a reader: to ask for help. Interestingly, however, he rated himself as a terrific reader.

Figure 3.4 Burke Reading Interview Results for Chad B.

1. When you are reading and come to something you don't know, what do you do?

   Ask for help

2. Do you ever do anything else?

   Ask a friend

3. Who do you know who is a good reader?

   Adriana (a school friend)

4. What makes him/her a good reader?

   I don't know

5. Do you think she/he ever comes to a word she/he doesn't know when reading?

   Yes

   If your answer is yes, what do you think she/he does about it?

   Asks for help

6. What do you think is the best way to help someone who doesn't read well?

   Ask someone for them (ask someone for help for them)

7. How did you learn to read? What do you remember? What helped you to learn?

   I don't know

8. What would you like to do better as a reader?

   Read words better, listen better

9. Describe yourself as a reader.

   I read good, read easy words good

10. Using a scale of 5 to 1 with 5 being a terrific reader, what overall rating would you give yourself as a reader?

    5

Source: Form adapted from *Reading Miscue Inventory: Alternative Procedures* (pp. 219–220), by Y. Goodman, D. Watson, and C. Burke, 1987, Katonah, NY: Richard C. Owens.

Developmental Reading Assessment (Beaver, 2001). Based on the information gained from surveys, and in keeping with the DRA guidelines, the examiner selected four DRA texts at Levels 1 through 4 for the formal assessment. These texts were in the kindergarten range and the equivalent of Guided Reading Levels A through C (Fountas & Pinnell, 1996). Chad's predictions about the Level 1 book provided evidence that this text would be at his independent level, so the examiner began with a Level 2 book, *Bath Time* (DeLapp, 2002a). His accuracy rate in this 34-word predictable text was 94%, with two miscues and two self-corrections. His first attempt for the word *purple* was *pink.* He looked at the picture and self-corrected the miscue. A bit later on, he substituted *purple* for *pink* but again looked at the picture and corrected the error. He had one omission (*I* at the beginning of a sentence) and one substitution: *bubbles* for *bath.*

Because he seemed comfortable, and because this text appeared to be at his instructional level, the examiner continued on to Level 3. Chad completed the picture walk for *Look at Me* (DeLapp, 2002c) and was able to make several feasible predictions. He read the text with 90% accuracy. His retelling was limited and required a good deal of prompting from the examiner. A summary of the DRA Observation Guide is provided in Figure 3.5.

Figure 3.5   Summary DRA Assessment for Chad B.

Text: *Look at Me: Level 3* (Grade Level Equivalent K, Guided Reading Level C)

Previewing and Predicting Response (after completing a picture walk):

Chad gathered enough information to make several appropriate predictions.

Oral Reading Miscues			
Page/Line	Text Words	Words Said	Error Type
10/1	said the boy	the boy said (counted as 3 errors)	Substitution
12/2	We	Will	Substitution
12/2	rope	rup	Substitution
12/3	said	sad	Self-correction

Total Errors: 5

Accuracy: 90%

Total Self-Corrections: 1

Source: Form adapted from *DRA Observation Guide,* by J. Beaver, 2002, Parsippany, NJ: Celebration Press.

Fluency

Chad read in short phrases most of the time with some intonation.

At Difficulty

Chad used picture clues heavily and some phonics knowledge (initial sound) when he came to difficult text. He paused at *slide* saying s—lide and at *skate* saying s—kate.

Comprehension (Score of 9: Very Little Comprehension)

Chad was able to list the characters and understood the setting when prompted. He was able to retell what happened at the very beginning of the story when asked, but provided minimal responses. He was able to relate his favorite part of the story: *When the girl said, "look at me, I can rollerblade,"* although the word *skate* was used in the text. He was not able to make any connections, and when asked, *"What did the story make you think of?"* he responded, *"Nothing."*

Additional Examiner Notes

I wonder whether Chad's retelling was poor because he was getting antsy and wanted to be done? We had only been working for 15 minutes at this time, but he seemed tired.

Session 3

Informal Writing Assessment. After reading the book *I Like Me* (Carlson, 1990), the examiner asked Chad to write a completion of the prompt "I like . . ." as many times as he could think of responses. He wrote five sentences (see Figure 3.6) and made multiple spelling errors.

The examiner wanted to see what spellings Chad would produce in an unprompted text and so asked him to write, unaided, about something he had done recently. He wrote one sentence ("I am working with my tractor.") and drew a picture (see Figure 3.7).

Figure 3.6 Informal Writing Assessment for Chad B.

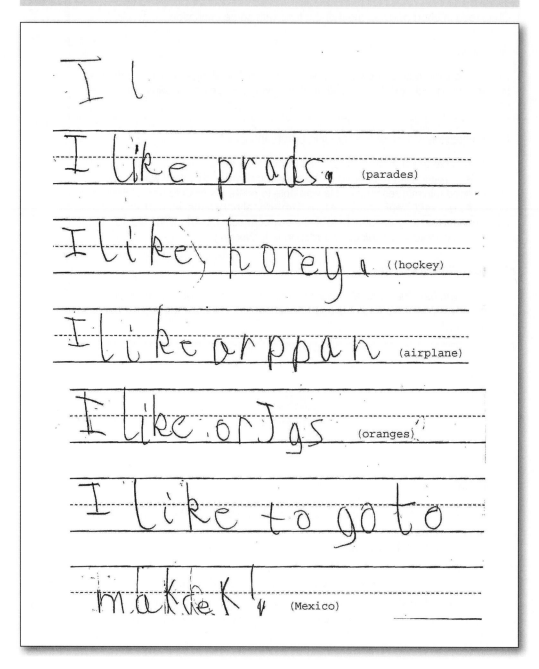

Figure 3.7 Unprompted Writing Sample of Chad B.

Session 4

Informal Letter Sounds Assessment. Based on the results of the writing task, the examiner decided to assess Chad's knowledge of letters and letter sounds. Chad identified all 26 of the uppercase letters and 25 of those in lowercase. When trying to identify some of the letter names, he sang the alphabet song. He did not recognize the letter *d*. He identified 20 of the 26 sounds. The errors he made were as follows:

- For E and Y, he said he didn't know the sounds.
- For T, he said *it*.
- For U, he said the long *e* sound.
- For X, he said *n*.
- For C, he said *ch*.

It took him a long time to complete this assessment.

Developmental Reading Assessment (Beaver, 2001). Although the Level 3 text Chad had read in Session 2 was at his frustration level, the examiner wanted to further explore his word recognition strategies and so selected a Level 4 text, *Get Your Umbrella* (DeLapp, 2002b). Chad completed the picture walk, making many appropriate predictions. He made miscues, including omissions, substitutions, and one insertion. He seemed to attend to beginning sounds or picture cues to help him identify words. His oral reading accuracy was at 87%. He read word-by-word in a monotone voice. Interestingly, he was able to retell all of the key events in sequence with only one prompt and referred to the characters by name. A summary of the DRA Observation Guide is provided in Figure 3.8.

Additional Information

Examiner Anecdotal Notes

After Session 1. While I was reading aloud to relax Chad before beginning with the more formal assessments, he began to get antsy and kicked his sandal off. I am not sure if he has to fiddle while he is listening or just has a hard time sitting. After the interest survey, I read aloud from a different book. While I read, he started playing with a pointer that I have that is in the shape of a flower. I continued to let him play with it because I wanted to see if he was still able to listen. He correctly answered all of the questions that I asked during and after reading.

Case Recap:

1. Review the case and the notes you have taken in response to the guiding questions one final time, and add or revise any information you may have missed.

2. Make a list of additional questions you have about the case. What further information do you need that might be explored in the case discussion?

3. Think about Chad's early language experiences. To what extent might his first language (Russian) be affecting his reading development?

Figure 3.8 Summary DRA Observation Guide for Chad B.

Text: *Get Your Umbrella* (Grade Level Equivalent K, Guided Reading Level C)

Previewing and Predicting Response (after completing a picture walk): Gathered enough information to make several appropriate predictions.

Oral Reading Miscues			
Page/Line	Text Words	Words Said	Error Type
2/1	rain	rain	Repetition*
2/1	said	said	Repetition
3/1	Kim	——	Omission
5/1	kitchen	chair	Substitution
5/2	it	is	Substitution
5/2	is	the	Substitution
5/2	——	umbrella	Insertion
5/2: The phrase in the text read *Here it is*. Chad said, *Here is the umbrella.*			
6/1	Dad	——	Omission
6/1	——	said	Insertion
Total Errors: 7—Accuracy: 87%			
Total Self-Corrections: 0			

*Repetitions are noted, but not counted as errors.

Fluency

Chad read in a monotone, mostly word-by-word but sometimes in short phrases.

He used some intonation and attended to punctuation some of the time.

At Difficulty

Chad used picture clues, attempted to sound out unknown words, and paused several times when reading.

Comprehension (Score 22: Very Good Comprehension)

Chad's retelling was complete and correct. He referred to the main characters by name and included many details from the story. His interpretation of the story was at the literal level. The examiner used only one prompt to guide Chad's retelling.

Additional Examiner Notes

Chad blew me away on this one. He told me every event in the order that it happened. I was amazed. When I asked him what his favorite part of the book was he said it was when Dad told Kim the sun was out.

Source: Form adapted from *DRA Observation Guide*, by J. Beaver, 2002, Parsippany, NJ: Celebration Press.

CASE 2: ASSESSMENT REPORT FOR KAYLA E.

Background Information

Child's name: Kayla E.
Current age: 8
Current grade level: End of Grade 2

Referral

Kayla's second grade teacher and her mother referred her to the Center for assessment.

Family and Medical History

Kayla, an eight-year-old girl, lives with her mother and stepfather in a small city with a population of 57,000. Her father lives and works on an American Indian reservation in the north central part of the state. She spends weekends with him occasionally. Kayla, a Native American, lived on the reservation with her grandmother for a time when she was younger. The primary language spoken in both homes is English. There are no physical concerns; however, she was tested for an emotional disorder the previous year and results indicated possible difficulties with anxiety, depression, and attentiveness.

Kayla's mother completed the survey *My Child as a Learner*. She described Kayla as a physically active child with a "great imagination." She noted that she lacks confidence in reading and no longer enjoys it. She does, however, enjoy telling stories and will expand on the real things that have happened to her. See Figure 3.9 for complete information.

School History

Kayla has just completed second grade in a K through fifth school located in a neighborhood in the north end of the city. She received Title I services in reading for all of Grade 1 and the first part of Grade 2. She was tested for learning disabilities and was found to have deficits in reading, writing, and speech. Her cognitive functioning, communicative status, motor ability, sensory status, and health and physical status were all reported to be within the average range. She now receives special education services for reading and speech.

Kayla's teacher reported that she has improved as a reader and writer since the beginning of the school year but is still at the emergent level. She noted that Kayla is not a risk taker; if unsuccessful, she "shuts down." (See the full survey response in Figure 3.10.)

Figure 3.9   Reading Center Parent Survey for Kayla E.: Child as Learner

1. What are your child's free-time interests?

   She loves sports: baseball, soccer, floor hockey, kickball, riding bike, skate boarding, and she also likes to watch the cartoon network.

2. What types of books does your child enjoy?

   Books about spiders, animals, Fantasy (Harry Potter)

3. What types of writing does your child do at home?

   She is always leaving notes for me or play notes when pretending to be spy.

4. What are your observations about how your child learns?

   She learns best in one/one settings. She is very visual and kinesthetic.

5. What are some other things you would like us to know about your child?

   She has a great imagination and loves to expand on "real" things that have happened.

6. In what ways do you think we can best help your child?

   I feel any extra reading practice, strategies, or fun would be great for her confidence and self-esteem. If she reads something and it doesn't make sense, she'll say it out loud and try to figure out what doesn't fit. She is not very confident at all. She often says she can't.

Source: Form adapted from *Practical Aspects of Authentic Assessment: Putting the Pieces Together* (pp. 206–207), by B. Hill and C. Ruptic, 1994, Norwood, MA: Christopher-Gordon.

Figure 3.10   Classroom Teacher Referral Form for Kayla E.

1. Please describe the nature of the child's reading and writing.

   Kayla is an emergent reader and writer. This is a big improvement since fall. She is quite a visual learner. She will take more risks in writing.

2. Please describe any strategies, materials, or activities that have been used with this child.

   Basic sight words, phonic skills, repetitive story lines, small group and one-on-one

3. What is the child's attitude toward reading and school in general?

   Not consistent in risk-taking. Wants to be successful and if isn't she shuts down.

(Continued)

Figure 3.10 (Continued)

4. Is this child receiving special services of any kind?

   LD: Reading and Speech-language: language expressive; concept, verb tenses, etc.

Any comments or suggestions?

Has low self-esteem in reading—is feeling more like a reader but needs early success to stay motivated.

Detailed Assessment Information

Session 1

Interest Survey. When the examiner asked Kayla to complete the *About Me* survey, she initially worked independently, but as soon as she encountered a word she did not know, she abruptly stopped and asked for help. With the examiner at her side, she completed the survey. She noted that her favorite book was *The Cat in the Hat* (Seuss, 1957). She told the examiner that the "*Cat In the Hat* books" are the only ones that she reads. She likes to spend her free time watching TV and playing sports. See the full survey response with Kayla's own spellings in Figure 3.11.

Attitudes About Reading and Writing. The examiner asked Kayla to complete the Garfield Reading and Writing Attitude Surveys and read each item to her. Kayla circled each item quickly and impatiently, wanting to end the task as quickly as possible. On the reading survey, her full scale percentile rank was 54; however, she showed a preference for academic reading (57th percentile) over recreational reading (50th percentile) when compared with midyear second grade students. Her percentile rank on the writing survey was 36 when compared with midyear second grade students. The most negative responses (scored 1 out of a possible 4) were for items that asked about making revisions in her writing.

Figure 3.11   *About Me* Interest Survey for Kayla E.

I live with *my mom and stepdad*.

When I get home from school I like to *woh* (watch) *TV*.

My favorite TV show is *dinse chanl*.

My favorite movie is *hare potr*.

I participate in sport called *soff Ball*.

I spend time on my hobby, which is *TV*

My favorite subject in school is *resis* (recess) *mahs* (math).

My favorite thing to read is *cat in the hat*.

Topics I like to read about include *cat in the hat*.

My plans for my future include *go Back to cile* school*.

Other things about me that I'd like to share are *spost* (sports) *tinisis* (tennis).

*This was the name of the school; the "c" should have been the letter "k" and the "e" a "y."

Burke Reading Interview. The examiner read the prompts from the reading interview and dictated Kayla's responses. Although she rated herself as a "terrific reader," other responses indicated that she used few strategies when faced with challenging text: "give up," "ask for help," or "pick another book." (See Figure 3.12 for the complete survey results.)

Session 2

High-Frequency Word List. The examiner began Session 2 by asking Kayla to read from a list of high-frequency words. This particular word list, used in the Reading Center for almost two decades, was subdivided into lists ranging from pre-primer through seventh grade. Kayla read all 42 words in the pre-primer list correctly. She read 91% of the primer list correctly and made the following errors:

- *down* for *did*
- *lunch* for *laugh*
- *now* for *new*

Figure 3.12 Burke Reading Interview Results for Kayla E.

1. When you are reading and come to something you don't know, what do you do?

   Nothing, give up

2. Do you ever do anything else?

   Ask for help

3. Who do you know who is a good reader?

   My teacher

4. What makes him/her a good reader?

   She can read chapter books.

5. Do you think she/he ever comes to a word she/he doesn't know when reading?

   No, I don't think.

   If your answer is yes, what do you think she/he does about it?

6. What do you think is the best way to help someone who doesn't read well?

   Ask a teacher

   Read a different "just right" book.

7. How did you learn to read? What do you remember? What helped you to learn?

   I don't know. In kindergarten we read books. My cousin read to me. My teacher helped me, telling us words, reading the pictures.

8. What would you like to do better as a reader?

   Memorize what I read and learn what words mean.

9. Describe yourself as a reader.

   Read the Cat in the Hat books.

10. Using a scale of 5 to 1 with 5 being a terrific reader, what overall rating would you give yourself as a reader?

    5

Source: Original form in *Reading Miscue Inventory: Alternative Procedures* (pp. 219–220), by Y. Goodman, D. Watson, and C. Burke, 1987, Katonah, NY: Richard C. Owens.

She omitted *what*. When she read the first grade list, she slowed down considerably even though the examiner encouraged her to move along. She read 75% of the words correctly but made several omissions and errors, as shown in the chart that follows:

Omissions	Errors
• around	• *eat* for *ate*
• cold	• *be* for *by*
• could	• *fat* for *far*
• every	• *ho* for *how*
• first	• *now* for *know*
• our	• *where* for *were*
• pretty	
• round	
• why	

Her frustration increased as she read through the second grade list, omitting 29 of the 59 words. She made one error, reading *dirt* for *draw*. Her accuracy rate was 49%.

Developmental Spelling Test. Because of the inconsistency of her spellings on the interest survey, the examiner wanted to determine Kayla's developmental stage and so administered the *Developmental Spelling Test* (Gentry & Wallace, 1993). The results of the test are displayed in Figure 3.13. Kayla is primarily at the *phonetic spelling* stage.

Figure 3.13 Developmental Spelling Test Results for Kayla E.

Word Dictated	Word Spelled	Stage
1. monster	mostr	Phonetic
2. united	unitdid	Phonetic
3. dress	dras	Phonetic/Transitional
4. bottom	Botm	Phonetic
5. hiked	hikt	Phonetic

(Continued)

Figure 3.13 (Continued)

Word Dictated	Word Spelled	Stage
6. human	hemin	Phonetic
7. eagle	egl	Phonetic
8. closed	clos	Phonetic
9. bumped	Bumt	Phonetic
10. type	tipt	Phonetic

Source: Adapted from *Teaching Kids to Spell,* by J. Gentry and J. Wallace, 1993, Portsmouth, NH: Heinemann.

Session 3

Informal Writing Assessment. The examiner also wanted to see what spellings Kayla would produce in her own text and so asked her to write a journal entry about anything she wanted. Her entry was about a dog named Casey (spelled *case*). She wrote the equivalent of seven sentences but used end punctuation only twice. Her misspellings were as follows:

- *Munda* for *Monday*
- *win* for *when*
- *gud* for *good*
- *vey* for *very*
- *spish* for *special*
- *lwisd* for *always*
- *ranovr* for *ran over*

She also used *he* for *him* twice. Her writing sample is provided in Figure 3.14.

Developmental Reading Assessment (DRA). Based on the information gained from surveys, and in keeping with the DRA guidelines, the examiner selected DRA texts at Levels 10 through 14 for the formal assessment. These texts were in the first grade range and the equivalent of Guided Reading Levels E through H (Fountas & Pinnell, 1996). From among these, Kayla selected *The Wagon* (Maione, 2006) as a "just right" book for her. She completed a picture walk and

Figure 3.14   Unprompted Writing Sample for Kayla E.

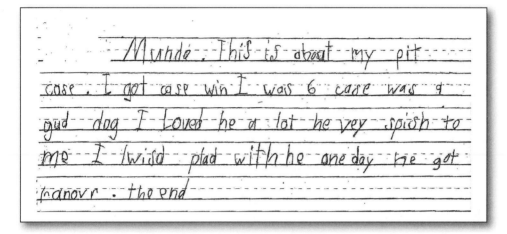

was able to label events and actions logically without prompting. Her accuracy rate for this 203-word text was 91%, with 18 miscues and two self-corrections. All but one of the miscues was a substitution. For the majority of miscues, she seemed to attend to the beginning sounds to identify the words. Her oral reading was rather monotone, and she yawned several times as she moved through the passage. Still, her retelling was complete. A summary of the DRA Observation Guide is provided in Figure 3.15.

Figure 3.15   Summary DRA Observation Guide for Kayla E.

Text: *The Wagon: Level 14* (Grade Level Equivalent 1, Guided Reading Level H)

Previewing and Predicting Response (after completing a picture walk):

Kayla gathered pertinent information and connected events and actions with no prompting.

Oral Reading Miscues			
Page/Line	Text Words	Words Said	Error Type
2/2	He	His	Substitution
2/2	was	used	Substitution

Figure 3.15 (Continued)

2/3	newspapers	new superpaper new papers	Substitution
3/3	a	——-	Omission
4/2	other	ol older other	Self-correction
4/4	He	The	Substitution
4/4	covered	gravel	Substitution
4/4	with	white	Substitution
4/4	dirt	dirty	Substitution
4/4	sticks	snake	Substitution
4/4	Line of Text: He covered it with dirt and sticks. Kayla's Reading: The gravel it white dirty and snake.		
5/4	dirty	rusty	Substitution
6/3	bucket	brush	Substitution
6/4	other	older other	Self-correction
7/1	They	then	Substitution
7/1	washed	was	Substitution
7/2	dents	dirts	Substitution
7/3	nice	new	Substitution
7/4	better	brand	Substitution
7/4	than	then	Substitution
7/4	new	now	Substitution
Total Errors: 18 Accuracy: 91% Total Self-Corrections: 2			

Fluency

Kayla read word-by-word and occasionally in short phrases and in a monotone.

Source: Adapted from *DRA Observation Guide,* by J. Beaver, 2002, Parsippany, NJ: Celebration Press.

At Difficulty

Kayla used picture clues heavily, paused often, and sometimes reread.

Comprehension (Score of 16: Good Comprehension)

Kayla was able to retell most of the events of the story in sequence and included many details without prompting. She responded with literal interpretation of the story and responded adequately to one teacher prompt. The second prompt, *What does this story make you think of?* elicited a lengthy story about a water-gun fight with her cousin that was not connected to the story.

Additional Examiner Notes

I think Kayla may perform better when she is not observed formally. She's hard on herself and gets mad at herself when she makes mistakes.

Case Recap:

1. Review the case and the notes you have taken in response to the guiding questions one final time, and add or revise any information you may have missed.

2. Make a list of additional questions you have about the case. What further information do you need that might be explored in the case discussion?

3. Consider whether there is a difference in Kayla's word identification skill when she reads words in extended texts versus word lists.

CHAPTER SUMMARY

This chapter focused on the importance of word identification in the reading process. Learning to identify words quickly and effortlessly is a critical element, and without it, the ultimate goal—reading for meaning—cannot be reached. It is important to remember, however, that studying words in isolation is not sufficient to improve children's reading of texts. A well-balanced instructional routine must also include plenty of reading in authentic texts and writing for real purposes. With such a routine, students like Chad and Kayla will have a better chance of gaining all of the skills necessary to develop into independent readers. The next chapter focuses on fluency, an element in reading development that has grown in importance in the last decade.

Terms highlighted in this chapter

decoding 65

predicting 65

rime 65

alphabetic principle 65

pre-alphabetic phase 67

full-alphabetic phase 67

automatic-alphabetic phase 67

miscue analysis 69

precommunicative spelling 72

phonetic spelling 72

conventional spelling 73

analytic phonics 74

syntactic cues 74

language experience charts 76

open sort 76

analogizing 65

onset 65

word structure 65

sight word 66

partial-alphabetic phase 67

consolidated-alphabetic phase 67

informal reading inventories 68

graphophonic cue 69

semiphonetic spelling 72

transitional spelling 72

synthetic phonics 74

analogy-based 74

semantic cues 74

closed sort 76

interactive writing 78

FINAL QUESTIONS FOR REFLECTION AND RESPONSE

1. Review the phases of word learning presented at the beginning of this chapter and determine which phase is predominant for Kayla and for Chad.

2. Using the information provided in this chapter or another source related to word identification instruction, design a lesson that would be appropriate for Kayla and for Chad.

3. Think about the elements related to reading performance, beyond word identification (fluency, vocabulary, comprehension, engagement). Which might also be problem areas for Chad and Kayla? Which might be strengths?

Journals Online

Visit the student study site at www.sagepub.com/combsstudy to access recent, relevant, full-text journal articles from SAGE's leading research journals.

REFERENCES

Barone, D., Hardman, D., & Taylor, J. (2006). *Reading first in the classroom*. Boston: Allyn & Bacon.

Barr, R., Blachowicz, C., Bates, A., Katz, C., & Kaufman, B. (2007). *Reading diagnosis for teachers: An instructional approach* (5th ed.). Boston: Allyn & Bacon.

Bean, W., & Bouffler, C. (1997). *Read, write, spell*. York, ME: Stenhouse.

Bear, D., Invernizzi, S., & Templeton, F. (2004). *Words their way* (3rd ed.). Upper Saddle River, NJ: Merrill Prentice Hall.

Beaver, J. (2001). *Developmental reading assessment: K–3 teacher resource guide: Revised*. Parsippany, NJ: Celebration Press.

Caldwell, J. S., & Leslie, L. (2009). *Intervention strategies to follow informal reading inventory assessment: So what do I do now?* Boston: Allyn & Bacon.

Carlson, N. (1990). *I like me*. New York: Puffin.

Clark, K. (2004). What can I say besides "sound it out"? Coaching word recognition in beginning reading. *The Reading Teacher, 57*(5), 440–449.

Clay, M. (1993). *An observation survey of early literacy achievement*. Portsmouth, NH: Heinemann.

Cunningham, P. (1999). What should we do about phonics? In L. Gambrell, L. M. Morrow, S. B. Neuman, & M. Pressley (Eds.), *Best practices in literacy instruction* (pp. 68–89). New York: Guilford Press.

Cunningham, P., & Cunningham, J. (1992). Making words: Enhancing the invented spelling-decoding connection. *The Reading Teacher, 46*(2), 106–115.

DeLapp, P. (2002a). *Bath time*. Parsippany, NJ: Celebration Press.

DeLapp, P. (2002b). *Get your umbrella*. Parsippany, NJ: Celebration Press.

DeLapp, P. (2002c). *Look at me*. Parsippany, NJ: Celebration Press.

Dolch, E. W. (1936). A basic sight vocabulary. *Elementary School Journal, 36*, 456–460.

Ehri, L. (2004). Teaching phonemic awareness and phonics: An explanation of the national reading panel meta-analysis. In P. McCardle & V. Chhabra, *The voice of evidence in reading research* (pp. 153–186). Baltimore: Paul H. Brookes.

Ehri, L. (2005). Learning to read words: Theory, findings, and issues. *Scientific Studies of Reading, 9*(2), 167–188.

Ehri, L., & McCormick, S. (2004). Phases of word learning: Implications for instruction with disabled readers. In R. Ruddell & N. Unrau (Eds.), *Theoretical models and processes of reading* (pp. 365–389). Newark, DE: International Reading Association.

Fountas, I., & Pinnell, G. (1996). *Guided reading: Good first teaching for all children*. Portsmouth, NH: Heinemann.

Fry, E. (2001). Instant word comprehensive test. In E. Fry (Ed.), *Informal reading assessments K–8* (pp. 27–33). Westminster, CA: Teacher Created Materials.

Gentry, J., & Wallace, J. (1993). *Teaching kids to spell*. Portsmouth, NH: Heinemann.

Gentry, R. (2006). *Breaking the code: The new science of beginning reading and writing*. Portsmouth, NH: Heinemann.

Goodman, Y., Watson, D., & Burke, C. (1987). *Reading miscue inventory: Alternative procedures*. Katonah, NY: Richard C. Owens.

Gunning, T. (2001). *Building words: A resource manual for teaching word analysis and spelling strategies*. Boston: Allyn & Bacon.

Harris, T., & Hodges, R. (1995). *The literacy dictionary: The vocabulary of reading and writing*. Newark, DE: International Reading Association.

Hill, B., & Ruptic, C. (1994). *Practical aspects of authentic assessment: Putting the pieces together*. Norwood, MA: Christopher-Gordon.

Kear, D. J., Coffman, G. A., McKenna, M. C., & Ambrosio, A. L. (2000). Measuring attitude toward writing: A new tool for teachers. *The Reading Teacher, 54*(1), 14–24.

Leslie, L., & Caldwell, J. (2000). *Qualitative reading inventory–3* (3rd ed.). Boston: Allyn & Bacon.

Lipson, M., & Wixson, K. (2003). *Assessment & instruction of reading and writing difficulty: An interactive approach* (3rd ed.). Boston: Allyn & Bacon.

Lyon, A., & Moore, P. (2003). *Sound systems: Explicit, systematic phonics in early literacy contexts.* Portland, MN: Stenhouse.

Maione, H. (2006). *The wagon.* Parsippany, NJ: Celebration Press.

Manzo, A., Manzo, U., & Albee, J. (2004). *Reading assessment for diagnostic-prescriptive teaching* (2nd ed.). Toronto, Ontario, Canada: Wadsworth/Thompson Learning.

McKenna, M., & Kear, D. J. (1990). Measuring attitude toward reading: A new tool for teachers. *The Reading Teacher, 43,* 626–639.

Mesmer, H., & Griffith, P. (2005). Everybody's selling it—But just what is explicit, systematic, phonics instruction? *The Reading Teacher, 59*(4), 366–376.

Morrow, L., & Morgan, L. (2006). Phonics: Explicit and meaningful instruction. In C. Cummins (Ed.), *Understanding and implementing reading first initiatives: The changing role of administrators* (pp. 31–41). Newark, DE: International Reading Association.

National Reading Panel. (2000). *Teaching children to read: An evidenced-based assessment of the scientific research literature on reading and its implications for reading instruction.* Washington, DC: National Institute of Child Health and Human Development.

Parette, H., Blum, C., Boeckmann, N., & Watts, E. (2009). Teaching word recognition to young children who are at risk using Microsoft PowerPoint coupled with direct instruction. *Early Childhood Education Journal, 36,* 393–401.

Pikulski, J. (1997). *Teaching word-identification skills and strategies: A balanced approach.*

Retrieved June 19, 2009, from http://www.eduplace.com/rdg/res/teach/

Pinnell, G. S., & Fountas, I. (1998). *Word matters: Teaching phonics and spelling in the reading/writing classroom.* Portsmouth, NH: Heinemann.

Samuels, J. (2002). Reading fluency: Its development and assessment. In A. Farstrup & S. Samuels (Eds.), *What research has to say about reading instruction* (pp. 164–183). Newark, DE: International Reading Association.

Seuss, D. (1957). *The cat in the hat.* New York: Random House.

Sherman, D., Kleimand, G., & Peterson, K. (2004). *Technology and teaching children to read.* Retrieved August 1, 2010, from http://www.neirtec.org/reading_report/

Snow, C., Burns, S., & Griffin, P. (1998). *Preventing reading difficulties in young children.* Washington, DC: National Academy Press.

Stahl, S. (1998). Teaching children with reading problems to decode: Phonics and "not-phonics" instruction. *Reading and Writing Quarterly, 14*(2), 165–168.

Strickland, K. (2005). *What's after assessment? Follow-up instruction for phonics, fluency and comprehension.* Portsmouth, NH: Heinemann.

Wall, H. (2008). Interactive writing beyond the primary grades. *The Reading Teacher, 62*(2), 149–152.

White, T. (2005). Effects of systematic and strategic analogy-based phonics on Grade 2 students word reading and reading comprehension. *Reading Research Quarterly, 40*(2), 234–255.

Woods, M., & Moe, A. (1999). *Analytical reading inventory* (6th ed.). Upper Saddle River, NJ: Simon & Schuster.

Zimmerman, B., Padak, N., & Rasinski, T. (2008). *Evidence-based instruction in reading: A professional development guide to phonics.* Boston: Pearson Education.

CHAPTER 4
FOCUS ON FLUENCY

She crossed her hands on her lap as if she were saying lessons, and began to repeat it, but her voice sounded hoarse and strange, and the words did not come the same as they used to do. . . . "I'm sure those are not the right words," said poor Alice, and her eyes filled with tears. . . .

—Lewis Carroll

INTRODUCTION

It is probably not difficult to bring to mind the slow, halting voice of a young child just beginning to develop the skills needed to read text in a meaningful way. It is also easy to visualize an older boy or girl whose reading is laborious and choppy and delivered in a worried monotone. This second child would rather be out the door—anywhere but where the sighs of his or her classmates again signal failure. We most likely smile at the memory of the younger reader because we know that with time and appropriate instructional support, her or his oral reading will become more fluent. Thinking about the second reader, however, may cause us some discomfort. We know that the older reader's performance is most likely the sign of a deeper reading problem, one not easily resolved (Caldwell & Leslie, 2009; Strickland, 2005). The child's ability or inability to read text fluently tells us something about how she or he is developing as a proficient reader.

In this chapter, you will meet Sherry and Dale. Sherry was in Grade 5, and Dale was at the end of third grade at the time of this assessment. As you read each case, you will discover that, while each has issues with reading fluency, the source of those issues is very different. The information provided in Sections I and II, and the interventions discussed in Section III, should help you make sense of their cases and guide you toward understanding their abilities and their needs related to word identification.

SECTION I: WHAT DO WE KNOW ABOUT READING FLUENCY?

What Is Reading Fluency?

According to Padak and Rasinski (2008), **fluency** is "the ability to read expressively and meaningfully as well as accurately and with appropriate speed" (p. 9).

Fluent readers have developed their decoding skills such that they recognize words automatically and accurately, allowing them to focus on the meaning of those words as well as the text as a whole (Rasinski, 2006; Hiebert, 2006). When reading orally, students show that they are focusing on meaning by using appropriate phrasing and expression (Kuhn, 2009). Fluency then serves as an indicator of the reader's word recognition skill as well as of comprehension of text (Fuchs, Fuchs, Hosp, & Jenkins, 2001; Kuhn & Stahl, 2004).

As noted by Padak and Rasinski (2008), fluency has three elements—accuracy, rate, and expression, or **prosody**—all of which must be considered to gain a true sense of a reader's fluency. The first element, reading accuracy, is the correct reading of words, and it relies on a child's sight word knowledge and decoding ability. Although we want students to read the words correctly, inaccurate reading alone may not point to a comprehension problem because making errors in words that do not change the overall meaning of the text will have little or no effect on comprehension (Caldwell & Leslie, 2009; Pinnell, Wixson, Campbell, Gough, & Beatty, 1995).

The second element, reading rate, is the speed at which a student moves through a given text. Rate will and should vary according to the reader's interest, purpose, background knowledge, and word recognition skills (Beers, 2003; Caldwell & Leslie, 2009). Rate is thought to be a reliable indicator of fluency and is strongly correlated with comprehension, at least for early readers (Torgeson & Hudson, 2006). Allington (2006), however, cautioned against considering rate as a sole indicator of either. Although word-by-word reading can signal the presence of a problem, speedy reading can also signify trouble. Children who read quickly without appropriate phrasing or expression, more or less barking at print, may have limited comprehension.

The third element, prosody, is the reading of text in a way that mimics the rhythmic patterns of language; its features include phrasing, intonation, and stress. Phrasing involves the appropriate parsing or chunking of texts. We do not speak word-by-word; rather, we group words into meaningful units. Fluent readers do the same. Intonation refers to a rising and falling of the pitch in the voice that conveys meaning. For example, a rising pitch at the end of a sentence regularly signals that a question has been read. Stress relates to the emphasis that is placed on words within sentences (Kuhn, 2009; Kuhn & Stahl, 2004). The same sentence can mean something very different depending on which words are emphasized:

"**I** love you": It is I who loves you, not that other person.

"I **love** you": The emotion I feel for you is love.

"I love **you**": It is you I love, not that other person.

Prosody—appropriate phrasing, intonation, and stress—provides an indication that the reader is actively deriving meaning from text and should be considered alongside accuracy and rate when determining overall fluency (Miller & Schwanenflugel, 2006; Torgeson & Hudson, 2006).

Several factors can influence fluency. A reader's inability to recognize automatically a significant number of high-frequency words and a weakness in quickly decoding less frequent words will affect fluent reading. In addition, unfamiliarity with the content and vocabulary and lack of interest in the topic will negatively affect the reading of a given text. This is noticeable with students who were fluent readers in early grades but have become more challenged by the unfamiliar content and heavy vocabulary loads in texts they encounter in later grades (Pikulski, 2006; Pressley, Gaskins, & Fingeret, 2006). Also, English language learners may stumble over text when concepts, expressions, vocabulary, or the culture of the classroom vary greatly from their own (Palumbo & Willcutt, 2006). Finally, fluent reading can be difficult to impossible for students with a reading disability related to a brain processing disorder or for those who are easily distracted and lose their place and focus frequently (Beers, 2003; Palumbo & Willcutt, 2006).

How Does Reading Fluency Develop?

Fluency development can be conceptualized using LaBerge and Samuels's (1974) **automaticity model.** In describing that model, LaBerge and Samuels (1974) suggested that individuals have limited amounts of attention or cognitive capacity available for complex tasks, and in order to deal successfully with all of the activities that make up a task, a certain number of them must become automatic. Certainly, reading is a complex task. The student who views words as units, processing them quickly and accurately, is said to have reached automaticity in word recognition (Beers, 2003; Fuchs et al., 2001). In addition, when a student also automatically groups those words into meaningful units and routinely uses punctuation to determine where to pause and where to place emphasis, cognitive capacity becomes available and facilitates focusing on the meaning of the text (National Institute of Child Health and Human Development, 2000; Kuhn & Stahl, 2004; Pressley et al., 2006; Palumbo & Willcutt, 2006).

Fluency develops over time and is situational: that is, not all readers are equally fluent with all texts. Even a skilled adult will exhibit disfluent reading when engaged with unfamiliar content (Pressley et al., 2006). According to the automaticity model of LaBerge and Samuels (1974), the emergent and beginning reader will always exhibit disfluency because her or his total attention will be focused on working through each sentence word by word. As the reader internalizes graphophonic skills and builds a rich oral and sight word vocabulary, fluency with text will increase (Pikulski, 2006).

According to Kuhn (2009), typically developing readers can be expected to be fluent with grade-level materials by the end of Grade 3. This does not mean that we should remain unconcerned with children who are developing fluency less well than their peers. Such concerns should prompt several questions:

- Do these children consistently process all words letter by letter, even those high-frequency words most readers have memorized earlier?
- Do they read familiar texts slowly and with effort?
- Are they reading in phrases or at a rapid pace but with little or no expression?
- Are they consistently unable to retell what they have read?

Children who struggle with fluency early on are likely to have trouble with reading comprehension as they move up the grades (Miller & Schwanenflugel, 2006). Reading, the very activity needed to become more fluent, becomes an increasingly painful and unsuccessful process, which they shun (Caldwell & Leslie, 2009).

SECTION II: HOW CAN WE ASSESS READING FLUENCY?

There are a number of measures that can be used to assess fluency. These include commercially prepared products such as Dynamic Indicators of Basic Early Literacy Skills (**DIBELS**) and reading inventories, as well as classroom procedures such as Curriculum-Based Measurement (**CBM**; Deno & Marston, 2006). Because accurate reading at an appropriate rate is a good predictor of reading comprehension, at least in the early grades (Fuchs et al., 2001; Riedel, 2009), teachers have begun to assess these elements only. However, some researchers warn against ignoring prosody or comprehension, both of which add to the information needed when trying to understand a student's reading difficulties (Allington, 2006; Kuhn, 2009; Topping, 2006). The first step in helping a struggling reader must be to gather as much information as possible to ascertain strengths and weaknesses; therefore, the assessment process outlined as follows includes measures of all elements of fluency and checks of comprehension.

1. A common first step when measuring fluency involves asking the child to read for one minute from an unfamiliar grade-level text that is 100 to 200 words in length. During the reading, the assessor notes the number of errors made as well as the number of words read and determines the words correct per minute (WCPM) score. This should then be compared to established norms, such as those offered by Rasinski (2004), to determine whether the child is making reasonable progress in relation to same-grade peers (see Table 4.1).

Table 4.1   Oral Reading Fluency (ORF) Norms

Grade	Fall (WCPM)	Winter (WCPM)	Spring (WCPM)
1		10–30	30–60
2	30–60	50–80	70–100
3	50–90	70–100	80–110
4	70–110	80–120	100–140
5	80–120	100–140	110–150
6	100–140	110–150	120–160
7	110–150	120–160	130–170
8	120–160	130–170	140–180

Source: From *Assessing Reading Fluency,* by T. Rasinski, 2004, Pacific Resources for Education and Learning: http://www.prel.org/media/137837/10_assessing-fluency.pdf

Kuhn (2009) suggested taking three 1-minute samples from both narrative and expository texts to increase reliability. Strickland (2005) recommended against using a stopwatch to time readers because it can be distracting and may send the message that reading is a race to the finish. Instead, she advised tape-recording the session and calculating the rate afterward.

2. The second step, a check of comprehension, is completed after the student finishes each 1-minute reading. This is accomplished by asking one or two general questions or by asking the student to retell the details of the passage.

3. The final step entails evaluating the student's prosody. This can be done informally by observing the student's use of punctuation and expression. Alternately, the assessor may choose to use a descriptive rubric such as the NAEP Oral Reading Fluency Scale (Daane, Campbell, Grigg, Goodman, & Oranje, 2005), which is included in Table 4.2. The information gleaned from this three-step process, especially when combined with an analysis of the errors made, will help the teacher or specialist decide whether the student's difficulty might be the result of a weakness in print skill, vocabulary knowledge, reading comprehension, or a combination of these and will provide direction for appropriate instruction.

The use of commercially prepared reading assessments is commonplace and provides an alternative to the process described previously. The Qualitative Reading Inventory (Leslie & Caldwell, 2000), the Analytical Reading Inventory (Woods & Moe, 1999), and the Developmental Reading Assessment (Beaver & Carter, 2003) have been used in the assessment of students whose case reports are presented in this book. All of them have some means to assess fluency.

Table 4.2   NAEP Oral Reading Fluency Scale, Grade 4: 2002

Fluent	Level 4	Reads primarily in larger, meaningful phrase groups. Although some regressions, repetitions, and deviations from text may be present, these do not appear to detract from the overall structure of the story. Preservation of the author's syntax is consistent. Some or most of the story is read with expressive interpretation.
	Level 3	Reads primarily in three- or four-word phrase groups. Some small groupings may be present. However, the majority of phrasing seems appropriate and preserves the syntax of the author. Little or no expressive interpretation is present.
Nonfluent	Level 2	Reads primarily in two-word phrases with some three- or four-word groupings. Some word-by-word reading may be present. Word groupings may seem awkward and unrelated to larger context of sentence or passage.
	Level 1	Reads primarily word-by-word. Occasional two-word or three-word phrases may occur—but these are infrequent and/or they do not preserve meaningful syntax.

Source: From *Fourth-Grade Students Reading Aloud: NAEP 2002 Special Study of Oral Reading* (NCES 2006-469) (p. 27), by M. C. Daane, J. R. Campbell, W. S. Grigg, M. J. Goodman, and A. Oranje, 2005, Washington, DC: Government Printing Office.

SECTION III: WHAT INTERVENTIONS MIGHT PROMOTE FLUENCY?

Effective fluency-related interventions share four common elements: modeling of fluent reading, providing "just in time" oral support, providing multiple opportunities to practice, and monitoring and offering feedback (Kuhn, 2009; Rasinski, 2003). All of the instructional strategies described here share these elements.

Repeated Reading. In a review of the literature, repeated reading procedures were the most commonly mentioned interventions for improving fluency as well as word recognition and comprehension (Samuels, 2006). In general, the student is asked to read aloud short but meaningful texts several times until she achieves satisfactory accuracy, rate, and comprehension (Palumbo & Willcutt, 2006). Selected texts should be of interest to the student and somewhat challenging, but they should still have a large percentage of high-frequency words and words with decodable patterns (Pressley et al., 2006). Once the appropriate

Providing "just in time" oral support can help students increase reading fluency.

level of text has been determined, the classroom teacher, an instructional assistant, a parent, or a higher ability reader can guide the student through this activity. A summary of the repeated reading procedure as provided in Kuhn's text, *The Hows and Whys of Fluency Instruction* (2009, pp. 85–88). is provided here:

- Select a challenging text and identify a 100- to 200-word passage.
- Provide a copy for you and one for the student.
- Ask the student to read the passage aloud while you record the rate (words read per minute) and the number of miscues to chart (an accuracy of 85–90% on initial reading indicates that the selected text is appropriate).
- Discuss the reading rate and review the miscues, and then establish a final goal for reading rate that is reasonable and helps the student understand that reading is not a race. Finally, tell students you will be asking them what the passage is about after the rereading.
- Ask the student to review the passage silently as this can build his or her comfort level with the text.
- Ask the student to reread the text while you record the new rate and number of miscues.
- The student should continue to read the passage up to five times or until the goal is met. Rereading more than five times is not productive and indicates that the text may be too difficult.

Wide-Oral Reading. Although the repeated reading procedure has long been an instructional staple, recent evidence suggests that supported wide-oral reading of texts may result in similar or higher gains in fluency (Kuhn, 2009; Reutzel, Jones, Fawson, & Smith, 2008; Roberts, Torgeson, Boardman, & Scammacca, 2008; Stahl, 2004). Stahl (2004) suggested that the amount of time spent reading connected text in a supported environment may be more important than the rereading of the same text. Kuhn (2009) noted that it may be easier to learn words when they are seen in a variety of texts and contexts versus the same text multiple times. It appears that wide-oral reading may be used as an alternative to the repeated reading procedure, with one caveat. The reading should be highly scaffolded. Independent reading will not provide the scaffolded instruction necessary to build the fluency of struggling readers, although independent silent reading can improve reading overall as long as the text is well matched to the student's independent level (Allington, 2006) and the time-on-task is modified to allow the lower ability reader to maintain attention and motivation (Samuels, 2006).

Assisted Reading. There are multiple interventions within this category. In each case, the reader is paired with a higher ability reader (teacher, peer, tutor, computer, or parent) during the activity. Three specific approaches will be detailed in this section. The first, the **Neurological Impress Method** (NIM), was developed by Heckelman in 1969 (Kuhn, 2009). The text to be read should be somewhat challenging but of interest to the student. The procedure for the activity is as follows:

- The instructor sits a little behind or beside the student.
- The student and instructor read aloud together in unison.
- While reading, the instructor keeps an appropriate pace and models a prosodic reading of the text.
- The student reads for at least five minutes initially to build stamina. Time on task can be increased as the student's confidence and ability develop.

A second approach, paired reading, is a collaborative effort between a student and tutor or classroom peer, depending on the type of procedure selected. In Duolog Reading (Topping, 2006), a higher ability reader (the tutor) is paired with a lower ability reader (the student). The Paired Repeated Reading Procedure (Nichols, Rupley, & Rasinski, 2009) matches classroom peers who share similar reading ability levels. Each approach is outlined in the paragraphs that follow.

In Duolog Reading (Topping, 2006, p. 121), the tutor, a higher ability reader, selects a text that is of interest to the student, but a little above his or her independent level. To ensure fluency gains, the pair should meet at least three times per week, for at least 10 minutes per session, for at least six weeks. Each session is conducted as follows:

- Both begin reading the text together in unison.
- Should the student miscue, the tutor corrects any error by reading the word correctly.
- The student repeats the word correctly, and they both continue reading.

- If the student feels confident enough to read alone, she or he signals the tutor nonverbally.
- The tutor stops reading.
- If the student makes an error, the tutor corrects the error by reading the word correctly.
- The student repeats the word correctly, and they both continue reading until the tutee signals her preference to read solo.
- If the student does not read a word within four seconds, the tutor treats it as a miscue and provides the word for the tutee.
- The pair should pause from time to time to discuss the meaning of the text.

For Paired Repeated Reading (Nichols et al., 2009, p. 5), the teacher pre-assigns pairs of readers who are at similar levels of ability and provides them with a short passage that is 100 to 150 words in length. The text may be somewhat challenging, but because the teacher will not be sitting beside the pair throughout the reading, the text cannot be so difficult that children are unable to work through it successfully. The steps in this procedure are as follows:

- Both children read the passage silently.
- The first student reads the passage aloud three times, while the listener assists when necessary.
- After each reading, the listener evaluates the reader using a student-friendly fluency evaluation form. (Such a form can be developed using the NAEP Oral Fluency Rubric as a guide, or an existing form can be used. See Nichols et al., 2009, p. 6.)
- After the third reading, students switch roles.
- The teacher circulates, providing encouragement and assistance and conducting informal assessments.

Small and Whole Group Approaches. It is not always possible for teachers to provide individualized support in the classroom setting. Three interventions, Echo Reading, Choral Reading, and Readers Theatre (Kuhn, 2009), offer fluency practice in whole or small group environments. In Echo Reading, the teacher reads a short portion of the text while the students read along. The students then read the text aloud, repeating the teacher's phrasing and expression. In Choral Reading, the teacher and students read the text together. Khun (2009) suggested using Choral Reading as a follow-up to Echo Reading on the same text.

Providing time and support for children to prepare for Readers Theatre performances can help them develop into confident, fluent readers.

Readers Theatre is a particularly engaging activity for all learners. It can promote the fluency of those who struggle with texts in an environment that provides a legitimate reason for students to repeatedly read the script (Tyler & Chard, 2000). In addition, scripts that focus on science or social studies can help children learn content as they work to improve their fluency. It is quite easy to find commercially developed scripts or to download scripts from Internet sources (e.g., www.storiestogrowby.com; www.scriptsforschools.com; www.aaronshep.com). Scripts can also be created from narrative texts or by the children themselves. There is no need for additional props or staging because the focus is on delivering the dialogue in an accurate and expressive manner. It is important to provide ample practice time and to ensure that the lines assigned to struggling readers are not above their **instructional reading level** (Worthy & Prater, 2002).

Phrased Text Lesson. The final intervention in this chapter can help students who tend to read texts in a labored fashion with little or no phrasing. Rasinski (2003) noted that because the phrase carries meaning, failing to read in meaningful units can impact comprehension. The Phrased Text Lesson is designed to be used with small groups of students and is taught over two consecutive days for 10 to 15 minutes each day. The steps are outlined here:

- In preparation, select short reading passages and mark or "cue" phrase boundaries for the reader. Single slashes within the sentence indicate short pauses. Double slashes are used to denote sentence boundaries, indicating a longer pause.
- Give the students a copy of the text; remind them of the importance of reading in phrases, not word by word, and explain the markings on the text.
- Read the text aloud several times, exaggerating phrases.
- Choral read the text several times, emphasizing good phrasing and expression.
- Ask students to read the passage with partners two or three times.
- Ask partners to perform orally for the group.
- On the next day, give students an unmarked copy of the same text and repeat the same procedure. (Rasinski, 2003, pp. 141–142)

Intervening With Technology. Technology tools that promote fluency development will most likely ask children to interact repeatedly with texts. A few resources are listed here.

- E-books: Electronic books are available as CDs or DVDs, or as downloadable files for e-readers such as the Kindle™ and the Apple iPad. There are also online resources and commercial programs available. For example, the Magic Keys (www.magickeys.com/books) site houses several children's stories. The student can read the text or, in a few cases, listen to or reread the text independently, clicking on the unfamiliar words for assistance.
- Podcasts: Teachers can help children make podcasts of them reading texts repeatedly to help them gain confidence in their growing fluency abilities. Also, teachers can create their own podcasts of children's books that match the interests of their students. They can then publish the podcasts to a preselected site that students can access at school or at home.
- iPod and iPad Applications: *K–12 Timed Reading Practice* is an application that consists of short, timed reading passages for students in Grades K through 4. Students read silently or aloud and click through the pages. When finished with the text, readers are shown their reading rate for that passage. Caution is warranted, though, since neither prosody nor accuracy is tracked. Still, this application provides for repeated reading of texts that may help increase fluency overall.

The case reports presented in this chapter will help you consider the issues related to fluency discussed in previous sections of the chapter. Your challenge is to consider what the basis of Sherry's and Dale's disfluencies might be and, thus, what instructional approaches might be employed to best address each student's weakness.

Guiding Questions

Section IV of the chapter will help you apply your understandings about fluency to two particular cases. Read each case quickly to get the gist of what it is about and to identify the issues. Read each case a second time, and when you come to a stop sign in the case, jot down your answers to the following questions:

- What important facts have been revealed at this point in the case?

- Based on what you know so far, what do you think might be going on? It may help to respond to the following prompt: Could it be that . . . ?

- What are the learner's strengths and needs?

- What further assessments or interventions might you try to confirm your ideas?

CASE 1: ASSESSMENT REPORT FOR SHERRY R.

Background Information

Child's name: Sherry R.
Current age: 11
Current grade level: Midyear Grade 5

Referral

Sherry's teacher requested that she be assessed. Parental permission was granted.

Family and Medical History

Sherry just recently celebrated her 11th birthday. No physical concerns were noted, although, at 5'8", she is quite tall for her age. Sherry lives in a single-parent home with her mother and two brothers. Her father regularly moves in and out of the house but was living with the family at the time of this assessment. The language spoken in the home is English.

Her mother has a debilitating back condition and is unable to attend school conferences; therefore, conferences are routinely conducted via phone. During a phone interview with the examiner, the mother responded to a four-item questionnaire about her daughter's skills and interests. She stated that she is very proud of her daughter's accomplishments and always looks forward to report card time. She reported that, overall, Sherry enjoys school, loves to draw, and is a good basketball player. See Figure 4.1 for her complete responses to the questions.

Figure 4.1   Parent Survey for Sherry R.: Child as a Learner

1. How does your child seem to feel about going to school?

   She's a little slow in the morning and sometimes tardy, but this has nothing to do with wanting to go to school. She loves school.

2. What are your goals for your child this year?

   I want her to keep progressing like she has been. She's my one child I don't need to worry about. I want her to do well.

3. What are your child's interests?

   She loves to draw. She gives her pictures (pastels and crayons) to her friends, to me, to her teacher and is very proud. She is also good in basketball and loves to play.

4. What types of activities do you do together?

   We're pretty busy, but we watch movies together. Sometimes Sherry and I go shopping and she helps her brother with his math sometimes.

Source: Form from *Practical Aspects of Authentic Assessment: Putting the Pieces Together* (p. 206), by B. Hill and C. Ruptic, 1994, Norwood, MA: Christopher-Gordon.

School History

Sherry is at midyear in Grade 5 in a small neighborhood elementary school serving about 240 children, one she has attended since kindergarten. Her teacher, Ms. Stern, provided information to the examiner through a phone interview. She noted that Sherry is very respectful of adults and her classmates and, although quiet by nature, has a large group of friends and is well liked. She loves art and usually chooses to draw during free time.

Ms. Stern added that although Sherry is academically successful, when she reads aloud, her voice is somewhat halted and the reading choppy. She struggles with what seem to be unfamiliar vocabulary words and tends to read slowly. During literature groups, it is difficult to tell whether she comprehends all that she reads because she rarely offers comments. When prompted directly, she is able to answer the question, but without depth. Because she is so quiet, it is hard to tell whether she does not comprehend the text or whether her quiet personality leads her to give limited responses.

Sherry received Title I support during Grade 3 due to concerns about her comprehension, vocabulary, and oral reading fluency. Instruction included work in decoding unknown words through syllabication and use of context clues, using appropriate phrasing when reading aloud, and retelling through journal writing. Even though her teachers reported that reading continued to be a challenge for her, she did not continue in Title I during Grade 4 because end-of-year reading scores placed her in the 67th percentile. She successfully completed Grade 4, and although reading fluency remains an issue in Grade 5, she continues to be successful academically.

When asked about the instructional approaches she employs in her classroom, Ms. Stern said the following:

Our school is dedicated to providing a rich language arts program. Literature groups are conducted throughout the year and include whole and small group instruction as well as partner and individual reading. Literature logs are maintained and reading instruction stresses literal and inferential comprehension, vocabulary, main ideas, and summarizing. The students are surrounded with books of every genre. I have a large classroom library. Writing workshop is a regular part of our school day. All steps in the writing process are taught and students share their work with each other.

Detailed Assessment Information

Session 1

At the beginning of the first session, Sherry was extremely quiet. Her answers for the interest inventory were short, more list-like, but as the session continued, she seemed to become more comfortable and her responses showed more depth.

Interest Survey. The examiner interviewed Sherry and recorded her responses. Sherry loves watching TV and wants to be an actress when she grows up. She plays basketball, takes flute lessons, and is in the Girl Scouts. She reads and writes outside of school. Her favorite school-related activity is math, while social studies is her least favorite (see Figure 4.2).

Figure 4.2 Interest Survey for Sherry R.

1. What kinds of things do you like to do outside of school?

   Watch TV, play with my puppy Destiny and dog Taz, math (I always do extra credit), read, draw.

2. What organized activities do you do outside of school?

   Basketball, Girl Scouts, flute lessons

3. What do you write about at home?

   Stories, usually fiction, and lists of things I need to do

4. What kinds of things do you like to read at home?

   Fiction books, the newspaper but I only glance through it.

5. What do you like to read about?

   Fairies, fantasy are my favorites

6. What do you want to be when you grow up?

   An actress in the movies or on TV, it doesn't matter

7. What are your parents' jobs? What kinds of things do they do at work?

   My mom doesn't work because of her bad back. Dad is a manager at a nursing home and he works with the clients.

8. What is your favorite subject at school? Least favorite?

   Math because it is easy and fun. Least favorite is social studies because I don't find it that interesting.

9. What would you like to learn about this year?

   I'd like to learn really long algebra. I look at my sister's (who is in high school) and I have no clue what it's about. I want to know more.

10. What's something about you that people at school might not know?

    I'd rather watch TV than do anything else.

11. Have you ever traveled? Where?

    Yes, we go to Scotland to visit my grandparents. Also, we go to New York City to visit Mom's family.

12. What else would you like me to know about you?

    I can't think of anything else.

Source: Form adapted from *Practical Aspects of Authentic Assessment: Putting the Pieces Together* (pp. 174–175), by B. Hill and C. Ruptic, 1994, Norwood, MA: Christopher-Gordon.

Writing Attitude Survey. The examiner recorded Sherry's responses to the Hill and Ruptic *Writing Attitude Survey* (1994, p. 181). Her comments revealed that she has a positive attitude toward writing as long as she is allowed to choose the topic. She enjoys sharing her work and getting ideas from others (see Figure 4.3).

Figure 4.3   Writing Attitude Survey for Sherry R.

1. How do you feel about writing?
   I like to write when it's not about a specific topic. I like to choose my own.

2. When and how did you learn to write?
   I learned in first or second grade, but I don't remember how. The teacher taught us. It just sort of happened.

3. What kinds of things do you write at school?
   Research reports, literature responses, history stories.

4. What kinds of writing do you do at home?
   Fiction stories and lists.

5. Why do you think it's important to be a good writer?
   To share work with others that they will like. Also, to get better grades.

(Continued)

Figure 4.3 (Continued)

6. How do you feel when you are asked to share your writing with others?

   It depends if I like it. If I do then I'm very excited for others to hear it.

7. How do you feel when others share their writing with you?

   I enjoy their new ideas. I feel like I can get a little help improving my own writing.

8. How do you feel about yourself as a writer?

   I'm not great at writing on specific topics. If I can choose my own then I can do a better job.

Source: Original form in *Practical Aspects of Authentic Assessment: Putting the Pieces Together* (p. 181), by B. Hill and C. Ruptic, 1994, Norwood, MA: Christopher-Gordon.

Reading Inventory. The examiner used the *Analytical Reading Inventory* (ARI; Woods & Moe, 1999) to assess Sherry's reading strengths and needs. As the first step, she administered the *Seven Questions About Reading* (Woods & Moe, 1999, p. 72) form (see Figure 4.4) and the *Reading Interview* (Woods & Moe, 1999, p. 73) (see Figure 4.5) and recorded Sherry's responses. Sherry expressed a positive attitude toward reading and understood its benefits. She was able to explain what she does well as a reader and

Figure 4.4   ARI Seven Questions About Reading Survey for Sherry R.

1. Why do you read?

   Some things you need to know and you can find them in books. Some things in books are not on TV and they are more fun.

2. What benefits do you see in reading? How do you think reading helps you?

   Easier to understand more things. Sometime people speak and you don't really know what they mean. They [books] explain things more clearly. You learn more than on TV. They're more educational. Books have the summary on back cover.

3. What do you do well as a reader?

I'm better at reading silently. When you read out loud—it's easier to read in your mind. You can lose your place when reading out loud. I like to read slow to understand. I can't do this aloud. Small, little pictures help you understanding what the book is about. If a word has clear syllables, I can figure it out, but if I've never seen a word before it's harder. It's harder to understand when reading out loud. Fiction is more fun.

4. Do you read at home? How often? What do you read?

I read at home—around 6 days a week. On Saturday I read more because I have more time. I usually read fiction. I like things about witches and fairies—fun imaginary things.

5. How does reading make you feel?

Depends on the book. If it's one I can't understand or get into it's not as fun. Good books make you want to read more and more and more. Some books are frustrating. Maybe too much detail about things I don't want to hear about like death. I think I read slow, but I understand it better that way.

6. What are some of your favorite books?

Standing in the Light; Mary Kate and Ashley books; the first Harry Potter book; The BFG; My Name is not Angelica.

7. Do you have a favorite author? Why do you enjoy this author's books?

No favorite author. I look at the title, cover, and read the back.

Source: Original form in *Analytical Reading Inventory* (6th ed., p. 72), by M. Woods and J. Moe, 1999, Upper Saddle River, NJ: Merrill.

added information on her weak areas, including a concern about reading aloud because she is slow. When asked what she does when she comes to an unknown word, she listed sounding out, skipping it, and asking someone else. When asked about word or paragraph comprehension, she stated that she would use a dictionary if she needed to or would ask one of her siblings for help. She was able to list the titles of favorite books and noted that she reads at home six days out of the week. Sherry provided a good deal of information about herself as a reader and offered some evidence that she reads independently on a regular basis; however, her word solving and comprehension strategies seem limited.

Figure 4.5 ARI Reading Interview for Sherry R.

Book Selection Strategies

1. Why do you check out a book to read?

   I look at the title, cover, and description on the back. On the cover I look at the person's face or the fantasy type artwork or the animals. It has to be an interesting title. Not just a name.

2. How do you know if you can read the book?

   I flip by the pages. If the words are really tiny and really long, I don't pick it. I try the hard words. If there are only one or two hard words then I know it's okay.

Before Reading Strategies

3. Now that you have a book to read, do you do anything before you start reading?

   Probably look at the names of the chapters to see what the book might be about.

During Reading Strategies

4. If you are alone and can't pronounce a word, what do you do?

   Try to sound it out then skip over it until someone is around to ask.

5. If you are alone and don't know what a word means, what do you do?

   Probably look it up in the dictionary or skip over it if I still understood generally what was going on. You don't really want to stop in the middle of reading.

6. What do you do if you don't understand a paragraph or an entire page?

   Probably go ask one of my brothers and sister to read it to me to help.

After Reading Strategies

7. Now that you've completed the book, what do you do?

   Try to find a new book. Probably wouldn't start it right away because you want the ending to have a chance to sink in—only if it was a really good one.

Source: Original form in *Analytical Reading Inventory* (6th ed., p. 73), by M. Woods and J. Moe, 1999, Upper Saddle River, NJ: Merrill.

Session 2

ARI Word Lists (Woods & Moe, 1999). The second step in the administration of the *ARI* involves asking students to read lists of isolated words that occur in the reading passages and to create a sentence from two or more words. The examiner began this phase of the assessment using Form C. Sherry read the Primer list through Level 2 correctly and with ease and confidence. At Levels 3 and 4 she continued to read confidently, although she made two errors in Level 3 (one self-corrected) and three errors in Level 4.

At Levels 5 and 6, she read more slowly and spent more time on the following words: *telegram, argument, region, manager, parallel, falter, privacy, microphone, vapor,* and *reluctant.* She parsed these longer words and then repeated them once or twice before moving on. Although she correctly read the shorter word *foam,* she repeated it three times before moving on. It was clear that these words were less familiar to her even though she was able to decode them.

The sentences that she created were tied to her own life experiences and provided ample evidence that she understood what the selected words meant. Overall, Sherry successfully identified and decoded words at several levels and did not seem distressed even when she slowed down to work words out. Her errors revealed that she focuses on the beginnings and ends of words (see Figure 4.6).

Figure 4.6 ARI Word List Results for Sherry R.

Level	# Words Correct	Errors		Sentence (Examiner-selected word is in bold.)
		Text	Student Read	
Primer	20/20	NA	NA	Examiner did not ask for sentences.
1	20/20	NA	NA	My friend Chelsea and her mother own a **balloon** business. In old days they used **wagons** to deliver stuff.
2	20/20	NA	NA	We have a **library** in our school. I don't **remember** much when I was one.

(Continued)

Figure 4.6 (Continued)

Level	# Words Correct	Errors		Sentence (Examiner-selected word is in bold.)
		Text	Student Read	
3	18/20	fright breath	fight/fright (self-corrected) breathe	My puppy **wiggles** when it's sleeping. My **fellow** classmates and me want to go to Darnell Lake.
4	17/20	vicious sample windshield	vigorously simple windshed	In the Electric Slide we have a lot of **motions** to learn. In gym, a couple of years ago, we used to go throw up the **parachute** and then sit under it while it sank.
5	18/20	kindle halt	kindly holt	On the Titanic they didn't use the **telegram**. In a movie I saw the person said that they had a **vision** from God.
6	17/20	midstream graceful particle	mainstream grateful particular	My brother Justin will be going to **college** next year. A lot of famous stars like to have **privacy**.

Session 3

The examiner decided to begin with the Level 4 passage. This deviated somewhat from the directions given in the ARI, which would have started Sherry at Level 2, the lowest level at which she made no errors. However, because Sherry made only two errors at Level 3, one of which was self-corrected, she read through the Level 3 and 4 word lists comfortably, and her sentences were creative and complex, the examiner elected to begin the passage assessment at Level 4.

ARI Passage Assessments (Woods & Moe, 1999). Sherry's prediction for the selection *The Sick Pony* was brief, and she restated what was written in the title and the first two sentences rather than indicating what the story might be about. Her oral reading was somewhat choppy, with multiple pauses, but she did group some words together into meaningful phrases, and she attended to end punctuation most of the time. Her rate was reasonable, although a bit behind what would be expected in a text that was one year below her grade level (Sherry at 95 WCPM on the fourth grade passage vs. the norm at 110–150 WCPM for Grade 5). Sherry had a total of 11 miscues and made two self-corrections. The miscues were primarily substitutions that were graphophonically similar to the word in the passage. She did not attend to the middle parts of words. Three of the substitutions, although syntactically correct, changed the meaning of the passage. There were also a few omissions and insertions, but these did not affect the overall meaning of the passage.

Sherry's retelling was complete with many details relayed in a logical order, and all of the story elements were included. She responded correctly to all of the comprehension questions; however, the examiner occasionally asked her to expand on her first response. Sherry appeared confident and relaxed throughout. Although her miscues indicated that this text was borderline frustrational, her comprehension was at an independent level; therefore, the examiner moved on to the next level.

Sherry's prediction for the fifth grade passage, *A Woman Race Car Driver*, was limited to a restating of the title and the first three sentences. She added, "I don't even know—it's probably about fuel or something—like how much fuel you get in your car." Sherry's oral reading was halting and choppy, with poor phrasing. She made no distinction between the narrator's voice and the dialogue of the driver. She read sentences that ended with exclamation marks in the same way as those ending with periods. Her rate was reasonable but still lagged behind grade level peers (Sherry at 104 WCPM vs. the norm at 110–150 WCPM for Grade 5). She had five miscues and three self-corrections. Two of the miscues and all of the self-corrections were substitutions and most were graphophonically similar to the words in the passage. For the most part, she appeared to attend to the beginnings of the words. Only one of the substitutions changed the meaning of the passage. The remaining miscues were omissions and insertions, which did not alter the meaning. The passage was at Sherry's instructional level for word recognition.

Sherry's retelling was complete and presented in a logical order, with many but not all of the details in the story. However, all story elements were present and she was able to give a succinct summary statement. She responded correctly to all of the comprehension questions but needed several prompts for the evaluation-related question. The passage was at Sherry's independent level for comprehension, and her emotional status remained calm and confident. (See Figure 4.7 for a summary of Sherry's responses to this text.)

Figure 4.7 Summary ARI Assessment for Sherry R.

Text: *Form C, Level 5: A Woman Race Car Driver* (Woods & Moe, 1999, pp. 157–159)

Prior Knowledge/Prediction Response:

After reading the title: *It's probably going to be about a woman racing in a car.*

After reading the first two sentences: *Probably about Shirley get, going to the top on fuel race car racing fuel cars. I don't even know, but it's probably about fuel or something about how much fuel you race with.*

Reading Rate/Accuracy Score: 104 WCPM (Norm for 5th grade peers for spring is 110–150)

Phrasing: The first paragraph of the passage that Sherry read is included below. It is coded to attempt to represent her oral phrasing. Each singular slash / represents a short pause; each double slash // represents a longer pause. The excerpt is typed as it appeared in the original work, staying true to where one line of text dropped down to the next. Although Sherry's oral reading was not completely devoid of expression, it was quite limited. All endings sounded the same. For example, she did not change expression to signal that a sentence had ended in an exclamation mark rather than a period.

A Woman Race // Car Driver

"I want to be / the fastest woman / top fuel / car / driver in the world," //

stated Shirley / Muldowney. // I want to go / 500 / miles / per hour!" / In those

days, // top fuel cars were the fastest, / the most powerful / and the most carefully

// built / machines in // the / car racing sport (Woods & Moe, 1999, p. 157).

Oral Reading Miscues				
Page/Line	Text Words	Words Said	Error Type	Meaning Change?
158/8	determination	de-ter-mi-na-tion	N	N
158/10	confidence	coughing	Substitution	Y
158/12	established	estimated	Self-correction	N
158/13	rushed	crashed	Self-correction	N
158/14	Victory Lane	Victory Line	Substitution	N
158/15	as	——	Omission	N
158/15	a	——	Omission	N
158/15	——	the	Insertion	N

158/15 (miscued line)	Text: . . . will think of me as a top race car driver. Sherry: . . . *will think of me the top race car driver.*			
158/16	as	——	Self-correction	N

Total Errors: 5 = Instructional Level

Total Meaning Change Errors: 1 = Independent Level

Total Self-Corrections: 3

Retelling:

Well—well the person, Shirley, wanted to be the fastest woman racer and she—so on race day she um she started racing really fast and she went 2—2—230 and then she got to 242 and that was like a record so she accomplished what she set out to and she won the race.

Thumbnail Summary:

Shirley wanted to set a record on being the fastest woman racer, and when it came race time she set a record and she was the fastest one.

Comprehension Questions:

[Plus (+) indicates the question was answered correctly. Minus (−) indicates it was answered incorrectly.]

+ Q: Who is the main character in this story?

Sherry: *Shirley*

Examiner: Can you think of her last name?

Sherry: [long pause] *I don't know.*

+ Q: What is Shirley's goal?

Sherry: *To be the fastest woman racer.*

Examiner: How fast did she want to go?

Sherry: *500 miles per hour.*

+ Q: What were top fuel cars like?

Sherry: *They were the fastest, most carefully machines put together.*

+ Q: What do you know about the phrase top challenger?

Sherry: *Top challengers I guess is the best.*

+ Q: What does the phrase top challenger have to do with the story?

Sherry: *Well, she wanted to be the best.*

(Continued)

Figure 4.7 (Continued)

+ Q: What do you know about the word speedometer?

Sherry: *I'm guessing that's what—it shows how fast you're going.*

+ Q: What does speedometer have to do with the story?

Sherry: *It shows how fast she was going?*

Examiner: And how fast did she go?

Sherry: *She went 242.*

+ Q: What happened when Shirley's determination kicked in?

Sherry: *She wanted to go faster.*

+ Q: In your opinion, what was so unusual about Shirley's being a top fuel driver?

Sherry: *Well probably that um, um [pause] she was a girl.*

+ Q: Why won't people think of her as "just a woman who drives a race car"?

Sherry: *'Cause she set a record.*

Examiner: Any other reason?

Sherry: *She probably got to her goal.*

Session 4

During this final session, the examiner asked Sherry to read the Level 6 narrative passage *Open Heart Surgery* silently. There was a clear pattern of limited phrasing and intonation in Sherry's oral reading, and Sherry had noted earlier in the interview phase of the assessment that she preferred reading silently. The examiner wanted to check for silent reading comprehension in more difficult text. Sherry's prediction was limited. Her retelling related most of the details in a logical order. She also answered all of the comprehension questions correctly, putting this passage at her independent level.

Because Sherry's disfluent reading did not seem to affect her comprehension of text at or near her grade level, the examiner decided to end the session with a conversation around Sherry's oral reading. She asked Sherry how she felt about herself as a reader and in what areas she would like to improve. Sherry immediately voiced a concern about reading aloud to her peers. She said, "I know I'm a good reader, but it doesn't sound like I am." She recalled having trouble with the name of the horse (Galiban) in the passage *The Sick Pony* and was concerned because she had to slow down each time she came to it. The examiner explained that a character name does not always need to be pronounced correctly to get the meaning of the story. Sherry replied, "Yeah, but it's harder to keep track of the characters if you can't say their name in your head." Sherry then stated a second goal. She wanted to be able to say bigger, unfamiliar words more quickly so she wouldn't have to stop reading in the middle of the sentence to figure it out.

Additional Information

Examiner Anecdotal Notes

Regarding Sherry's miscues, when she is faced with an unfamiliar word, she slows down, looks at the beginning few letters, and then seems to make up a word that is graphophonically similar but not always semantically correct. In these instances, I think she may be relying on context to understand the passage and ignores words she doesn't know.

Case Recap:

1. Review the case and the notes you have taken in response to the guiding questions one final time, and add or revise any information you may have missed.

2. Make a list of additional questions you have about the case. What further information do you need that might be explored in the case discussion?

3. Think about the factors that influence reading performance beyond fluency. Which might be problem areas for Sherry? Which might be strengths?

CASE 2: ASSESSMENT REPORT FOR DALE D.

Background Information

Child's name: Dale D.
Current age: 9
Current grade level: End of Grade 3

Referral

Dale's third grade teacher, Mr. Tomlinson, requested that he be assessed.

Family and Medical History

Dale is an only child and lives with his mother and father in a small midwestern city. English is their primary language. Dale's mother runs a children's daycare center from her home. She reported that Dale has asthma and seasonal allergies. At the time of the assessment, he was taking daily medications for allergies and using inhalers for his asthma.

Mrs. D. completed a survey about her son as a learner. She listed several physical activities he enjoys and commented that he was curious about everything. She stated that he gets frustrated easily and that she wants him to enjoy reading, not hate it. She also noted that, while she did not object to his coming to the reading program, it was at her mother-in-law's and Dale's teacher's insistence that she agreed to his attending. Finally, she reported that Dale receives speech services in school but did not provide any details. See Figure 4.8 for the complete survey.

Figure 4.8 Parent Survey for Dale D.: Child as Learner

1. What are your child's free-time interests?
   He loves to draw, play hockey, basketball, ride his bike, swim, roller blade, skateboard, ride his scooter. He enjoys his Game Boy. TV shows. He love the Disney channel.

2. What types of books does your child enjoy?
   Chapter Books Sports Kids Illustrated.

3. What types of writing does your child do at home?
   Cursive

4. What are your observations about how your child learns?

He's curious about everything. But then he's almost 10 yr. old.

5. What are some other things you would like us to know about your child?

Dale gets frustrated easily. When he's tired, it's hard for him to get his mind going. It's hard to work him. I want him to enjoy reading not to hate it. All I heard was that this was an excellent program for him to get into for reading. So I am hoping It'll help him to read a bit better. He's already a good reader. But my (mother-in-law) insisted he be in this. As well as his teacher. I love my son, so whatever helps him & works. I am anxious to hear how he does.

Source: Form adapted from *Practical Aspects of Authentic Assessment: Putting the Pieces Together* (pp. 205–207), by B. Hill and C. Ruptic, 1994, Norwood, MA: Christopher-Gordon.

School History

Dale has just completed third grade at Beth Forsythe Elementary, a small neighborhood K through fifth school. His special education teacher, Ms. Brainard, completed a survey related to Dale's reading strengths and weaknesses. She noted that his end of Grade 3 Guided Reading Level is at L-M (Fountas & Pinnell, 1996), approximately one year behind the benchmark. She indicated that Dale is weak in the areas of fluency and comprehension and that his writing skills are also limited. He went to Reading Recovery for a time in second grade but was discontinued (no reason for the discontinuance was noted in the report). During Grade 3, he received special education services for reading, spelling, written language, and math one hour per day, four days per week. This included instruction in phonics, specifically digraphs, blends, and word endings. She noted that he is a hard worker and likes to read, but that he has difficulty staying focused when working in small groups or independently. See Figure 4.9 for a more detailed review.

Figure 4.9   Teacher Referral Form for Dale D.

1. Please describe the nature of the child's reading and writing.

Dale has been making steady progress with his reading skills. He is now reading at Guided Reading L-M. He has been working on increasing his fluency. He uses picture clues, context clues, and letter clues to help him decode new words. Dale needs to increase his reading fluency and comprehension skills. His writing skills are more limited. He expresses his thoughts in short, simple sentences. He has a limited writing vocabulary. Dale has a shortened classroom spelling list. He does well on his weekly spelling tests but has some difficulty transferring these correct spellings into his written work.

(Continued)

Figure 4.9 (Continued)

2. Please describe any strategies, materials, or activities that have been used successfully with this child.

   Dale did go to Reading Recovery for a time last year. The LD Specialist used Reading A-Z and some special leveled reading packets from the Media Center. Also some trade books have been used with him. We work on new vocabulary words before reading. He has continued to learn phonics skills: digraphs, consonant blends, and word endings. The Neurological Impress Method and chorus reading have been used with him to help increase his fluency. The language experience method has been used for his writing. He has some attentional difficulties at times if in a group of 2 or 3 or working independently.

3. What is the child's current reading level?

   Informal miscue—L-M

4. Is this child receiving special services of any kind not detailed in 2 above?

   Dale receives one hour per day (4 days a week) of learning disabilities services in the areas of reading, spelling, written language, and math. He also receives speech and language services—using correct syntax and articulation.

5. What is the child's attitude toward reading and school in general?

   Dale is a hard worker. He likes to read. He studies his spelling words at home. He comes ready to work.

6. Why do you think this child may benefit from this program?

   He could really benefit from the one-on-one instruction.

Detailed Assessment Information

Session 1

About Me Survey. The examiner gave Dale a short survey to complete as a way of learning about him and helping him become more comfortable. He had arrived at the assessment session with a stuffed animal, a wolf, that he said he brings along whenever he gets scared. He listed hockey, watching the Disney channel, drawing, and being with friends as favorite things. He left the line related to his favorite thing to read blank, but he did write that he liked reading about sports. He made several spelling errors: *firends/firens* for *friends, hoey* for *hockey, spourtes* for *sports,* and *raising giye* for *racing guy.*

Attitudes About Reading and Writing. Dale completed the *Garfield Elementary Reading Survey* (McKenna & Kear, 1990) and the *Garfield Writing Attitude Survey* (Kear, Coffman, McKenna, & Ambrosio, 2000). His total raw score on the reading survey, 24, was so low that it was at level 0 in the percentile rankings for the third grade. After he had finished responding to the survey independently, the examiner read each of the statements aloud to Dale to be sure he understood the questions. He did not change his responses. He assigned all items a score of 1 or 2 (on a scale of 1–4) with the exception of Item 4: *How do you feel about getting a book for a present,* which he gave a score of 3.

He ranked in the first percentile on the writing attitude survey. He scored all but three items at 1 and 2. The three items he scored at 3 out of a possible 4 were *How would you feel about writing a letter stating your opinion; How would you feel if you were an author who writes books;* and *How would you feel about becoming an even better writer than you already are?* Because Dale's responses indicated an extremely negative attitude toward reading and writing, the examiner followed up with forms that she hoped would provide more detail, *What I Think About Reading* (Strickland, 2005) and *What I Think About Writing* (Strickland, 2005). Dale's responses were extremely limited and supported the previous surveys. Dale did not like reading or writing and did not see them as important. (See Figure 4.10 for the results.)

Figure 4.10 Reading and Writing Survey Results for Dale D.

What I Think About Reading (Strickland, 2005, p. 22)	*What I Think About Writing* (Strickland, 2005, p. 23)
When did you learn to read? Who taught you? *my grandma*	When did you learn to write? Who taught you? *my tacher*
How often do you read? *No*	What do you like to write at home? *nothing*
What do you enjoy reading in school or at home? *sportes*	What do you like to write about at school? *nothing*

(Continued)

Figure 4.10 (Continued)

What I Think About Reading (Strickland, 2005, p. 22)	What I Think About Writing (Strickland, 2005, p. 23)
Do you have books of your own? If so, what are the titles of some of them? *yes*	What makes a person a good writer? *peradis* [practice]
Who is your favorite author? Your favorite book? *Mostertrockes* [monster trucks]	Who do you think is a good writer? Why is she good? *chelse* [Chelsea]
Do you like people to read aloud to you? *no case it git bord* [no cause it gets boring]	What are some topics you like to write about? *bikes*
Do you like to read aloud or silently? Why? *read to yourslef case* [cause] *it's better*	Do you like to share your writing with other people? Why or why not? [no response]
Do you go to the library? *some times*	Do you like to read the writing of other people in your class? Why or why not? [no response]
What do you think a good reader is? What do good readers do? *pereds* [practice] *reading*	What do you think about writing? *Bad*
Do you think you are a good reader? Why or Why not? *no, case* [cause] *I dont pereds* [practice]	Do you think writing is important? Why or why not? *riting is not inaportin* [important]
Do you think it's important to read? Why or why not? *no you dont have to read*	
What do you want to learn about reading? *no*	

Developmental Reading Assessment (Beaver, 2001). Based on the information gained from the surveys, the examiner selected DRA texts ranging from Levels 18 to 24 for the formal assessment. These texts were in the second grade range and the equivalent of Guided Reading Levels J through L (Fountas & Pinnell, 1996). Dale selected the Level 24 text, *Thin as a Stick* (Vaughan, 2002). In keeping with the directions for the assessment, Dale read the first two pages of the text aloud, made a prediction, and then read the text silently before he completed a retelling and responded to comprehension questions. He was unable to make a prediction, responding at first with, "I don't know." When the examiner prompted Dale further, he referred back to the pictures to predict. During the silent reading, he yawned and sighed a few times. His retelling required a great deal of prompting, and he relied heavily on the pictures, not the text, as he responded to the examiner's questions.

Finally, the examiner asked Dale to read pages 5 through 7 aloud. His oral reading was slow, word-by-word, and without expression. He paid little attention to end punctuation, often not stopping at all. His oral reading fluency score on this text was 63 WCPM (vs. the norm for spring of third grade, 80–110 WCPM). He made multiple miscues (90% accuracy rate overall) that were graphically similar to the beginnings of the words in the text, but seldom semantically appropriate. This text was at Dale's frustration level, so the examiner decided to ask him to respond to a Level 20 text during the next session.

Session 3

Developmental Reading Assessment (Beaver, 2001). The examiner provided Dale with a Level 20 text, *Turtle's Big Race* (Trumbauer, 2002), for this session. The procedures for administering the assessment were the same as those used in the Level 24 text. This time, however, Dale's miscues were fewer (97% accuracy rate) and his retelling more complete, though he still needed several prompts. Initially, Dale provided the wrong ending to the story, but after reading aloud the final pages, he revised his response and gave the correct ending. His oral reading was choppy, with limited phrasing, and was delivered in a monotone voice. He paid a bit more attention to end punctuation and read the word "Ouch!" with appropriate expression. His oral reading fluency score was 77 WCPM for this Grade 2 text. Figure 4.11 provides a detailed summary of the results of this assessment.

Figure 4.11   Summary DRA Assessment for Dale D.

Text: *Turtle's Big Race* (Trumbauer, 2002): *Level 20* (Grade Level Equivalent 2, Guided Reading Level K)

Previewing and Predicting Response (after reading the first page): *They're going to have a race. They're fighting over the pond and whoever wins gets the pond.*

Oral Reading Miscues (pages 6–7 of text)			
Page/Line	Text Words	Words Said	Error Type
6/1	stuck	stook	Substitution
6/2	with	in	Self-correction
6/4	wanted	went	Substitution
6/6	bit	bite	Substitution
6/7	shouted	shout	Substitution
6/9	up into	he to	Self-correction
6/11	grassy	grass	Substitution
7/4	the pond	the was	Self-correction
7/5	looked	asked	Self-correction
7/11	his	the	Self-correction
7/12	grassy	grass	Substitution

Total Errors: 6

Accuracy: 97%

Total Self-Corrections: 5

Reading Rate/Accuracy Score: 77 WCPM (Norm for 3rd grade peers for spring is 80–110 WCPM with grade level material)

Phrasing and Fluency

Dale read word-by-word with a few short phrases.

He used little intonation and attended to punctuation infrequently.

Phrasing: The first paragraph of the passage used for Dale's oral reading check is included here. He had already read the passage silently. It is coded to attempt to represent his oral phrasing. Each single slash / represents a short pause; each double slash // represents a longer pause. Because Dale's phrasing was almost nonexistent, I have underlined those groups of words that he did read as a meaningful unit. The excerpt is typed as it appeared in the original work, staying true to where one line of text dropped down to the next. Dale read without expression and seldom paused at the ends of sentences.

*But / Turtle / had / a // plan. He / stuck / out / his / long /
neck / and / grabbed / Beaver's / tail / with / his / jaws. /
Beaver / felt / something. He / didn't / look / back
Because / he / wanted / to / win / the / race. They
were / almost / to / the / other / side / of the pond.
Turtle / bit / down / very hard / on / beaver's tail.*

<u>Strategies Used With Difficult Text</u>

Dale used picture clues when he came to difficult text and attended to the initial sounds to help problem solve words.

<u>Comprehension (Little to Some Comprehension)</u>

Dale's retelling included some key events with a few important details. He referred to the main characters by name. The examiner used multiple prompts and questions, to aid him in recalling the details of the story. After the first reading he provided an incorrect ending, but corrected this after he reread the ending aloud.

Source: Adapted from *DRA Observation Guide*, by J. Beaver, 2002, Parsippany, NJ: Celebration Press.

Additional Information

Examiner Anecdotal Notes

After Session 3. Dale's reading engagement level is weak. He couldn't list one of his favorite books. His oral reading is also very monotone and word-by-word. I think that issues with his speech may contribute to his monotone reading since this is how he talks in normal conversation. I was discouraged by his slow reading and weak comprehension. I think that he lacks confidence in himself and the answers he gives. He doesn't believe that he is a good reader, and he is very unsure of himself.

Case Recap:

1. Review the case and the notes you have taken in response to the guiding questions one final time, and add or revise any information you may have missed.

2. Make a list of additional questions you have about the case. What further information do you need that might be explored in the case discussion?

3. Think about the factors that influence reading performance beyond fluency. Which might be problem areas for Dale? Which might be strengths?

CHAPTER SUMMARY

This chapter provided you with a brief discussion of fluency and its role in the reading process. As you analyzed and discussed the case reports for Sherry and Dale, you likely concluded that both struggle with fluency, though the reasons for their difficulty differ markedly. As you think about how you might help these readers, it is important to understand the sources of their disfluency because simply teaching children to read faster will not lead to deeper comprehension (Allington, 2006; Rasinski, 2006; Topping, 2006). Disfluent reading is an outward indicator that children are not reading texts in meaningful ways, and all areas of reading, including vocabulary knowledge, comprehension, word skill, and engagement, must be considered when designing targeted instruction. Without targeted support, readers like Dale fall farther and farther behind and learn to avoid reading altogether, while those like Sherry lose confidence and fail to realize their own reading strengths. The next chapter addresses vocabulary—a necessary element in the development of skilled and independent reading.

Terms highlighted in this chapter

fluency 108	prosody 109
automaticity model 110	DIBELS 111
CBM 111	Neurological Impress Method (NIM) 115
instructional reading level 117	

FINAL QUESTIONS FOR REFLECTION AND RESPONSE

1. After reading the information in this chapter and the cases, what role do you believe fluency plays in the development of proficient reading?

2. Compare and contrast the cases of Sherry and Dale with other readers you have known who have had difficulties with fluency. Why is it important to understand the reason for their disfluency?

3. What interventions, in addition to those provided in this chapter, do you believe might be most effective in helping Sherry and Dale improve their fluency?

Journals Online

Visit the student study site at www.sagepub.com/combsstudy to access recent, relevant, full-text journal articles from SAGE's leading research journals.

REFERENCES

Allington, R. (2006). Fluency: Still waiting after all these years. In J. Samuels & A. Farstrup (Eds.), *What research has to say about fluency instruction* (pp. 94–105). Newark, DE: International Reading Association.

Beaver, J. (2001). *Developmental reading assessment: K–3 teacher resource guide: Revised.* Parsippany, NJ: Celebration Press.

Beaver, J., & Carter, M. (2003). *DRA: Developmental reading assessment.* Parsippany, NJ: Celebration Press.

Beers, K. (2003). *When kids can't read, what teachers can do: A guide for teachers, 6–12.* Portsmouth, NH: Heinemann.

Caldwell, J. S., & Leslie, L. (2009). *Intervention strategies to follow informal reading inventory assessment: So what do I do now?* Boston: Allyn & Bacon.

Daane, M. C., Campbell, J. R., Grigg, W. S., Goodman, M. J., & Oranje, A. (2005). *Fourth grade students reading aloud: NAEP 2002 special study of oral reading (NCES 2006-469).* Washington, DC: U.S. Department of Education. Institute of Education Sciences, National Center for Education Statistics.

Deno, S., & Marston, D. (2006). Curriculum-based measurement of oral reading: An indicator of growth in fluency. In J. Samuels & A. Farstrup (Eds.), *What reaserach has to say about fluency instruction* (pp. 179–203). Newark, DE: International Reading Association.

Fountas, I., & Pinnell, G. (1996). *Guided reading: Good first teaching for all children.* Portsmouth, NH: Heinemann.

Fuchs, L., Fuchs, D., Hosp, M., & Jenkins, J. (2001). Oral reading fluency as an indicator of reading competence: A theoretical, empirical, and historical analysis. *Scientific Studies of Reading, 5*(3), 239–256.

Hiebert, E. (2006). Becoming fluent: Repeated reading with scaffolded texts. In J. Samuels & A. Farstrup (Eds.), *What research has to say about fluency instruction* (pp. 204–226). Newark, DE: International Reading Association.

Hill, B., & Ruptic, C. (1994). *Practical aspects of authentic assessment: Putting the pieces together.* Norwood, MA: Christopher-Gordon.

Kear, D. J., Coffman, G. A., McKenna, M. C., & Ambrosio, A. L. (2000). Measuring attitude toward writing: A new tool for teachers. *The Reading Teacher, 54*(1), 14–24.

Kuhn, M. (2009). *The hows and whys of fluency instruction.* Boston: Allyn and Bacon.

Kuhn, M., & Stahl, S. (2004). Fluency: A review of developmental and remedial practices. In R. Ruddell & N. Unrau (Eds.), *Theoretical models and processes of reading* (pp. 412–453). Newark, DE: International Reading Association.

LaBerge, D., & Samuels, S. (1974). Towards a theory of automatic information processing in reading. *Cognitive Psychology, 6,* 293–323.

Leslie, L., & Caldwell, J. (2000). *Qualitative reading inventory–3* (3rd ed.). Boston: Allyn & Bacon.

McKenna, M., & Kear, D. J. (1990). Measuring attitude toward reading: A new tool for teachers. *The Reading Teacher, 43,* 626–639.

Miller, J., & Schwanenflugel, P. (2006). A longitudinal study of the development of reading prosody as a dimension of oral reading fluency in early elementary school children. *Reading Research Quarterly, 43*(4), 336–354.

National Institute of Child Health and Human Development. (2000). *Report of the National Reading Panel: Teaching children to read: An evidence-based assessment of the scientific research literature on reading and its implications for reading instruction: Report of the subgroups.* Washington, DC: U.S. Government Printing Office.

Nichols, W. D., Rupley, W., & Rasinski, R. (2009). Fluency in learning to read for meaning: Going beyond repeated readings. *Literacy Research and Instruction, 48*(1), 1–13.

Padak, N., & Rasinski, T. (2008). *Evidence-based instruction in reading: A professional development guide to fluency.* Boston: Allyn & Bacon.

Palumbo, T., & Willcutt, J. (2006). Perspectives on fluency: English-language learners and students with dyslexia. In J. Samuels & A. Farstrup (Eds.), *What research has to say about fluency instruction* (pp. 159–178). Newark, DE: International Reading Association.

Pikulski, J. (2006). Fluency: A developmental and language perspective. In J. Samuels & A. Farstrup (Eds.), *What research has to say about fluency instruction* (pp. 70–93). Newark, DE: International Reading Association.

Pinnell, G. P., Wixson, K., Campbell, J., Gough, P., & Beatty, A. (1995). *Listening to children read aloud: Data from NAEP's integrated reading performance record (IRPR) at Grade 4.* Washington, DC: National Center for Education Statistics.

Pressley, M., Gaskins, I., & Fingeret, L. (2006). Instruction and development of reading fluency in struggling readers. In J. Samuels & A. Farstrup (Eds.), *What research has to say about fluency instruction* (pp. 47–69). Newark, DE: International Reading Association.

Rasinski, T. (2003). *The fluent reader: Oral reading strategies for building word recognition, fluency, and comprehension.* New York: Scholastic.

Rasinski, T. (2004). *Assessing reading fluency.* Retrieved May 20, 2009, from http://www.prel.org/products/re_assessing-fluency.htm

Rasinski, T. (2006). Fluency: An oft-neglected goal of the reading program. In C. Cummins (Ed.), *Understanding and implementing reading first initiatives: The changing role of administrators* (pp. 60–71). Newark, DE: International Reading Association.

Reutzel, R., Jones, C., Fawson, P., & Smith, J. (2008). Scaffolded silent reading: A complement to guided repeated oral reading that works. *The Reading Teacher, 62*(3), 194–209.

Riedel, B. (2009). The relations between DIBELS, reading comprehension, and vocabulary in urban first-grade students. *Reading Research Quarterly, 42*(4), 546–562.

Roberts, G., Torgeson, J., Boardman, A., & Scammacca, N. (2008). Evidence-based strategies for reading instruction of older students with learning disabilities. *Learning Disabilities Research & Practice, 23*(2), 63–69.

Samuels, J. (2006). Toward a model of reading fluency. In J. Samuels & A. Farstrup (Eds.), *What research has to say about fluency instruction* (pp. 24–46). Newark, DE: International Reading Association.

Stahl, S. (2004). What do we know about fluency? In P. McCardle & V. Chhabra (Eds.), *The voice of evidence in reading research* (pp. 187–211). Baltimore, MD: Paul H. Brooks.

Strickland, K. (2005). *What's after assessment? Follow-up instruction for phonics, fluency and comprehension.* Portsmouth, NH: Heinemann.

Topping, K. (2006). Building reading fluency: Cognitive, behavioral, and socioemotional factors and the role of peer-mediated learning. In J. Samuels & A. Farstrup (Eds.), *What research has to say about fluency instrtucion* (pp. 106–129). Newark, DE: International Reading Association.

Torgeson, J., & Hudson, R. (2006). Reading fluency: Critical issues for struggling readers. In J. Samuels & A. Farstrup (Eds.), *What research has to say about fluency instruction* (pp. 130–158). Newark, DE: International Reading Association.

Trumbauer, L. (2002). *Turtle's big race.* Parsippany, NJ: Celebration Press.

Tyler, B., & Chard, D. (2000). Using readers theatre to foster fluency in struggling readers: A twist on the repeated reading strategy. *Reading & Writing Quarterly, 16*(2), 163–168.

Vaughan, R. (2002). *Thin as a stick.* Parsippany, NJ: Celebration Press.

Woods, M., & Moe, J. (1999). *Analytical reading inventory* (6th ed.). Upper Saddle River, NJ: Merrill.

Worthy, J., & Prater, K. (2002). "I thought about it all night": Readers theatre for reading fluency and motivation. *The Reading Teacher, 56*(3), 294–297.

CHAPTER 5
FOCUS ON VOCABULARY

"When I use a word," Humpty Dumpty said in rather a scornful tone, "it means just what I choose it to mean—neither more nor less."

—Lewis Carroll

Guiding Questions

Sections I through III of this chapter will help build your knowledge related to vocabulary and will prepare you to read and discuss the cases. As you read the sections, consider the following questions:

- What does it mean to know a word?

- How do we acquire new vocabulary?

- How can we assess vocabulary?

- What interventions might improve vocabulary?

INTRODUCTION

Vocabulary matters, and its relationship to reading comprehension has been firmly established (Beck, McKeown, & Kucan, 2008; Blachowicz, Fisher, & Watts-Taffe, 2006; Cummins, 2006). It is widely known that word knowledge predicts comprehension (Fisher, Frey, & Lapp, 2009; Pearson, Heibert, & Kamil, 2007). Although we do not know the causal link (Kamil, 2004), many presume a shared relationship (Carlo et al., 2004). A strong vocabulary makes reading easier and more engaging, which leads to wider reading, which builds larger vocabularies. Sadly, the reverse is also true. Learners who struggle to comprehend text because of limited vocabularies are not avid readers, and so an important avenue for building word knowledge is blocked.

In this chapter, you will meet Darrell and Brandie. In both cases, their classroom teachers noted that they believed low vocabulary knowledge was a problem that contributed to the children's difficulties with reading comprehension. As you read each case, decide to what extent you agree with the teachers and consider what evidence there is to support your opinion. The information provided in Sections I and II and the interventions discussed in Section III should help you make sense of their cases and guide you toward understanding their abilities and their needs related to word identification.

SECTION I: WHAT DO WE KNOW ABOUT VOCABULARY DEVELOPMENT?

What Does It Mean to Know a Word?

Vocabulary researchers have described five aspects of word knowledge: **incrementality**, **multidimensionality**, **polysemy**, **interrelatedness**, and **heterogeneity**. Each of these aspects is defined here.

- *Incrementality.* Word learning occurs in small steps over time, and each time a word is encountered, a bit more about it is understood (Pearson et al., 2007; Spencer & Guillaume, 2006).
- *Multidimensionality.* Nagy and Scott (2000) described this as knowing many things about a given word, including its spoken form, written form, grammar, frequency in the language, denotative and connotative meanings, antonyms, synonyms, and appropriate affixes, as well as collocations (other words that occur frequently with it).
- *Polysemy.* This refers to the multiple meanings of words. Indeed, a word with several meanings can be especially confusing to a struggling reader since it is easier to attribute the wrong meaning to the word (Barr, Blachowicz, Bates, Katz, & Kaufman, 2007).
- *Interrelatedness.* Words are not isolated units. Knowledge of a given word is dependent on knowledge of other words associated with it (Nagy & Scott, 2000).
- *Heterogeneity.* Knowing a word is dependent on the word's function and structure (Pearson et al., 2007). As noted by Graves (2009), knowing a function word such as *the* differs substantially from knowing a concrete noun such as *ladder* or an abstract noun like *democracy* (p. 13).

Coming to know a word is a continuous, lifetime process (Cummins, 2006). It is affected by our experiences, which differ culturally and developmentally (Barr et al., 2007). It is also affected by the types of encounters, both formal and informal, we have with a word over time (Blachowicz & Fisher, 2006). It is much more complex than merely being able to provide a definition; knowing a word requires knowing many things about that word.

How Do We Acquire New Vocabulary?

The two vocabularies most frequently referred to in the literature are *receptive* and *expressive*. Our receptive vocabulary consists of all the words that we understand when a person speaks or when we encounter words in text. Our expressive vocabulary, on the other hand, consists of all those words we can produce in speaking or writing (Kamil, 2004). In general, our **receptive vocabulary** is larger than our **expressive vocabulary**, and we can understand many more words than we typically use in our speech or writing (Pearson et al., 2007).

Researchers have noted that we move in stages from no knowledge of a word to rich, nuanced knowledge through repeated exposures (Blachowicz & Fisher, 2006; Kamil, 2004). While many of these exposures may be incidental, the richer and more meaningful our encounters with words, the greater our vocabularies will be (Blachowicz et al., 2006). For younger children, this means immersing them in language-rich environments where they encounter new words daily. Reading to children and engaging them in discussion helps build both receptive and expressive vocabularies (Cummins, 2006). For older children, wide reading experiences will help them reinforce understandings of familiar words and build new vocabularies (Fisher et al., 2009).

According to Nagy and Scott (2000), children learn 2,000 or more words per year incidentally, but learning new words at a rate such as this is inhibited if language experiences are limited. Blachowicz et al. (2006) noted that by age three most children have acquired wide differences in vocabulary knowledge. Learners from low socioeconomic groups and English language learners are especially at risk (Spencer & Guillaume, 2006). Children from low-income families are more likely to have fewer words in their receptive and expressive vocabularies than those from middle- and upper-income families (Labbo, Love, & Ryan, 2007). English language learners often lack the required depth of

Reading to and talking with children is an essential activity that will help build their vocabularies.

knowledge about English words and have had little exposure to mainstream **academic vocabulary** (Carlo et al., 2004). Incidental exposure to words will not advance the vocabularies of these children; instead, intentional and intense **scaffolded instruction** is required to address their needs (Blachowicz & Fisher, 2006).

SECTION II: HOW CAN WE ASSESS VOCABULARY?

The connection between vocabulary and comprehension is obvious, but it is not always possible to know when a limited vocabulary is the key stumbling block to comprehension. Barr et al. (2007) noted that, when a student is experiencing comprehension difficulties and there does not seem to be an underlying print-skill deficit, it is possible that poor vocabulary may be involved. In such situations, direct assessment of a student's word knowledge may be helpful.

In their 2007 edition of *Reading Diagnosis for Teachers: An Instructional Approach*, Barr and her colleagues (2007) outlined a four-step process for assessing a student's vocabulary. This is done as an additional assessment only after the student has failed to successfully comprehend a passage. The steps are as follows:

1. Select three to eight words from the previously read passage. The words should be important to an understanding of the passage.

2. For each word, ask the student: What does ____ mean? or What is an _____? or other probing questions. In the case of words with multiple meanings, include contextual information so that the student has an opportunity to supply the intended definition. If the student's initial response is unsuccessful or limited, ask for an object or situation to which the word would apply or ask the student to use the word in a sentence.

3. Analyze the student's responses.

   a. Generally, if the student does not know as many as half the words presented, you should consider vocabulary knowledge a general area of weakness.
   b. Consider the extent to which the selected words may have blocked comprehension. To do this, look back at incorrect answers from the comprehension questions and determine whether the answer was incorrect because of an unknown word.

4. Additional assessment may be helpful in determining to what extent lack of vocabulary knowledge impaired the student's understandings of the passage. Return to the passage and select additional words that you suspect the student did not know. Repeat Steps 2 and 3 (pp. 125–127).

Clearly, a student may have limited word knowledge in relation to a single passage and still be able to comprehend other passages. While it is important to get a sense of an individual's word knowledge, it is always important to assess such words as they appear within passages rather than in isolation. Barr and her colleagues' (2007) approach to vocabulary assessment can provide rich information since it allows students to meet words in context.

Graves (2009) suggested the use of multiple-choice items to assess vocabulary knowledge. Words to be assessed can be selected from available word list sources such as *The First 4000 Words* (Graves, Sales, & Ruda, 2009). Alternately, the teacher can select words from grade-level fiction and nonfiction texts that children will likely encounter during the school year. Multiple-choice tests can be constructed using two formats. First, the word to be tested can appear in isolation and serve as the question stem (the beginning part of the question). The options as suggested by Graves (2009) should contain the following elements:

- The correct answer should be clear and concise.
- The distractors (remaining options) should be clearly wrong.
- The options should be about the same length and use the same syntax. (p. 89)

For example, an assessment of the word *opinion* might look like this:

1. opinion
   a. habit
   b. belief
   c. ability

In the second format, suggested by Blachowicz and Fisher (2006), the word to be tested can appear within context in either a sentence or paragraph. Students are asked to select the best synonym from a list of four words. Such an assessment of the same target word, *opinion*, might look like this:

2. Anna agreed with Janet's *opinion* about the movie. It was awful and a waste of their time and money.

   a. habit
   b. belief
   c. ability
   d. example

Whether you use a quick assessment such as a multiple-choice test or a lengthier one like the four-step process described previously, when students repeatedly demonstrate problems with word knowledge, vocabulary instruction will help improve comprehension.

SECTION III: WHAT INTERVENTIONS MIGHT IMPROVE VOCABULARY?

As noted by Barr et al. (2007), if a student does not know 50% or more of the words encountered in a text, vocabulary can be considered an area of concern. If there is enough evidence to suspect that a weakness in vocabulary is contributing to the student's difficulties, boosting word knowledge will likely improve his or her comprehension of texts. The final section in this chapter provides a description of a few instructional interventions that will help build students' vocabulary.

The Storybook Strategy. We know that wide reading will help our students (Barone, Hardman, & Taylor, 2006; Blachowicz et al., 2006; Fisher et al., 2009; Manzo, Manzo, & Thomas, 2006), and so any approaches that encourage students to increase the amount of time spent in books will be beneficial. Since it is not likely that these children will elect to spend their free time reading, teacher read alouds, when structured to focus specifically on vocabulary, can have a positive impact on their learning.

The Storybook Strategy described by Hickman, Pollar-Durodola, and Vaughn (2004) is an example of a read-aloud format that increases children's time with books while intentionally building vocabulary and comprehension skills. Although their article discusses this strategy in relation to English language learners, it is easy to see how the elements can be used with other learners who need additional instruction in vocabulary. An overview of the strategy is provided here. (For a more detailed presentation, refer to the Hickman et al. [2004] article in *The Reading Teacher.*)

At the heart of the Storybook Strategy is the read aloud, an activity that is a staple in the elementary classroom. Narrative and nonfiction texts may be used and should be at one or two levels above most students' instructional levels. The teacher should consider selecting a series of texts around a theme since this increases the chances that students will have multiple encounters with similar vocabulary across texts. Once the texts are selected, the teacher should separate each into short passages of 200 to 250 words and select three interesting and challenging vocabulary words for each passage.

Hickman et al. (2004) suggested that **Tier 2 words**, as described in *Bringing Words to Life: Robust Vocabulary Instruction* (Beck, McKeown, & Kucan, 2002), will be the most useful. These are words more commonly encountered in texts than in everyday conversation (e.g., *accurate, participate, extraordinary*). A careful study of these words improves students' comprehension because they can be used across a variety of contexts and situations. In contrast, **Tier 1 words** are basic words that are well known and rarely need instruction (e.g., *home*), and **Tier 3 words** are low-frequency words with particular and narrow meanings (e.g., *bungalow*).

Once the vocabulary words have been selected, the teacher is ready to implement the strategy over three to five days. The following five elements are essential to this special type of read aloud:

1. Introduce the story and preview the vocabulary. Provide short explanations of each target word in language that is familiar to the students. Be sure that the definitions are clear and accurate and that they focus, at least initially, on the meaning within the context of the story.

2. Read the passage out loud, focusing on prosody, and then guide students in a discussion that encourages them to use the targeted vocabulary words.

3. Reread the passage, focusing attention on the vocabulary words by having students signal when they hear the word. After the rereading, have students create their own sentences using the words.

4. Engage the students in a dialogue about the story and vocabulary in relation to their own experiences to extend comprehension and processing of vocabulary. The conversation is facilitated by the teacher, and students must do most of the talking.

5. Summarize what was learned about both the story and the vocabulary words, and challenge the students to use the new words throughout the day. Prior to beginning a new passage the next day, review what was learned the day before (Hickman et al., 2004, pp. 725–727).

Vocabulary Self-Collection Strategy. We also know that **word consciousness** helps students continue to build their receptive and expressive vocabularies.

Blachowicz and colleagues (2006) described word consciousness as "an awareness of words and their meanings, an awareness of the ways in which meanings change and grow, and an interest in and motivation to develop new word knowledge" (p. 527). One activity that can help children build word consciousness is the Vocabulary Self-Selection Strategy (VSS; Haggard, 1982). In 2002, Ruddell and Shearer conducted a study with at-risk middle school students; results provided evidence that their self-chosen words were challenging and important and that they remembered those words longer than those that were part of a predetermined spelling curriculum.

VSS is a student-centered interactive strategy that is relatively easy to implement in the classroom or when working with individual children. Ruddell and Shearer (2002) described procedures for its use within a language arts class. Each Monday, students brought in one word that they thought should be part of the spelling/vocabulary list for that week. As part of the nomination process, they told where they found the word, explained what they thought it meant, and told why it should be studied. The teacher also nominated one word per week. The class discussed each word and refined its definition as they finalized the list for the week, usually consisting of not more than five to

The process of selecting and studying words engages students in ways that help build a deeper understanding of those words.

seven words. The final set of words was recorded in students' vocabulary journals. From Tuesday to Friday, the words were studied through discussion, completion of semantic organizers, and other interactive activities. The focus was on exploring each word to build deep, complex understandings. On Friday, students were tested on their ability to spell the words correctly, provide a definition, and use it in a meaningful sentence. Every three weeks, previous words were reviewed and randomly selected for retesting. Although this instructional framework for the VSS appears to be quite traditional, the addition of student choice and plenty of opportunity to explore the words over time increased students' curiosity about and understanding of words that were important to them.

Two Techniques for Vocabulary Instruction in Content Areas. Targeted vocabulary instruction of carefully selected Tier 2 words (Beck et al., 2002) that are important to specific content fields is critical to bolster comprehension of subject-matter texts. However, the National Reading Panel's (2000) review of the research in vocabulary instruction did not lead them to advance a single method of instruction. Rather, because there were so few studies on any given approach, the panel suggested that a variety of direct and indirect methods that provide multiple exposures to words be used. In this section, two instructional techniques appropriate for use in content-area instruction, repeatedly suggested in the literature and detailed in Michael Graves's book *Teaching Individual Words* (Graves, 2009), will be outlined.

The *Four Square* technique (Graves, 2009, pp. 51–52) provides students with an opportunity to explore a word using multiple elements related to that word. The final product is a grid with four quadrants. The key word or concept is written in the upper left quadrant, and the teacher provides a student-friendly definition of the word. Students, in collaboration with the teacher and each other, record examples of the key word or concept and write these in the upper right quadrant. Next, they offer nonexamples and write these in the lower right. Finally, students provide their own definitions in the lower

Table 5.1 Four Square for *Restful*

Word
    restful
	Examples
	    listen to music, walk on the beach, take a nap

Definition
    relaxing, quiet,
    peaceful
	Nonexamples
	    banging drums, giving a speech, taking a test

left quadrant and share these with peers. See Table 5.1 for an example. It is possible to ask students for elements other than examples and nonexamples. Johns and Berglund (2006) suggested that students make a personal connection and list antonyms as substitutions.

The semantic mapping technique (Graves, 2009, pp. 47–48), sometimes called List-Group-Label (Readence, Moore, & Rickelman, 2000), allows students to tap into prior knowledge as they explore and categorize words according to their meanings and characteristics. It is enjoyable and requires the active engagement of students. After the key word or concept is presented to students, they work in small groups and list as many words as they can think of that are related to the target word. As students read their words, the teacher writes them on chart paper or a whiteboard. Depending on the students' prior understandings of the concept, the teacher might group the words in broad categories as students supply them or challenge students to do this work in small groups. Finally, students supply a category or label for the shorter lists of words they have constructed. Because the intent of this activity is to activate students' prior knowledge as well as build their understandings of target words, it is an effective comprehension-building strategy as well.

Intervening With Technology. Wide reading promotes vocabulary development as well as fluency, so any software or Internet resources that engage children with texts that might be a bit challenging for them is likely to increase their receptive vocabularies. Those resources noted in Chapter 4 as well as Storyline Online (www.storylineonline.net), a video streaming site where members of the Screen Actors Guild read quality children's literature aloud, will engage readers. The following is a list of other resources.

- *Learning Vocabulary Can Be Fun* (www.vocabulary.co.il): An Internet site with a number of games for K–12 students. Games are available in category areas such as analogies, homophones, root words, and syllables. While the site offers a wide variety of games, most are best used for practice with words children have already been introduced to.
- *Vocabulary Games* (http://www.vocabulary.co.il/): This site offers a number of vocabulary games and activities that will entertain children while providing practice with words that are listed across a number of categories ranging from idioms to root words to homophones.
- *Cast UDL Book Builder* (http://bookbuilder.cast.org/): This website serves many purposes, including building vocabulary. Teachers and students can create their own books, adding text, images, and audio content. The glossary section is especially useful for building vocabulary knowledge. The book's creator can determine which words should be defined

and click on the glossary tab. A definition and sample sentence can be entered in student-friendly language, and an image can be uploaded. When the students read the text, they can click on the underlined vocabulary words and the glossary entry that was created earlier will pop up.

- *iPod and iPad Applications:* The *Word List App* is a tool for older learners (middle school and up). Clicking on the "Select Word" button provides definitions and sample sentences on flip cards. The "Take Test" button sends students to a multiple choice quiz, and immediate feedback is given and the definition is reviewed. The "Progress Chart" shows the number of words explored and, of those, the number that have been correctly defined in the "Take Test" area. This application has the capacity to provide repeated independent practice with almost 2,000 words, but it needs to be used in conjunction with other vocabulary-building activities in order to ensure that the student truly knows and is able to use the words learned.

SECTION IV: THE CASES

The two assessment case reports presented in this chapter were selected because teachers and examiners felt that limited vocabulary knowledge was an issue in the students' comprehension problems. While there may be other areas of concern as well, as you read the cases, consider whether or not you believe that targeted vocabulary instruction might help Darrell or Brandie improve their comprehension of texts.

Guiding Questions

Section IV of the chapter will help you reflect on what you have learned about vocabulary development and apply your understandings to two particular cases. Read each case quickly to get the gist of what it is about and to identify the issues. Read each case a second time, and when you come to a stop sign in the case, jot down your answers to the following questions:

- What important facts have been revealed at this point in the case?

- Based on what you know so far, what do you think might be going on? It may help to respond to the following prompt: Could it be that . . . ?

- What are the learner's strengths and needs?

- What further assessments or interventions might you try to confirm your ideas?

CASE 1: ASSESSMENT REPORT FOR DARRELL A.

Background Information

Child's name: Darrell A.
Current age: 9
Current grade level: End of Grade 3

Referral

Both Darrell's parents and his teacher requested that Darrell be assessed.

Family and Medical History

Darrell, a nine-year-old, lives with both parents and a younger sister in a small city. The primary language spoken in the home is English. No physical health concerns are noted at this time; however, when he was younger, he had frequent ear infections.

Darrell has been diagnosed with Attention Deficit Hyperactivity Disorder (ADHD) and takes medication daily. He exhibits some anxiety in school-based settings and has hand tremors when the difficulty level of a task increases.

Darrell's parents completed two surveys. In the first, they provided information about their son as a learner (see Figure 5.1), and in the second, they focused on reading-related behaviors (Figure 5.2). In general, the parents were concerned about Darrell's lack of comprehension and noted that, while he seems to be able to identify words, he has trouble understanding what he has read.

Figure 5.1   Parent Survey for Darrell A.: Child as Learner

1. What are your child's free-time interests?
   Swimming, fishing, playing computer, playing PlayStation, watching TV, and listening to music.

2. What types of books does your child enjoy?
   He enjoys nonfiction books.

(Continued)

Figure 5.1 (Continued)

3. What types of writing does your child do at home?

   Darrell doesn't do much writing at home. We have a hard time getting him to practice.

4. What are your observations about how your child learns?

   Darrell seems to take awhile before he understands things.

5. What are some other things you would like us to know about your child?

   Seems to do better in reading when it is more one-on-one then in front of peers.

6. In what ways do you think we can best help your child?

   Darrell is having trouble with compensation in reading he reads well & can sound out words well and does very well in spelling.

Source: Form adapted from *Practical Aspects of Authentic Assessment: Putting the Pieces Together* (pp. 205–207), by B. Hill and C. Ruptic, 1994, Norwood, MA: Christopher-Gordon.

Figure 5.2 Parent Survey for Darrell A.: Child as Reader

1. Does your child enjoy reading?

   We try to incourage Darrel to read at home he does very little at home. He does enjoy reading at school.

2. When did your child begin to read?

   He was slow at learning and unsure how he learned we started trying to teach him at home before starting school.

3. Does your child read for enjoyment?

   He seems to do mainly for necessary reasons.

4. Does your child own books?

   We have many books they are kept on a book shelf Just for the kids and we make regular trips to the library. He has a library card and visits the school and Public library on regular basis.

5. Do others in your family read for enjoyment?

   His sister (7) enjoys reading she reads all the time.

6. What are your child's strengths related to reading?

   can sound out words great and reads well but comprehension is poor.

7. How can we support your child's reading?

   Just to learn to comprehend what he reads.

School History

Darrell is in a third grade classroom. The school is located on the central west side of town in a community of working- and middle-class people. His teacher, Mrs. Rowen, reported that he is reading a year below grade level and has difficulty with comprehension and vocabulary concepts. She indicated that he receives additional help in reading for 30 minutes daily (see Figure 5.3). She notes he is a happy child and easy to work with. Classroom instruction includes reading to him when the class is dealing with texts above his instructional level.

Figure 5.3 Teacher Referral Form for Darrell A.

1. Please describe the nature of the child's reading and writing.

   Darrell is reading at 95% accuracy at a 'K' level which is about one year below grade level. Instructionally he reads at an 'L' level, still below grade level. He's decoding & fluency are good here, however he really struggles with comprehension. Vocabulary concepts cause difficulties. He struggles with more complex sentence structure.

(Continued)

Figure 5.3 (Continued)

2. Please describe any strategies, materials, and/or activities that have been used successfully with this child.

   I find that having him read with someone else & discussing the story as he reads is most helpful. We read to him from books above his level to build vocabulary and background knowledge.

3. What is the child's attitude toward reading and school in general?

   He's a very easy going happy child. He's very easy to work with. He reports that he understands reading better if we talk about it. He is very interested in factual materials.

4. Is this child receiving special services of any kind?

   He receives additional reading help for 30 minutes every day from a Title I reading teacher. Right now we are using a reading workshop format. Darrell is in LD Math at present and has issues with organization.

Any comments or suggestions?

Really encourage him to ask questions when he does not understand (in discussion or in reading).

Detailed Assessment Information

Session 1

Interest Survey. The examiner asked Darrell to complete a 12-question interest survey (Hill & Ruptic, 1994, pp. 175–176). In summary, he enjoys making snow forts, learning about dinosaurs, and participating in gym class. His least favorite subject is math: when asked for a reason, he said, "Because, I hate it." The only topic that he likes to read about is fishing. Darrell's handwriting was very difficult to decipher.

Attitudes About Reading and Writing. Darrell completed the Garfield Elementary Reading Survey (McKenna & Kear, 1990) and the Garfield Writing

Attitude Survey (Kear, Coffman, McKenna, & Ambrosio, 2000). He ranked in the 94th percentile on the reading attitude survey. There were no significant differences in the raw scores between recreational and academic reading. He scored in the 89th percentile on the writing attitude survey. It should be noted that Darrell completed the surveys with a group of children. He was observed looking around the table to see how the other children were responding before circling a Garfield figure on his own survey.

Session 2

Informal Read Aloud. Because initial information indicated that Darrell was below grade level in reading and might exhibit anxiety when tasks were too difficult, the examiner asked him first to read aloud from a text he had self-selected in the Reading Center library. As he read from *Sugarbush Spring* (Chall, 2000), he seemed to struggle with the vocabulary. He relied on the pictures to work out the word meanings and stopped frequently to ask questions about the words. He did not exhibit anxiety or frustration, but it was clear that this mid-third-grade text was causing him difficulties.

Developmental Reading Assessment (Beaver, 2001). Based on the information gained from parent and teacher surveys and the informal read aloud, and in keeping with the DRA guidelines, the examiner selected DRA texts ranging from Levels 24 through 30 for the formal assessment. These texts were in the second- or third-grade range and the equivalent of Guided Reading Levels L through N (Fountas & Pinnell, 1996). Darrell selected the Level 28 text as a "just right" book for him. He read it quickly and easily. His miscues were rare, and his comprehension was at an independent level (Barr et al., 2007), so the examiner asked him to read the Level 30 text, *Tiger's Whirlwind Day* (Pfeffer, 2004). Darrell was highly successful with this text as well. He added the word *thunder* to *storm* consistently. He did not know the word *insisted* (he said *inhist*) and asked for the meanings of the words *rippled* and *whirlwind*. All other errors were self-corrected. His retelling was complete, and he responded to the inference questions correctly.

Session 3

Developmental Reading Assessment (Beaver, 2001). The examiner asked Darrell to read and respond to a Level 34 text, *Summer Discovery* (Stanley, 2004). This was the next level up in the DRA series. Darrell read this text with 98% accuracy, but his comprehension was very low. He seemed to rely heavily on the pictures, and he struggled with vocabulary throughout. A summary of the DRA Observation Guide is provided in Figure 5.4.

Figure 5.4 Summary DRA Assessment for Darrell A.

Text: *Summer Discovery* (Stanley, 2004): *Level 34* (Grade Level Equivalent 3, Guided Reading Level O)

Previewing and Predicting Response (after reading the first page): *He doesn't want them to find out. Mom gives notes but likes the notes.* Darrell appears nervous when responding.

Oral Reading Miscues			
Page/Line	Text Words	Words Said	Error Type
13/4	five	fine	Substitution
13/7	hadn't	had	Substitution
13/8	did	didn't	Self-correction
13/8	she	he	Self-correction
13/9	mothballs Darrell said, "I don't know what that is."	mouthballs	Substitution
13/10	dad's	dad	Substitution
13/13	it	——	Omission
13/14	Peck's	Perk's	Substitution
13/17	little	——	Self-correction
Total Errors: 6—Accuracy: 97%			
Total Self-Corrections: 3			

Fluency

Darrell read in longer phrases and at an adequate rate but sometimes in a monotone.

He used some intonation and attended to punctuation some of the time.

Strategies Used With Difficult Text

Darrell reread and used picture clues when he came to difficult text.

Comprehension (Little to Some Comprehension)

Darrell's retelling included some key events with a few important details. He referred to the main characters using pronouns instead of names. The examiner used multiple prompts and questions, but Darrell had a very difficult time recalling the details of the story.

Adapted from *DRA Observation Guide: Summer Discovery, Level 34* (Beaver, 2002)

Additional Examiner Notes

I could tell that during his silent reading portion, he was not reading everything. He took about eight seconds to read a page with 90 words on it. I asked him if he might have accidentally missed a few pages. He said he might have and reread from near the beginning but the same thing happened. Most of his comprehension was from picture clues, and he misinterpreted quite a few things. There were also a few vocabulary words that stumped him.

Session 4

Vocabulary Assessment. The examiner followed the steps for the *Individual Vocabulary Assessement* (outlined in Barr et al., 2007, pp. 125–127). Because Darrell had exhibited problems with vocabulary words in the DRA text *Summer Discovery* (Stanley, 2004), the examiner selected another text at the same level, *Be Nice to Josephine* (Horvath, 1970/1997). The following seven words were selected: *longingly, disgust, vacant, mumbled, squirmed, unexpected,* and *holiday.* The phrase *blood is thicker than water* was also selected. The examiner asked Darrell to read the story. While he did not appear nervous, his hands were shaking as he read, and he read in a quiet whisper. He appeared to be studying the pictures carefully. As soon as the examiner left Darrell's side, he completed the remaining five pages of the story in less than a minute. His retelling was weak, he included few details even after many prompts, and a number of events were misinterpreted. Out of the eight vocabulary items, Darrell was able to respond correctly three times to the probe "What does _____ mean?" (See Figure 5.5 for Darrell's responses.)

Additional Information

Examiner Anecdotal Notes

After Session 3. I had Darrell try to read a DRA Level 30 book silently just to see if what happened last time (skipping over much of the story) had

Figure 5.5 Darrell's Responses to Vocabulary Assessment

Prompt used: What does _____ mean?

WORD	DARRELL'S RESPONSE
1. longingly	*looked for; see something that's small*
2. discussed	*discussed*
3. vacant	*I don't know.*
4. mumbled	*quiet talk*
5. squirmed	*wiggly*
6. unexpected	*didn't know it was going to happen*
7. holiday	*baseball days? day?*
8. blood is thicker than water	*family is better than water*

something to do with that particular session. He did do better at first but started skimming the pages again by page eight. I chose three words to assess vocabulary, boarded, glum, *and* dirty look. *He knew two of the three. He said* glum *meant bored. Darrell read loud a selected passage at a 97% accuracy rate, but his comprehension was very low and he misinterpreted some events. He also said, "I'm just guessing the characters 'cause I don't know them."*

Case Recap:

1. Review the case and the notes you have taken in response to the guiding questions one final time, and add or revise any information you may have missed.

2. Make a list of additional questions you have about the case. What further information do you need that might be explored in the case discussion?

3. Think about the elements, beyond vocabulary, discussed in other chapters. Might any of these also be problem areas for Darrell? Might any be areas of strength?

CASE 2: ASSESSMENT REPORT FOR BRANDIE C.

Background Information

Child's name: Brandie C.
Current age: 10
Current grade level: End of Grade 5

Referral

Both Brandie's parents and her teacher requested that Brandie attend the Reading Center Program.

Family and Medical History

Brandie is 10 years old and lives with her parents in a small town about 22 miles from a small midwestern city. The primary language spoken in the home is English. No physical health concerns are noted at this time.

Brandie's mother completed a six-question survey about her child as a learner. She noted that Brandie does not enjoy reading and that although she can read all of the words accurately in a given text, she does not comprehend what she has read. She also stated that Brandie may have test anxiety and considers test-taking very difficult. See Figure 5.6 for the full report.

Figure 5.6   Parent Survey for Brandie C.: Child as Learner

1. What are your child's free-time interests?
   Brandie likes are projects such as drawing and painting. She likes to play outside with her friends and likes to watch TV.

2. What types of books does your child enjoy?
   We have lots of books at home but she is not an avid reader. She does her reading what is required for school. Her favorites would be about animals.

(Continued)

Figure 5.6 (Continued)

3. What types of writing does your child do at home?

   Her writing is basically what she does for school work. She tells me she doesn't like to write reports as this requires picking out the most important information and she says she gets too much information as its hard to pick out what is the most important for her.

4. What are your observations about how your child learns?

   I feel Brandie either understands what she's doing or not. If she gets it—she understands—if she doesn't—she doesn't understand. There is no in between. Spelling is no problem learning, but subjects that require reading and finding things in paragraphs are hard for her.

5. What are some other things you would like us to know about your child?

   I notice when she reads, she reads the words wonderfully but when she is done and I ask her what she's read, she doesn't really know. She reads the words but doesn't comprehend what she is reading at the same time.

6. In what ways do you think we can best help your child?

   Brandie has made great strides this year, although she needs help comprehending what she is reading, since every subject has reading with it. I also notice when we study for the tests she knows everything we have studied but if on the test the teacher has reworded a question of how we have studied she doesn't know how to pick out the key words that it is still what we have studied to her it is something different. She is a great kid. And wants to do well. We, as parents want to give her every opportunity to help her gain skills to ease her anxiety re: tests and aid her in her everyday school work. She does well when we study with her and her tests are hard for her. Her classroom and Title 1 reading and math teachers feel she has test anxiety. She does prefer to have tests read to her as she says if she takes it she reads things several times and tends to over analyze it. Mrs. Horn says that many times she had the right answer but then erased it. And changed it to something else. We look forward to your program!

Source: Form adapted from *Practical Aspects of Authentic Assessment: Putting the Pieces Together* (pp. 205–207), by B. Hill and C. Ruptic, 1994, Norwood, MA: Christopher-Gordon.

School History

Brandie has just completed fifth grade at Middle Valley Elementary School. Her classroom teacher, Mrs. Horn, reports that Brandie lacks comprehension due, at times, to low vocabulary. She struggles more with nonfiction text and has difficulty summarizing and picking out important information. Mrs. Horn also notes that Brandie's parents are extremely supportive (see Figure 5.7).

Figure 5.7 Teacher Referral Form for Brandie C.

1. Please describe the nature of the child's reading and writing.

   When reading fiction she reads more fluently with more confidence. When she reads NF she's less fluent and more choppy and she lacks comprehension at times due also to low vocabulary. Summarizing the text is difficult and this is also apparent in her writing. Struggles with writing important information in her own words and wants to copy.

2. Please describe any strategies, materials, and/or activities that have been used successfully with this child.

   Some graphic organizers have been used for example: beginning, middle, end and key points. Partner reading, read alouds for novels, etc. have been used also. Test are being read to her since March. She's receiving Title I services and interactive editing has been successful in her NF content area subjects, mostly Social Studies.

3. What is the child's attitude toward reading and school in general?

   Brandie wants to do well and is a very hard working student. She likes school but is very unsure of herself with academics.

4. Is this child receiving special services of any kind not detailed in 2 above?

   Parents are very, very, supportive!

5. Why do you think this child may benefit from this program?

   Brandie would gain fluency with her oral reading. She would also gain confidence in herself and her ability to pick out key information. I think she would develop skills and strategies to help her figure out words she doesn't know or understand.

Detailed Assessment Information

Session 1

Interest Survey. The examiner asked Brandie to complete a brief survey to record her interests. In summary, she enjoys art and lists her hobbies as drawing and painting. She loves horses and enjoys reading about animals. In the future, she intends to be a veterinarian. She plays basketball in school and plays drums in the school band. Although Brandie was very quiet during the session, she discussed her written answers with the examiner and added that she collects rocks and seashells.

Burke Reading Interview (Goodman, Watson, & Burke, 1987). After completing the interest survey, the examiner gave her the 10-question interview. She found this second survey more difficult and spent a great deal of time on each question. It seems that Brandie sees reading as a process of sounding out and memorizing words (see Figure 5.8).

Figure 5.8 Burke Reading Interview Results for Brandie C.

1. When you are reading and come to something you don't know, what do you do?

   I try to sound it out or have someone help me.

2. Do you ever do anything else?

   think of it

3. Who do you know who is a good reader?

   my grandpa

4. What makes him/her a good reader?

   he puts expression into his reading

5. Do you think she/he ever comes to a word she/he doesn't know when reading?

   no

   If your answer is yes, what do you think she/he does about it?

6. What do you think is the best way to help someone who doesn't read well?

   Try to teach them.

7. How did you learn to read?

   in school

8. What do you remember?

   reading was somewhat easy for me when I was younger

9. What helped you to learn?

hearing someone read

10. What would you like to do better as a reader?

Memorize what I read and learn what words mean.

11. Describe yourself as a reader.

I have some trouble pronouncing words.

12. Using a scale of 5 to 1, with 5 being a terrific reader, what overall rating would you give yourself as a reader?

3 or 4

Source: Original form in *Reading Miscue Inventory: Alternative Procedures* (pp. 219–220), by Y. Goodman, D. Watson, and C. Burke, 1987, Katonah, NY: Richard C. Owens.

DRA Student Reading Survey *(Beaver & Carter, 2006).* In preparation for the DRA, the examiner asked Brandie to complete the DRA Grades 6–8 Survey. (This survey was chosen rather than the one for Grades 4–5 because Brandie would soon be entering Grade 6.) She responded more quickly to this survey but wrote very little text. In the area of *Wide Reading,* Brandie noted that she doesn't read much and is not currently reading anything, although she does like animal books. In the area of *Self-Assessment/Goal Setting,* she sees herself as a good speller and predictor. Her single goal is to remember what she's read by "sounding out words and getting them right."

Session 2

Writing Survey (Strickland, 2005). Originally, Brandie was to have completed an informal writing survey during Session 1, but because it took her so long to complete the other surveys, the examiner decided to wait until Session 2. Brandie did not seem to have as much difficulty with this one as she had with those related to reading. Overall, her responses indicate that her attitude toward writing is quite positive. She made some interesting spelling errors (*wrighting, exsiting, beaucause*). For her complete responses, see Figure 5.9.

Developmental Reading Assessment (Beaver & Carter, 2003a). Based on the information gained from surveys, the examiner selected a DRA nonfiction text at Level 50, *Storm Chasers.* This text was in the fifth grade range and the

Figure 5.9 *What I Think About Writing* Survey Results for Brandie C.

1. When did you learn to write? Who taught you?
   Around kindergarten. My parents, grandparents, and my teacher.

2. What do you like to write at home?
   I like to make cards at home.

3. What do you like to write at school?
   I like to make books in school.

4. What makes a person a good writer? What do good writers do?
   When they right exsitment in it. When they proofread and spell right

5. Who do you think is a good writer? Why is he or she good?
   My parents. beaucause

6. What are some topics you like to write about?
   I like to right funny things.

7. Do you like to share your writing with other people? Why or why not?
   Yes, because then they might think of something similar to that.

8. Do you like to read the writing of other people in your class? Why or why not?
   Yes, because it might be an exsiting wrighting.

9. What do you think about your writing?
   I like it because when I write I might think of something when I write.

10. Do you think writing is important? Why or Why not?
    Yes, because when you get older you'll have to right a lot.

Source: Original form in *What's After Assessment: Follow-Up Instruction for Phonics, Fluency and Comprehension* (p. 23), by K. Strickland, 2005, Portsmouth, NH: Heinemann.

equivalent of Guided Reading Levels U through W (Fountas & Pinnell, 1996). Brandie completed the oral reading portion of the assessment first. Her rate of reading at 90 words per minute was somewhat slow. She read with some expression and made only four miscues, none of which altered meaning (two insertions, two repetitions). Her oral reading accuracy was 98%.

Next, Brandie completed the prediction section of the Student Booklet. She predicted that she would learn about storms and asked three questions she thought the text might address: *How many different storms are their? How many tornadoes can go at a time? How do storms start?* Brandie reread the entire text and then completed the questions in the student booklet. It took her a long time to complete the booklet. She spent 30 minutes working on the first question, a summary, and constantly flipped back through the text to add more information. Rather than a summary, she wrote a series of facts, most copied directly from different sections of the text. Her responses to the remaining questions were scant, with the exception of Item 5 (*Metacognitive Awareness*). The whole process seemed to overwhelm and exhaust her. While her DRA score for oral reading was at the independent level, her comprehension skills and strategies score was at the intervention or frustration level. For a summary of her responses to the questions in the booklet, see Figure 5.10.

Figure 5.10   After Reading Student Booklet Response for Brandie C.

Text: *Storm Chasers* (Beaver & Carter, 2003b): *Level 50* (Grade Level Equivalent 5, Guided Reading Levels U–W)

Summary: Scored 1 of 4 possible points: Wrote 1 or 2 facts in own language and/or copied from the text. Written responses are included below:

Taking pictures of lightening is dangerous. Lightening kills about 100 people each year in the United States. It could strike several miles in front of a storm. (These were the 1st three sentences of paragraph 1, from page 3 of original text.)

Only about one in ten chases are actually tornadoes (sentence 2 on page 5). *Chasers have to be able to change routes as quick as the storm.* (This was a close paraphrase of sentence 8 on page 5 of the original text.)

Each year about 1,000 tornadoes are found here, in the United States (a close paraphrase of sentence 1 on page 6). *They kill about 80 people and injure more than 1,500* (sentence 2 from page 6 of original text). *Hurricanes can be more than 200 miles wide* (sentence 2, paragraph 2, from page 8 of original text).

Literal Comprehension: Scored 1 of 4 possible points: provided little information from the text and/or included incorrect information. Questions and responses are included below:

Q: What are the reasons storm chasers chase storms?
A: *To worn people.*

(Continued)

Figure 5.10 (Continued)

Interpretation: Scored 1 of 4 possible points: Little or no understanding of important text implications

Q: What qualities do you think help make a storm chaser successful?

A: *Storm chasers would have to be fast and careful so they don't get struck.*

Q: What in the text makes you think that?

A: *They would have to be in the hospital for a long time probably.*

Reflection: Scored 2 of 4 possible points: vaguely related or less significant message or information; general or no statement(s) to support opinion

Q: What do you think is the most important thing you learned from this text?

A: *That lightning can strike several miles in front of a storm.*

Q: Tell why.

A: *Because I never knew that.*

Metacognition: Scored 2 of 4 possible points: Gave a brief explanation of the use of 1 or more strategies; made vague or general statements

Strategies Used: Used text and graphic features to determine importance; reflected as to why things happened. Question and student response included below:

Q: Tell how you used these strategies by giving examples of what you did as you read the text.

A: *I looked at the title and the front picture and the question popped in my head. On pg. 6 I never knew about that stuff like the way a tornado goes and warmer and cooler air.*

Source: Adapted from *Teacher Observation Guide: Storm Chasers, Level 50,* by J. Beaver and M. Carter, 2003d, Parsippany, NJ: Celebration Press.

Session 3

Developmental Reading Assessment (Beaver, 2006). The examiner decided to focus this assessment session around a fiction Level 40 text, *All the Way Under* (Sreenivasan, 2003). The text was in the fourth grade range and the equivalent of Guided Reading Levels Q through R (Fountas & Pinnell, 1996). Brandie's completed oral reading rate at 129 words per minute was adequate. She read with some expression and made only four miscues. None altered meaning (three substitutions, one insertion), and all were self-corrected. Her reading accuracy was 99%, putting her at the independent level in this category.

After the oral reading, Brandie completed the two questions related to before reading predictions. She wrote one prediction: "The girl probably will go under water, and see that it isn't scary," and asked three questions (two virtually the same) she thought the text might answer: "How old is she? Why won't she go under water? How old is Katie?" Brandie needed a good deal of time to complete the student booklet after reading the text. She revisited the story before writing her answers, although not as much as she had in the nonfiction text. Her summary provided the plot line of the story, but none of the characters was mentioned by name. Her responses to the remaining questions were sufficient to yield a score of 12, putting this text at her instructional level in the area of comprehension skills and strategies. See Figure 5.11 for a summary of her responses to the questions in the booklet.

Figure 5.11   After Reading Student Booklet Response for Brandie C.

Text: *All the Way Under* (Sreenivasan, 2003): *Level 40* (Grade Level Equivalent 4, Guided Reading Levels Q–R)

Summary: Scored 2 of 4 possible points: Provided partial summary generally in own language, with some important characters/events. Written response included below:

The girl was scared of the water. Her cousin came, grabbed her hand and walked her into the water. Then a big wave came and washed her under. Then something grabbed her leg and she thought it was an octupous so she yelled for help. When the lifegaurd pulled her out and they saw that it was seaweed.

Then the lifegaurd showed her to put her head under water so then she decide's to go under water by herself.

Literal Comprehension: Scored 2 of 4 possible points: Included some information from the text. Questions and student responses included below:

Q: What is Sonya's problem?

A: *She's scared of water.*

Q: How is it solved?

A: *The lifegaured showes her to go under water so then she decides to go under by herself.*

Interpretation: Scored 2 of 4 possible points: Some understanding of important text implications, but provided little or no details. Questions and student responses included below:

Q: What do you think Sonya learns?

A: *Not to be scared of the water.* (had written and then erased *and seaweed*)

Q: What happens in the story to make you think that?

A: *When she'd go under water with any help.*

(Continued)

Figure 5.11 (Continued)

Reflection: Scored 2 of 4 possible points: Vaguely related or less significant message or information; general statement with no support. Questions and student responses included below:

Q: What do you think is the most important event in this story?

A: *Not to be scared of the water and seaweed.*

Q: Tell why.

A: *Because there's nothing to be scared of if someone's with you.*

Metacognition: Scored 2 of 4 possible points: Brief explanation of the use of one or more strategies; vague or general statements.

Strategies Used: Questioning. Questions and student responses included below:

Q: Give examples from this story to show what you did to help you understand it.

A: *I thought about it just before I read it. I have a question. Why is she scared of the water?*

Source: Questions taken from *DRA4–8 Teacher Observation Guide: All the Way Under, Level 40,* by J. Beaver and M. Carter, 2003c, Parsippany, NJ: Celebration Press.

Session 4

Vocabulary Assessment. Because Brandie's teacher had indicated that vocabulary was a problem, especially with nonfiction text, the examiner elected to conduct a vocabulary assessment and followed the steps for the *Individual Vocabualary Assessement* (outlined in Barr et al., 2007, pp. 125–127). She choose a fourth grade social studies text and excerpted a section about changes in the west. Brandie had difficulty with the comprehension questions and spent a lot of time revisiting the text for the anwers. Her retelling was incomplete, and she correctly answered only 83% of the questions. She offered acceptable definitions for only three of the nine vocabulary words, giving her a score of 44% in this area (see Figure 5.12 for Brandie's responses).

Figure 5.12   Brandie's Responses to Vocabulary Assessment

Prompt used: What does _____ mean?

WORD	RESPONSE
1. profit:	*when people give up stuff to sell*
2. fares:	*——*
3. freight:	*scared of somebody*
4. congress:	*I can't remember—I know it is from* SS (Social Studies)
5. plains:	*grassy hills and crops that farmers grow*
6. steel plow:	*use it to farm the sod*
7. settlers:	*people moved from someplace and they came to this land and settled in there and build houses and soon it becomes a big town.*
8. breadbasket:	*where wheat was grown to feed the whole country*

Additional Information

Examiner Anecdotal Notes

After Session 4. Brandie could not answer the comprehension questions without looking back. She answered by reading directly from the text. She wasn't able to give answers in her own words. She was good at finding where the answers were in the reading though. She struggled with the vocabulary words I assessed. The words definitely played a big part in her understanding of the text.

Case Recap:

1. Review the case and the notes you have taken in response to the guiding questions one final time, and add or revise any information you may have missed.

2. Make a list of additional questions you have about the case. What further information do you need that might be explored in the case discussion?

3. Think about the elements, beyond vocabulary, discussed in other chapters. Might any of these also be problem areas for Brandie? Might any be areas of strength?

CHAPTER SUMMARY

This chapter provided you with information about vocabulary development and instruction. In addition, the cases of Brandie and Darrell helped to build a context for you in which to consider the role vocabulary plays in the reading process. The more words that children know deeply, the more skilled they will be at unlocking the meaning across a variety of texts. While vocabulary knowledge is not the only skill required for comprehension, it is an essential one. The next chapter discusses comprehension and its importance in the reading process.

Terms highlighted in this chapter

incrementality 146	multidimensionality 146
polysemy 146	interrelatedness 146
heterogeneity 146	receptive vocabulary 147
expressive vocabulary 147	academic vocabulary 149
scaffolded instruction 149	Tier 2 words 152
Tier 1 words 152	Tier 3 words 152
word consciousness 152	

FINAL QUESTIONS FOR REFLECTION AND RESPONSE

1. Review the five aspects of word knowledge presented at the beginning of this chapter. Describe the ways you might develop instruction for Brandie and Darrell (or your own students) that would ensure that you are addressing each of these aspects.

2. If Brandie and Darrell were students in your classroom, how might you develop instruction that specifically targeted their weaknesses in vocabulary?

3. Consider the cases that you have read in other chapters. Do you believe that problems in vocabulary knowledge might be a factor in the students' literacy development? What evidence did you find that leads you to this conclusion?

Journals Online

Visit the student study site at www.sagepub.com/combsstudy to access recent, relevant, full-text journal articles from SAGE's leading research journals.

REFERENCES

Barone, D., Hardman, D., & Taylor, J. (2006). *Reading first in the classroom.* Boston: Allyn & Bacon.

Barr, R., Blachowicz, C., Bates, A., Katz, C., & Kaufman, B. (2007). *Reading diagnosis for teachers: An instructional approach* (5th ed.). Boston: Allyn & Bacon.

Beaver, J. (2001). *Developmental reading assessment: K–3 teacher resource guide: Revised.* Parsippany, NJ: Celebration Press.

Beaver, J. (2002). *Teacher observation guide: Summer discovery, Level 34.* Parsippany, NJ: Celebration Press.

Beaver, J. (2006). *DRA2: Developmental reading assessment: Teacher guide, Grades K–3.* Parsippany, NJ: Celebration Press.

Beaver, J., & Carter, M. (2003a). *DRA: Developmental reading assessment.* Parsippany, NJ: Celebration Press.

Beaver, J., & Carter, M. (2003b). *Student booklet: Storm chasers, Level 50.* Parsippany, NJ: Celebration Press.

Beaver, J., & Carter, M. (2003c). *Teacher observation guide: All the way under, Level 40.* Parsippany, NJ: Celebration Press.

Beaver, J., & Carter, M. (2003d). *Teacher observation guide: Storm chasers, Level 50.* Parsippany, NJ: Celebration Press.

Beaver, J., & Carter, M. (2006). *Developmental reading assessment: 4–8* (2nd ed.). Parsippany, NJ: Celebration Press.

Beck, I., McKeown, M., & Kucan, L. (2002). *Bringing words to life: Robust vocabulary instruction.* New York: Guilford Press.

Beck, I., McKeown, M., & Kucan, L. (2008). *Creating robust vocabulary: Frequently asked questions and extended examples.* New York: Guliford Press.

Blachowicz, C., & Fisher, P. (2006). *Teaching vocabulary in all classrooms* (3rd ed.). Upper Saddle River, NJ: Merril Prentice Hall.

Blachowicz, C., Fisher, P., & Watts-Taffe, S. (2006). Vocabulary: Questions from the classroom. *Reading Research Quarterly, 41*(4), 524–539.

Carlo, M., August, D., McLaughlin, B., Snow, C., Dressler, C., Lippman, D., et al. (2004). Closing the gap: Addressing the vocabulary needs of English-language learners in bilingual and mainstream classrooms. *Reading Research Quarterly, 39*(2), 188–215.

Chall, M. W. (2000). *Sugarbush spring.* New York: Harper Collins.

Cummins, C. (2006). *Understanding and implementing reading first initiatives: The changing role of administrators.* Newark, DE: International Reading Association.

Fisher, D., Frey, N., & Lapp, D. (2009). *In a reading state of mind: Brain research, teacher modeling, and comprehension instruction.* Newark, DE: International Reading Association.

Fountas, I., & Pinnell, G. (1996). *Guided reading: Good first teaching for all children.* Portsmouth, NH: Heinemann.

Goodman, Y., Watson, D., & Burke, C. (1987). *Reading miscue inventory: Alternative procedures.* Katonah, NY: Richard C. Owens.

Graves, M. (2009). *Teaching individual words: One size does not fit all.* New York: Teachers College Press.

Graves, M. F., Sales, G. C., & Ruda, M. (2009, April 12). *The first 4000 words.* Retrieved 2010, from http://www.thefirst4000words.com/

Haggard, M. R. (1982). The vocabulary self collection strategy: An active approach to word learning. *The Journal of Reading, 26,* 203–207.

Hickman, P., Pollar-Durodola, S., & Vaughn, S. (2004). Storybook reading: Improving vocabulary and comprehension for English-language learners. *The Reading Teacher, 57*(8), 720–730.

Hill, B., & Ruptic, C. (1994). *Practical aspects of authentic assessment: Putting the pieces together.* Norwood, MA: Christopher-Gordon.

Horvath, B. (1997). *Be nice to Josephine.* Parsippany, NJ: Celebration Press. (Original work published 1970)

Johns, J., & Berglund, R. (2006). *Strategies for content area learning* (2nd ed.). Dubuque, IA: Kendall/Hunt.

Kamil, M. (2004). Vocabulary and comprehension instruction: Summary and implications of the national reading panel findings. In P. McCardle & V. Chhabra (Eds.), *The voice of evidence in reading research* (pp. 213–234). Baltimore: Paul H. Brookes.

Kear, D. J., Coffman, G. A., McKenna, M. C., & Ambrosio, A. L. (2000). Measuring attitude toward writing: A new tool for teachers. *The Reading Teacher, 54*(1), 14–24.

Labbo, L., Love, M. S., & Ryan, T. (2007). A vocabulary flood: Making words "sticky" with computer response activities. *The Reading Teacher, 60*(6), 582–588.

Manzo, A., Manzo, U., & Thomas, M. (2006). Rationale for systematic vocabulary development: Antidote for state mandates. *Journal of Adolescent & Adult Literacy, 49*(7), 610–619.

McKenna, M., & Kear, D. J. (1990). Measuring attitude toward reading: A new tool for teachers. *The Reading Teacher, 43,* 626–639.

Nagy, W., & Scott, J. (2000). Vocabulary pocesses. In M. Kamil, P. Mosenthal, D. Pearson, & R. Barr (Eds.), *Handbook of reading research* (pp. 269–284). Mahwah, NJ: Lawrence Erlbaum.

National Reading Panel. (2000). *Teaching children to read: An evidenced-based assessment of the scientific research literature on reading and its implications for reading instruction.* Washington, DC: National Institute of Child Health and Human Development.

Pearson, D., Heibert, E., & Kamil, M. (2007). Vocabulary assessment: What we know and what we need to learn. *Reading Research Quarterly, 42*(2), 282–296.

Pfeffer, W. (2004). *Tiger's whirlwind day.* Parsippany, NJ: Celebration Press.

Readence, J., Moore, D., & Rickelman, R. (2000). *Prereading activities for content area reading and learning.* Newark, DE: International Reading Association.

Ruddell, M. R., & Shearer, B. (2002). "Extraordinary," "tremendous," "exhilarating," "magnificent": Middle school at-risk students become avid word learners with the vocabulary self-collection strategy. *Journal of Adolescent & Adult Literacy, 45*(5), 352–363.

Spencer, B., & Guillaume, A. (2006). Integrating curriculum through the learning cycle: Content-based reading and vocabulary instruction. *The Reading Teacher, 60*(3), 206–219.

Sreenivasan, J. (2003). *All the way under.* Parsippany, NJ: Celebration Press.

Stanley, E. (2004). *Summer discovery.* Parsippany, NJ: Celebration Press.

Strickland, K. (2005). *What's after assessment? Follow-up instruction for phonics, fluency and comprehension.* Portsmouth, NH: Heinemann.

CHAPTER 6
Focus on Comprehension

"It seems very pretty," she said when she had finished it, *"but it's RATHER hard to understand! . . . Somehow it seems to fill my head with ideas—only I don't exactly know what they are!"*

—Lewis Carroll

Guiding Questions

Sections I through III of this chapter will help build your knowledge related to comprehension and will prepare you to read and discuss the cases in Section IV. As you read, consider the following questions:

- What is reading comprehension?

- What factors influence comprehension?

- What are key characteristics of proficient and struggling comprehenders?

- How do we assess reading comprehension?

- What instructional interventions might be used to improve comprehension?

INTRODUCTION

Helping readers comprehend is at the heart of the literacy work teachers and specialists do. It is the end goal for them and their students. Gambrell, Block, and Pressley (2002) described reading comprehension as the process of "acquiring meaning, confirming meaning, and creating meaning from written texts. . . . In sum, comprehension is the process of meaning making" (pp. 4–5). If learners are not able to unlock the meaning of texts, if they are unable to make connections with what they already know, if they are not able to understand and integrate the words, phrases, paragraphs, and ideas across a text, then they are not really reading.

The two students you will read about in this chapter are Kari and Selena. Both struggle with comprehension. Your challenge as you read each case will be to decide whether or not a lack of skill in the area of comprehension alone is the issue. It may be that other elements related to the reading process are also affecting their ability to comprehend text. Consider their cases carefully because your decision will direct how you might intervene with readers like Kari and Selena. If you decide that comprehension weaknesses are the predominant issue, the information provided in Sections I and II of this chapter, along with interventions discussed in Section III, will help you think about what approaches might be the best to promote literacy growth in each of the children. If you think that other elements, such as word identification or vocabulary, are involved, the information in chapters related to those elements should guide your thinking about which interventions to employ.

Section I: What Do We Know About Comprehension?

What Is Reading Comprehension?

Definitions provided in the literature share an understanding of comprehension as a constructive, interactive process, an "elaborate dance" (Rasinski & Padak, 2008, p. 5) that takes place between the reader and the text (Hacker, 2004; National Reading Panel, 2000; Pardo, 2004; Rand Reading Study Group, 2004; Sweet & Snow, 1998). The process is driven by and dependent on several things, including decoding ability (Pressley, 2000; Paris & Hamilton, 2009), vocabulary knowledge (Fisher, Frey, & Lapp, 2009), and the reader's prior knowledge and experience, which is tied to his or her community and culture (Barr, Blachowicz, Bates, Katz, & Kaufman, 2007; Barton & Sawyer, 2003; Harris & Hodges, 1995).

Block (1999) described the development of comprehension as a "crafting process" (p. 99) and added that the teacher is an active participant in helping students work "artistically" (p. 99) with authors and texts. Central to the crafting process is readers' ability to employ strategies that will enable them to connect the language in the text to their own language and knowledge. Research in comprehension conducted over the last two decades has identified a number of strategies, also referred to as *cognitive* or *thinking strategies* (National Reading Panel, 2000), that readers use routinely in flexible and adaptable ways to "foster, monitor, regulate and maintain comprehension" (Dole, Duffy, Roehler, & Pearson, 1991, p. 242). The strategies most commonly discussed in the literature are questioning, summarizing, creating mental images, self-monitoring comprehension, activating prior knowledge, making inferences, predicting, and determining importance (Duke & Pearson, 2002; Fisher et al., 2009; Fordham, 2006; Gambrell et al., 2002; Keene & Zimmermann, 2007; May, 2001; McKenna & Dougherty Stahl, 2009; Reutzel, Camperell, & Smith, 2002; Wilhelm, 2001; Zimmermann & Hutchins, 2003).

Other strategies that occur less frequently in the literature but are still deemed important to effective comprehension include synthesizing (Fisher et al., 2009; Keene & Zimmermann, 2007; Zimmermann & Hutchins, 2003), connecting (Fisher et al., 2009; Fordham, 2006), setting a purpose (Fisher et al., 2009; Wilhelm, 2001), and evaluating (Fordham, 2006; Gambrell et al., 2002). None of the strategies noted above is innate; rather, each must be taught and practiced until it becomes effortless and reading automatic (Afflerbach, Pearson, & Paris, 2008).

What Factors Influence Comprehension?

According to Pressley (2000), comprehension is a multifaceted process that is developmental in nature. Three overarching elements that affect comprehension development are the reader, the text, and the context (see Figure 6.1). Factors within each of these interact to determine what a learner will understand at any particular time.

The Reader

Reutzel et al. (2002) discussed three reader variables that impact the ability to extract meaning from text. The first is the reader's oral language and vocabulary development. In general, they noted, children who do not acquire sufficient **expressive** and **receptive language skills** early in life experience comprehension difficulties later on.

Figure 6.1 Elements Affecting Comprehension Development

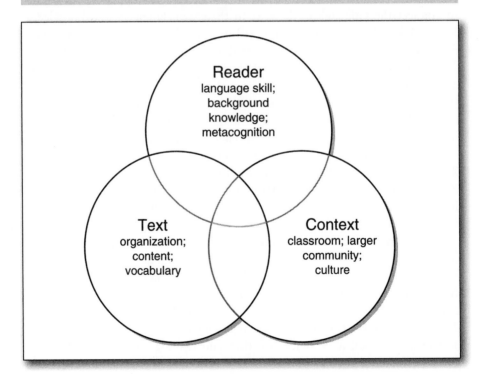

The second reader-related variable affecting comprehension is background knowledge. Proficient readers use their background knowledge to connect what they know to what they are reading. They engage actively with texts, making inferences, creating images, and asking and answering questions. Poor readers with limited background knowledge rarely challenge or identify inconsistencies in texts. This results in misinterpretations about what they read. Alternatively, some poor readers rely too heavily on their meager background knowledge. They draw on unrelated information that results in a misreading of the text and comprehension failure.

The third reader-related variable discussed by Reutzel and colleagues (2002) involves motivation (which will be discussed more thoroughly in Chapter 7) and self-regulation. Proficient readers' confidence with and ability to employ successful strategies independently increases their motivation and persistence with difficult text and fosters a desire to engage in reading independently. On the other hand, readers who struggle have low expectations for success, which exacerbates their ability to read strategically and limits their willingness to persist with challenging texts. Worse still, they begin to believe that their reading difficulties are related to something they cannot change.

Self-regulation is an aspect of metacognition. Metacognitive awareness is a critical factor in reading success that involves the reader's knowledge about and control over the strategies necessary for successful comprehension (Lipson & Wixson, 2003). As noted by Schmitt and Sha (2009), reading with meaning requires a balancing act between metacognitive knowledge and regulation (see Figure 6.2). Proficient readers know about strategies (declarative knowledge) that contribute to comprehension success, know how (procedural knowledge) to use the strategies, know when and where (conditional knowledge) to use them, and employ the strategies selectively "on the run," using a problem-solving process that sustains meaning.

The Text

Texts can provide a variety of challenges and can be easier or harder to read depending on those challenges. If the reader is unfamiliar with the genre, internal organization, and structure of a text, gaining meaning will be a challenge (Sweet & Snow, 1998). If the **content load**—the amount of content presented—is heavy and the ideas within the content are highly complex, comprehension can prove challenging. If the vocabulary is unfamiliar to the reader as well, the reading becomes laborious and comprehension is compromised. Eventually, the reader gives up. This is true even for the proficient reader. Although texts need

Figure 6.2 Metacognitive Balancing Act Influencing Comprehension

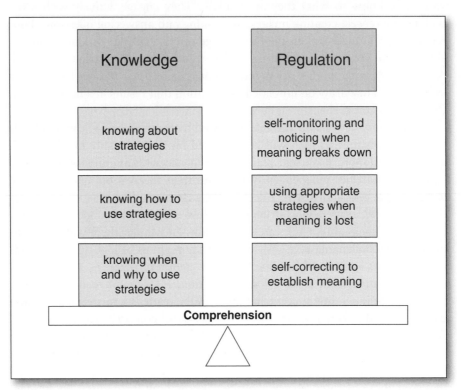

to be sufficiently challenging to ensure growth, if we repeatedly assign texts that are simply too hard, the opposite effect will result (Fisher et al., 2009).

The Context

Comprehension is affected by a learner's social construction of knowledge within the classroom as well as the community and the culture in which the learner lives (Barr et al., 2007). The specific curriculum and classroom activities along with student to teacher and student to student interactions will have an impact on what a learner comprehends. The classroom where students are engaged in rich in-depth discussions using multiple texts across various genres will yield a very different understanding from the classroom where students are assigned a single text to read and a series of questions to answer independently.

Clearly, learning does not happen solely within the confines of the classroom or school building. Other factors, including socioeconomic status, family and social group membership, and larger cultural beliefs and understandings will affect comprehension (Rand Reading Study Group, 2004; Sweet & Snow, 1998). The child who has a bedroom filled with books, a computer with Internet access, and parents who read and discuss stories and news will engage with texts in a very different way from the child who has had more limited literacy materials and experiences. Likewise, the child who lives within a family that has a rich interactive storytelling tradition will approach texts in a different way from the child whose family expects children to be quiet and unobtrusive during family gatherings. The language spoken in the home and the cultural background of the child must also be considered. If either differs significantly from the texts the child encounters in school, problems in comprehension are inevitable. Learning and literacy occur within a cultural and historical setting that helps to shape a reader's abilities and motivations and to define the level of success in the school activities in which the child will engage (Sweet & Snow, 1998).

What Are Key Characteristics of Proficient and Struggling Comprehenders?

The preceding paragraphs provided some information that helps us to understand the differences between proficient and struggling readers. Table 6.1 adds to this information by presenting a synthesis from the literature that contrasts the typical characteristics of successful readers with those of readers who struggle (Barone, Hardman, & Taylor, 2006; Duke & Pearson, 2002; Hacker, 2004; Keene, 2002; Ketch, 2005; National Assessment of Educational Progress, 1998; Pressley, 1999; Snow, Griffin, & Burns, 2005; Wilhelm, 2001).

Table 6.1 Contrasting Characteristics of Proficient and Struggling Comprehenders

Proficient Comprehenders	Struggling Comprehenders
• Generally read from first page to last, though they may jump around looking for information they think might be in the text or look back for clarification • Read selectively, deciding what to read carefully, what to read quickly, what not to read, and what to reread	• Often plow right through a text, decoding words but not comprehending • Act as though reading the last word of a passage is the only goal • Do not compare information with prior knowledge and fail to alter current understanding in light of new information

(Continued)

Table 6.1 (Continued)

Proficient Comprehenders	Struggling Comprehenders
• Have clear goals in mind and evaluate as they read to determine whether the text is meeting their goals • Predict the content, monitor whether their predictions are accurate, and make adjustments when they are not • Activate prior knowledge before, during, and after reading • Infer, question, and visualize as they read • Retell, synthesize, and reflect on the ideas in the text, constructing summaries and reasoning about whether the ideas in the text are sensible • Select, when comprehension is compromised, the correct strategy from among many in their repertoire to overcome roadblocks and restore meaning	• Believe that some ideas will remain vague • Skip over unfamiliar words • Fail to detect the errors or, if detected, fail to resolve them • Read on, when comprehension is compromised, and hope that understanding will magically occur • Fill gaps in understanding by inserting personal experiences • Believe that good readers never encounter obstacles and never ask for help • Give up

Awareness of these characteristics can help us identify learners who are struggling. Once identified, however, additional detailed assessment is essential in order to target the particular strategies and skills the learner needs to develop into a proficient comprehender of texts.

Section II: How Do We Assess Reading Comprehension?

A reader can fail to comprehend a text for many reasons. In addition to the factors, skills, and strategies noted previously, it is possible that limited decoding ability, poor sight word knowledge, or limited fluency is getting in the way of understanding the text (Rasinski & Padak, 2008). If any of these three is a primary culprit, instruction needs to be designed to address them specifically. (Chapters 3 and 4 address these elements in detail.) If, however, print skill and fluency is adequate and vocabulary knowledge seems sufficient, the processes involved in comprehension itself should be assessed (Barr et al., 2007). **Retelling,** questioning, and **think alouds** are the most common tools used to assess a learner's comprehension skill and strategy use.

Retelling is a very common post-reading assessment procedure that provides information about a learner's basic understanding of the text and reveals what information was valued (McKenna & Dougherty Stahl, 2009). It is simple and quick to implement and requires little preparation (Rasinski & Padak, 2008). Retellings may be oral or written, open-ended or prompted. Lipson and Wixson (2003) suggested doing both. Begin with an open-ended retelling in order to gain insight about how the learner processes text. Simply ask the reader to tell everything she or he remembers about what was just read. After allowing the student ample time to recall information, use prompts and questions such as "Where did the story take place? Who was the story about? What happened before/after . . . ?" to elicit more detail. When analyzing a retelling of narrative or expository texts, consider to what extent the student has included the items listed in Table 6.2.

There are two cautions to be made when using retellings to determine comprehension of text. First, it is possible that poor comprehension may be due to weaknesses in print skill or fluency. To control for these factors, Rasinski and Padak (2008) suggested that the assessor read aloud stories or expository excerpts as part of the assessment process. Second, retellings rely heavily on a learner's verbal skills and vocabulary. Deficiencies in these areas could lead to a mistaken judgement about the reader's understanding of the text. Barr and colleagues (2007) recommended that a retelling always be followed with a set of questions to determine the extent of the learner's comprehension skill.

Table 6.2   Retelling Elements

Narrative Text	Expository Text
All major plot elements are provided accurately and in order (setting, problem, plot details, resolution).	All main ideas and one or two details for each are included.
All major characters are named.	Organization of the retelling follows the organization of the text (chronological, compare/contrast, problem/solution, cause/effect, listing).
Any minor details or characters may be included, but not as a substitute for the main story.	Vocabulary used in the text, especially those words tied to key concepts, is used correctly.

Source: Adapted from Reading A–Z, at http://www.readinga-z.com/newfiles/strat/rubric_strat.html

Asking questions is the most frequently used procedure to determine comprehension of text. Barr and colleagues (2007) noted that questioning is essential to all assessment. "Because questions serve as cues or prompts, readers can usually remember much more about a passage in response to questioning than they can reproduce in a free recall" (pp. 205–206). Therefore, a good set of questions can provide the examiner with a more valid estimate of the reader's comprehension skill than retelling alone.

McKenna and Dougherty Stahl (2009) described three levels of questions most commonly used when assessing a learner's comprehension of text:

- Literal: questions that require the reader to recall a specific fact that has been explicitly stated in the reading selection (e.g., What were the three little pigs' houses made of?)
- Inferential: questions that lead the reader to make logical connections among facts in a text to reach a conclusion that is not specifically stated (e.g., What would you make your house out of if you were one of the pigs?)
- Critical: questions that call on the learner to make value judgments based on his or her own value system (e.g., Do you think it was OK for the third little pig to trick the wolf?)

McKenna and Dougherty Stahl (2009) further noted that the ability to assess the full extent of a learner's comprehension skill is dependent on the types of questions asked; therefore, a good post-reading assessment must include all three levels. In addition, they cautioned that questions that readers can answer correctly without having adequately comprehended a text fail to assess reading comprehension. Questions should target information in the text that is not likely to rely on the student's prior knowledge alone. Many **informal reading inventories,** such as the Qualitative Reading Inventory (QRI) (Leslie & Caldwell, 2000), Analytical Reading Inventory (ARI) (Woods & Moe, 1999), and Developmental Reading Assessment (DRA) (Beaver & Carter, 2006), include questions at all three levels.

The think-aloud strategy is a powerful procedure for revealing the strategies and processes a reader employs while moving through text. In the think-aloud procedure described by Lipson and Wixson (2003), the assessor asks the reader to stop at predetermined points during the reading of the text and discuss what she or he was thinking about or doing as she or he read that particular section. Wilhelm, in *Improving Comprehension With Think-Aloud Strategies* (2001), provided a checklist of strategies called My Think-Aloud Moves (pp. 169–171). As readers move through the text, they stop each time they make a mental move and check it off on the checklist. Readers then add a comment relating why and how they made that particular move. The mental moves included in the checklist are connecting, making predictions, making inferences, visualizing, and summarizing. Regardless of the procedure used, the think-aloud strategy is an effective performance-based assessment that provides evidence of a reader's use of comprehension strategies before, during, and after reading.

Comprehension can also be assessed through a learner's written responses to open-ended questions or freely written reflections; however, Snow et al. (2005) cautioned against using this process alone since the comprehension of young students or those who are not yet fluent writers can be severely underestimated.

Cloze assessment can reveal whether or not a student will be able to comprehend the material in a text. It involves deleting words from a prose selection of about 300 words. Generally, every fifth word is deleted—with the exception of the first sentence in the selection, which remains intact. Students read the text and replace the missing words based on the surrounding context (McKenna & Dougherty Stahl, 2009). In scoring the results, credit is given for exact matches only. A score of 60% or greater indicates that the text is at the child's independent reading level. A score ranging from 40% to 60% indicates that the text is within the child's instructional level, and a score below 40% indicates that the text is at the frustration level for the child.

Finally, graded word lists can provide a very rough estimate of comprehension but are no substitute for the real thing. McKenna and Dougherty Stahl (2009) noted that word lists are best used as a text-level starting point from which a more detailed assessment of a reader's comprehension of text can be administered. Many informal reading inventories use word lists in this way.

SECTION III: WHAT INSTRUCTIONAL INTERVENTIONS MIGHT IMPROVE COMPREHENSION?

As noted earlier in the chapter, a reader can fail to comprehend a text for many reasons, including weak background knowledge, poor decoding ability and sight word knowledge, limited vocabulary knowledge, poor fluency, and inadequate skills and strategies for understanding texts (Rasinski & Padak, 2008). It is important to identify the primary sources of the comprehension problem in order to provide appropriate instruction. This section of the chapter outlines four proven instructional interventions that can build skill and strategy use and improve comprehension overall: retellings, think alouds, **Comprehension Strategy Instruction (CSI)**, and **Reciprocal Teaching.**

Engaging children in activities that build their background knowledge before reading will enhance their comprehension of texts.

Retellings. Early in this chapter, retelling was described as a tool for assessing children's understanding of text. It is also an excellent instructional tool. Teaching children to engage routinely in quality retellings will improve their ability to summarize. The National Reading Panel (2000) determined that eight research-supported instructional methods improve comprehension, and among these was summarizing. Summarizing requires readers to identify key elements in a text (important ideas, events, and details in expository text or characters, setting, events, problem, and solution in narrative text) and to prioritize and organize them into an objective retelling (Ellery, 2009). Hoyt (2008) provided the following instructional sequence for teaching children to retell or summarize text:

1. Explain the importance of retelling and how it helps readers understand texts.

2. Model retelling multiple times during shared reading or read-aloud experiences and be explicit so that students understand that a retelling is focused and does not include everything.

3. Self-evaluate the retelling in front of the students and ask them to evaluate the retelling as well.

4. Use graphic organizers to provide cues that support the retelling.

5. Begin with shorter passages both narrative and expository and then move to longer selections.

6. Provide plenty of practice time for students—working with partners and small groups to read and retell. Provide partners with retelling guides, so they can evaluate each other's retelling.

7. Help students own the process by encouraging them to retell privately while they are reading independently. To facilitate this, stop students during independent reading time and ask them to retell silently in their heads before reading on (pp. 71–74).

Think Alouds. A second well-researched strategy for improving comprehension is the think aloud. You will recall this technique is used to assess comprehension as well. As the name implies, a think aloud is the process of making the reader's thoughts transparent and public by saying them aloud while reading (Duke & Pearson, 2002). It creates a record of the ways a reader employs strategies, makes decisions, and understands a text as she or he moves through it (Wilhelm, 2001). According to Wilhelm (2001), think alouds help struggling readers to

- Understand that reading should make sense.
- Move beyond a view of reading as simple decoding.
- Use many different strategies.
- Vary strategy use with different types of texts.
- Share ways of reading with peers and teachers.
- Learn about themselves and their thinking and reading. (pp. 33–34)

In his book *Improving Comprehension With Think-Aloud Strategies,* Jeffrey Wilhelm (2001) lists the following procedure for teaching the think-aloud process:

1. Choose a short section of text or short text.

2. Decide on a few strategies to highlight and let the text guide your choices.

3. State your purposes for reading, making sure to include a purpose related to the selection itself and strategy learning.

4. Read the text aloud and think aloud as you do so.

   - Use verbs such as *I wonder, I think, I predict, I bet,* or *I'm confused* to reveal your thinking.
   - Use phrases such as *I'm going to reread, I'll have to read further,* or *I don't know* to demonstrate the reading strategies you are using and, as important, to show struggling readers that expert readers work through text; they don't magically understand it.

5. After completing a think aloud of a section of text ask students to return to the beginning and underline the words and phrases that they think helped them use a particular strategy.

6. Ask students to make a list of the cues and signals in the text that prompted their use of a particular strategy.

7. Ask students to identify other real-world and reading situations in which they could use these same strategies.

8. Reinforce the think-aloud process with guided practice so students internalize it. (pp. 42–50)

Comprehension Strategy Instruction (CSI). Explicitly teaching the strategies that effective readers use helps struggling readers increase their comprehension of text and their willingness to persevere through difficult material (Gambrell et al., 2002; Paris & Hamilton, 2009). The steps used in CSI have been developed from cognitive models of thinking and learning (McKeown, Beck, & Blake, 2009), and they follow the **Gradual Release of Responsibility Model** proposed by Pearson and Gallagher (1983). This model has three phases to support and ensure student learning. In Phase 1, the teacher is fully responsible for the lesson and provides explicit instruction in strategy use through modeling. During Phase 2, the teacher slowly gives the students responsibility through guided practice. In Phase 3, the students take full responsibility, independently practicing the strategy to develop skill and fluency.

While researchers provide varying lists of comprehension strategies, the most commonly occurring in the literature include the following:

- Monitoring for comprehension (knowing when meaning is lost and using strategies such as ignore the problem and keep reading, reread, seek help, look at graphics or illustrations, etc., to regain understanding)
- Asking questions
- Summarizing
- Synthesizing across texts and other sources
- Activating prior knowledge

- Determining importance
- Creating sensory images
- Drawing inferences
- Predicting (Keene & Zimmermann, 2007; National Reading Panel, 2000; Pressley, 2000; Rasinski & Padak, 2008; Wilhelm, 2001)

Modeling the ways to implement comprehension strategies is a critical element of CSI.

The ultimate goal of CSI is that readers reach a level of automaticity with the strategies. At this point, the strategies become part of the repertoire of skills an effective reader uses to make meaning of text (Fisher et al., 2009). Wilhelm (2002) suggested the following five-step process for strategy instruction, which closely mirrors the procedures in the retelling and think-aloud interventions described earlier:

1. Goal Setting: Identify a strategy to teach the students who currently need it. Explain what the strategy is and why it is important.

2. Modeling: Demonstrate the strategy in real contexts; model how and when to apply the strategy.

3. Teacher-Led Collaboration: Use the strategy, and at different points in the reading, cue students to use the strategy.

4. Student-Led Collaboration: Direct students to use the strategy in small groups. Peers assist each other, and the teacher intervenes as needed.

5. Student Independence: Direct students to use the strategy on their own while the teacher assesses their progress toward independence. (p. 21)

While teaching the strategies is useful in improving struggling readers' comprehension, it is important to note that CSI should not be overemphasized such that it becomes the curriculum (Fisher et al., 2009; Wilhelm, 2001). The point of instruction is for students to draw on appropriate strategies as needed to maintain meaning—not to be able to pass a test about the strategies. Too much focus on strategy use during reading, once students have achieved a level of independence, can leave them less aware of the content of the ideas presented in the text and, ironically, reduce comprehension (McKeown et al., 2009).

Reciprocal Teaching. The final instructional intervention presented in this chapter was developed by Annemarie Palinscar in 1982, and it engages students in learning about and using four comprehension strategies at once: predicting, questioning, clarifying (comprehension monitoring), and summarizing (Duke & Pearson, 2002). It is an especially powerful instructional tool for helping struggling readers understand the concept that proficient readers apply multiple strategies flexibly as they move through text (McKenna & Dougherty Stahl, 2009). The teacher and students read and discuss segments of text together in a prescribed manner. In keeping with the Gradual Release of Responsibility (Pearson & Gallagher, 1983), the teacher explicitly models each strategy and slowly releases the responsibility to the students.

McKenna and Dougherty Stahl (2009) described the following process for Reciprocal Teaching:

1. Preview the reading selection (subtitles, pictures, bold-faced items, and graphic aids) and make a *prediction*.

2. Read a predetermined selection of the text.

3. Discussion leader: Ask students to share any problems they had with comprehension and allow others to *clarify* words and ideas that were confusing.

4. Discussion leader: Ask a *question* about important information in the text for students to discuss. Invite students to generate other questions and discuss possible answers.

5. Discussion leader: *Summarize* the text and make a *prediction.*

6. Reading continues to the next predetermined point, at which time another student leads the discussion. (p. 178)

Linda Hoyt (2002) developed Reciprocal Cards that can be used with students as they engage in the process of Reciprocal Teaching. In Version I, five of the eight cards contain a question prompt that focuses the students on attending to the four strategies:

1. Who would like to share the first prediction? (predicting)

2. Were there any words you thought were interesting or had questions about? (clarifying)

3. Where there any ideas you thought were interesting or confusing? (clarifying)

4. Did you have "I Wonder . . . ?" questions in this passage? What are some questions we might find on a test about this passage? (questioning)

5. Please think about this passage for a moment and prepare to share what you learned. (summarizing) (pp. 236–238)

The first card also directs the students to get ready to read and to prepare to make a prediction, and the eighth card indicates who will be the next discussion leader.

In Version II, each of four cards contains a series of prompts that promote thinking about one of the four strategies: predicting, clarifying, questioning, and summarizing. Version II cards may be used with readers who are not quite as confident or independent since they provide more information and support than the Version I cards. The cards can be found in Hoyt's book *Make It Real: Strategies for Success With Informational Texts* (2002).

Intervening With Technology. Interactive e-books that include tools for students to check for the definition or decoding of words help to support comprehension. Illustrations, animations, and sounds that support the meaning of the text (rather than being peripheral to it) also help bolster comprehension (Northeast and the Islands Regional Technology in Education Consortium, 2004). These and other technology-related resources are listed below.

- *Raz-Kids* (www.raz-kids.com/): This is a website that contains many leveled interactive books. Students can listen to a book while watching highlighted text, or they can read independently with some support by clicking on underlined words. This site is part of Learning A-Z.com, a resource that offers a variety of instructional tools related to literacy development. There is a subscription fee.

- *Starfall* (www.starfall.com): This site has a number of interactive books to support young readers. The stories are nicely illustrated. Not all stories have audio, but for those that do not, children can still click on words to hear them pronounced.

- *Graphic organizers* (http://printables.scholastic.com): Well-designed graphic organizers can build background and organizational knowledge that will aid comprehension. In addition, organizers that are either blank or partially completed can help children maintain meaning as they navigate through text or summarize and respond to texts after reading. The Scholastic website offers a number of organizers that can be down-loaded for free. Bubbl.us (http://bubbl.us/) is a free web application that allows students to create their own concept maps individually or in groups. Googledocs (https://docs.google.com/) is a free web-based set of tools that allow for the creation and sharing of documents. For example, teachers can use the presentation tool to create graphic organizers and share them with students, who can complete them individually or collaboratively.

- *Into the Book* (http://reading.ecb.org.): This is a web-based resource focusing on eight comprehension strategies (using prior knowledge, making connections, questioning, visualizing, inferring, summarizing, evaluating, and synthesizing). There is a teacher area and a student area. Students learn about the strategies and then try them out with online interactive texts.

- *iPod and iPad Applications:* A variety of electronic texts are available as applications. When combined with other tools such as graphic organizers or lessons related to comprehension strategy instruction, children can build their comprehension skills. It is important, however, to read the summary information about a text before downloading since there is a great variety in the quality and cost of these texts.

SECTION IV: THE CASES

The following case reports demonstrate difficulties with comprehension. Your challenge is to consider what comprehension issues might be causing difficulty for Selena and Kari, as well as what instructional approaches might be employed to further clarify your predictions and thinking. As you come to each stop sign, jot down answers to the following four questions in relation to the chapter's theme, comprehension, to help you prepare to discuss the cases.

Guiding Questions

Section IV of this chapter will help you reflect on what you have learned about comprehension and apply your understandings to two particular cases. Read each case quickly to get the gist of what it is about and to identify the issues. Read each case a second time, and when you come to a stop sign in the case, jot down your answers to the following questions:

- What important facts have been revealed at this point in the case?

- Based on what you know so far, what do you think might be going on? It may help to respond to the following prompt: Could it be that . . . ?

- What are the learner's strengths and needs?

- What further assessments or interventions might you try to confirm your ideas?

CASE 1: ASSESSMENT REPORT FOR SELENA H.

Background Information

Child's name: Selena H.
Current age: 8
Current grade level: Beginning of Grade 3

Referral

Selena's teacher requested that she be assessed. Parental permission was granted.

Family and Medical History

Selena is eight years old and lives with her biological mother and maternal grandmother. Selena's mother and grandmother are African American; her father is white. He lives in the southern United States and has no contact with the family. Selena's mother attends night school, works full-time at a nursing home, and works part-time at a fast-food restaurant.

Selena is in good health overall but has a mild case of asthma. Her vision and hearing, as reported by the school nurse, are within the normal range.

Selena's mother completed the survey *My Child as a Learner.* She wrote that they like to play games and go places together. She reported that Selena enjoys school and tries very hard to learn. If frustrated, she will seek help before giving up. Selena also enjoys coloring, watching TV, and reading to her younger cousins. Her mother tries to fit reading in, but between work and night school, she spends less than an hour a week reading with Selena. Her goal for her daughter is for her "to do the best she can and make it into fourth grade."

School History

Selena attends a large inner-city public school with students from diverse cultural and ethnic backgrounds. Over 90% of the student body receives free or reduced-price breakfast and lunch. She has 16 students in her third grade classroom, three of whom receive special education services.

Selena's teacher reported that phonics, writing, and math are taught in whole group settings. Reading instruction, on the other hand, is taught in a small group setting. The reading teacher pushes in and provides one-on-one instruction for children during reading time. In addition, 15 minutes is set aside each day for silent reading, and students read books of choice. Selena's teacher noted that Selena is a well-behaved student who enjoys socializing with her peers. She often volunteers to answer questions during instruction and when asked a question will usually guess the answer rather than respond with, "I don't know."

Detailed Assessment Information

Session 1

Interest Survey. Selena dictated her responses to the examiner. She was comfortable and chatty during the interview. She listed playing tag, jumping rope with friends, watching TV, and reading as activities she does out of school. Writing at home is limited to spelling practice. At home, she reads books about animals and dinosaurs. Arthur and Cinderella are her favorite story characters. Math and spelling are her favorite school subjects, and writing is her least favorite. See Figure 6.3 for the complete survey results.

Figure 6.3 Interest Survey for Selena H.

1. What kinds of things do you like to do outside of school?

   Play jump rope with my friends. Play tag and read.

2. What organized activities do you do outside of school?

   I have a club at my house and I play soccer.

3. What do you write about at home?

   I write about how nice my teacher is.
   I practice my spelling test at home.

4. What kinds of things do you like to read at home?

   I read books like Cinderella. I like to read about animals.

5. What do you like to read about?

   I like to read about Arthur and like to read to my cousin about dinosaur books.

6. What do you want to be when you grow up?

   A nurse.

7. What are your parents' jobs? What kinds of things do they do at work?

   Grandma works at the Ramada Inn. She makes beds and does housekeeping.
   Mom works at the nursing home and Arby's. She makes food and drinks.

8. What is your favorite subject at school? Why? Least favorite? Why?

   Math and spelling is my most favorite because it's fun and helps you learn to read.
   Writing because I can't concentrate. There is too much noise.

9. What would you really like to learn about next year? Why?

   Time tables, learn to write in cursive because if I don't learn how to write in cursive I can't spell in cursive, and if I don't learn my times tables I can't become a teacher.

(Continued)

Figure 6.3 (Continued)

10. What's something about you people at school might not know?

    I help the first graders with work.

    I can run fast.

11. Have you ever travelled? Where?

    I've been to New York City.

12. What else would you like me to know about you?

    I can count by 2's, 10's, 1's and 5's.

    I know how to make things like ice cream sticks.

Source: Original form in *Practical Aspects of Authentic Assessment: Putting the Pieces Together* (pp. 174–175), by B. Hill and C. Ruptic, 1994, Norwood, MA: Christopher-Gordon.

Attitudes About Reading and Writing. Selena completed the Garfield Reading and Writing Attitude Surveys (Kear, Coffman, McKenna, & Ambrosio, 2000; McKenna & Kear, 1990) independently while the examiner observed. Selena's percentile rank on the Reading Attitude Survey was 79, with a small preference in recreational reading (81st percentile) over academic reading (74th percentile). On the Writing Survey, her full-scale percentile rank was 66. For both surveys, Selena seemed to be very interested in coloring the Garfield figures and commented several times that she was not sure what the questions meant.

Session 2

ARI Word Lists (Woods & Moe, 1999). The examiner began the administration of the Analytical Reading Inventory (ARI) by asking Selena to read from Form A of the word lists to determine a starting place in the reading passages. Selena read the Primer and Level 1 lists at an independent level with ease and confidence. She made one error on the Primer list, reading *now* for *know.* She made two self-corrections in the Level 1 list (*wish* and *ready*). The sentences she created, "The *man* works at the bakery store and made a birthday *cake* for my friend" and "The *cat* is *crying*," provided sufficient evidence that she understood the meanings of the target words.

Selena made six errors at Level 2 as shown in the chart below:

Text	Selena's word
fair	fur
field	felled
bad	bed
reach	read
song	songs
planet	plant

The sentence she created was syntactically but not semantically accurate: "The fourth grade has instruments and plays a song." The examiner asked Selena to read the Level 3 word list but did not ask her to create a sentence because she miscued on 10 of the 20 words. Errors indicated that she relied on initial and occasionally medial sounds to work out the words.

Text	Selena's word
written	writer
patient	patent
manage	manase
bush	brush
gingerbread	kingerbrand
planet	plant
museum	mushroom
ill	I'll
engine	enough

Session 3

ARI Passage Assessments (Woods & Moe, 1999). The highest level at which Selena read all of the words correctly was Level 1, so the examiner selected a narrative passage at that level, *The Crowded Car,* to continue the assessment. In this passage, the main character, Terry, got into a small car carrying something in a paper bag for show-and-tell. Bill, Ann, and Sue got into the car as well, and each was carrying a paper bag. After Sue got into the car, Terry remarked that the car was getting fat and the children laughed.

After reading the title of the passage, Selena made the following prediction: "All the people are in the car and are all smooshed together." She read the first two sentences and added this to her prediction: "A boy has a little car for show-and-tell. The car is going to be too crowded and big people can't fit in." Selena's prediction revealed some prior knowledge about the subject of the passage, but she made an error in saying that the boy had a little car for show-and-tell. The paper bag, not the car, was the object for show-and-tell.

This passage contained 79 words, nine sentences, and two paragraphs. Selena's oral reading was choppy, and she repeated several words. She had two miscues, a repetition (repetitions of two or more words are coded as miscues in the ARI), and a substitution, *no* for *now.* This passage was at Selena's independent level for word recognition.

Selena did not alter her prediction statement, maintaining in her retelling that the car was the object that Terry was bringing to school for show-and-tell. Her retelling contained few details; however, she answered four of the five comprehension questions correctly, missing only the critical-level question. She was unable to provide an explanation as to why she thought Terry's joke was funny. Even with the limited retelling, this passage was at Selena's instructional level for comprehension. (See Figure 6.4 for a complete summary of Selena's responses to this text.)

The examiner decided to continue with a Level 2 narrative passage, *The Baseball Star.* In this story, the narrator recalled a time when he was at bat. He missed the first two pitches but hit the third and ran "like the wind" while the crowd cheered. Selena's predictions revealed that she had limited prior knowledge about the topic. This passage contained 117 words, 17 sentences, and three paragraphs. She read this text word by word with poor phrasing and intonation. She had eight miscues. All were substitutions. Most of these were graphophonically similar; however, all of them were syntactically unacceptable. Only one substitution, *baseball* for *ball,* was semantically acceptable. This passage was at the outer edges of Selena's instructional level for word recognition.

Figure 6.4 Summary ARI Assessment for Selena H.

Text: *Form A, Level 1: The Crowded Car* (Woods & Moe, 1999, pp. 82–86)

Prior Knowledge/Prediction Response:

After reading title: *All the people are in the car and are all smooshed together.*

After reading the first two sentences: *A boy has a little car for show-and-tell. The car is going to be too crowded and big people can't fit in.*

Fluency:

Selena read word by word, repeated words and phrases because she was monitoring the meaning or self-correcting, and used punctuation to divide text into units of meaning. Her overall rating for fluency was 3 = poor phrasing/intonation/reasonable pace.

Oral Reading Miscues				
Line	Text Words	Words Said	Error Type	Meaning Change?
3	into the car	into the car	Repetition	N
6	Now	no	Substitution	Y
Total Errors: 1				
Total Meaning Change Errors: 1				

Cueing Systems:

Miscues were graphophonically similar. One of the two did not match syntactically and represented a meaning change in the text.

Retelling:

The boy Terry had a little car for show-and-tell, and all these friends came in and Terry said, "This car is getting fat and his friends laughed."

Retelling Summary:

Few details, logical order

Story Elements:

Main Characters: Recalled some with probing

Time and Place: Recalled some with probing

Problem: Recalled

Plot Details: Some recall

(Continued)

Figure 6.4 (Continued)

Turning Point: Recalled
Resolution: Recalled

Comprehension Questions:

[Plus (+) indicates the question was answered correctly. Minus (–) indicates it was answered incorrectly.]

+ Q: Who is the main character in this story? (RIF: Retells in Fact)
  Terry

+ Q: What does each child have? (RIF: Retells in Fact)
  Paper bags

+ Q: What do you know about Show and Tell? (CAR: Connects Author and Reader)
  Kids take something to school and talk about it.

+ Q: What is the problem in the story? (PIT: Puts Information Together)
  The car is crowded.

+ Q: Why did the children laugh? (PIT: Puts Information Together)
  Terry said the car is getting fat.

– Q: Do you think Terry's joke was funny? (EAS = Evaluates and Substantiates)
  Yes, because he told a joke.

Reader Text Relationships:
From the Text: Adequate (2 of 2 questions answered correctly)
From Head to Text: Adequate (3 of 4 questions answered correctly)

Scoring Guide Summary:
Word Recognition: Independent Level
Comprehension: Instructional
Emotional Status: Calm and confident

Selena's retelling was extremely limited, and it appeared that she might have thought the story was about basketball, not baseball. She said, "He shoot the ball really far and he became a baseball star." She answered only two of the seven comprehension questions correctly, missing all inferential and one of two critical level questions. This passage was at Selena's frustration level for comprehension. (See Figure 6.5 for a complete summary of Selena's response to this text.)

Figure 6.5 Summary ARI Assessment for Selena H.

Text: *Form A, Level 2: The Baseball Star* (Woods & Moe, 1999, pp. 84–86)

Prior Knowledge/Prediction Response:

After reading the title: *If you played baseball when you were little, when you grow up you can become a baseball star and get 19 points.*

After reading the first two sentences: *He gets strike one and it's all about baseball.*

Fluency:

Selena read word-by-word; repeated words and phrases because she was monitoring the meaning or self-correcting; and used punctuation to divide text into units of meaning. Her overall rating for fluency was 3 = poor phrasing/intonation/reasonable pace.

Oral Reading Miscues				
Line	Text Words	Words Said	Error Type	Meaning Change?
1	Whiz	Wise	Substitution	Y
2	being	begin	Substitution	Y
4	Whiz	Wise	Substitution	Y
4	ball	baseball	Substitution	N
6	kill	skill	Substitution	Y
7	it	the	Substitution	Y
9	I	It	Substitution	Y
9	a	all	Substitution	Y

Total Errors: 8

Total Meaning Change Errors: 7

Cueing Systems:

Most miscues were graphophonically similar to the word in the passage, but few were syntactically matched. Most miscues altered the meaning of the passage.

Retelling:

He shoot the ball really far and he became a baseball star.

(Continued)

Figure 6.5 (Continued)

Retelling Summary:
Almost no details recalled

Story Elements:
Main Characters: Recalled main character as "he"
Time and Place: No recall
Problem: No recall
Plot Details: No recall
Turning Point: No recall
Resolution: No recall

Comprehension Questions:
[Plus (+) indicates the question was answered correctly. Minus (−) indicates it was answered incorrectly.]

− Q: Who is the main character in this story? (RIF: Retells in Fact)
  I don't know.

− Q: After strike one, how do you think the batter felt? (CAR: Connects Author and Reader)
  Sad because he didn't strike the ball

+ Q: After strike two, what did the batter plan to do? (RIF: Retells in Fact)
  Hit the ball and be a star.

− Q: What did it mean when the batter said, "I'll kill the ball!" (CAR: Connects Author and Reader)
  He was mad because he didn't get three strikes in a row.

− Q: Why was the last pitch good? (PIT: Puts Information Together)
  He shooted the ball way high and ran to first, second, third, fourth and home base.

− Q: Do you think it was good or bad to hit the ball right out of the park? (EAS = Evaluates and Substantiates)
  Bad because he could have smashed someone's house.

+ Q: How do you think the batter felt after hitting the ball? (EAS = Evaluates and Substantiates)
  He felt good because he was a winner.

Reader Text Relationships:

From the Text: Not adequate (1 of 2 questions answered correctly)
From Head to Text: Not adequate (1 of 5 questions answered correctly)

Scoring Guide Summary:

Word Recognition: Independent level
Comprehension: Frustration
Emotional Status: Calm but unsure

Session 4

To begin this session, the examiner selected another form of a Level 2 narrative passage, *My Pet Mouse,* and asked Selena to read the short text silently. In this story, the narrator's pet mouse was running about making a mess of the snacks that her mother had put out for a visiting neighbor. The neighbor eventually saw the mouse. Selena's predictions revealed that she had some prior knowledge about the topic. Her retelling was extremely limited, and some of the information she provided was incorrect. She said that the mouse went to the neighbor's house when in fact the neighbor had come to visit the narrator's home. She answered four of the six comprehension questions correctly. She missed one inferential and one critical-level question. This passage was at Selena's instructional level for comprehension.

The final passage the examiner asked Selena to read was a Level 2 expository text titled *Hearing Sounds.* The passage described how the ear hears sounds that are made through vibrations in the air caused by a moving object. Selena's predictions were logical based on the title and the first two sentences in the text. This passage contained 120 words, 14 sentences, and three paragraphs. Her reading was slow and choppy. She omitted almost an entire line in the second paragraph, a phrase elaborating on the definition of the word *vibrate,* but otherwise made four miscues. All were substitutions. She read two words as plurals (*sounds* for *sound* and *vibrates* for *vibrate*) and substituted *ear* for *air* and *of* for *if.* This passage was at Selena's instructional level for word recognition.

Selena's retelling was limited, and even though the examiner followed up with several probes, Selena was unable to recall much of the information in the text. She missed four of the six comprehension questions and provided little detail that linked to the passage. This passage was at Selena's frustration level for comprehension. (See Figure 6.6 for Selena's retelling and response to comprehension questions.)

Figure 6.6 Summary ARI Assessment for Selena H.

Text: *Form A, Level 2: Hearing Sounds* (Woods & Moe, 1999, pp. 176–178)

Prior Knowledge/Prediction Response:

After reading the title: *When you think you hear something but you don't.*
After reading the first two sentences: *It's about musical instruments.*

Retelling:

Selena: *Vibrating sounds.*
Examiner: *What about vibrating sounds?*
Selena: *It's like if the bell, if the room, if the air breathes the bell rings.*
Examiner: *Say that one more time.*
Selena: *If the air is blowing very hard the bell rings.*
Examiner: *What was this story telling you about vibrating sounds?*
Selena: *That if . . . it can hear loud and real sounds.*
Examiner: *What part of the body were they talking about?*
Selena: *E-A-R-S?*
Examiner: *Yes, that's how you spell it. Do you know what part of your body that is?*
Selena: *I guess I thought it was airs.*
Examiner: *But it's ears, your ear. What do your ears do?*
Selena: *Listen*

Comprehension Questions:

[Plus (+) indicates the question was answered correctly. Minus (–) indicates it was answered incorrectly.]

+ Q: What part of the body detects sound? (RIF: Retells in Fact)

   Ears

– Q: What do you know about the phrase "something vibrates"? (CAR: Connects Author and Reader)

   This is a hard one. It's something that if people, if no, if the air's moving the bells they go ding dong.

What does the phrase "something vibrates" have to do with this text?
   Um things were vibrating.

– Q: What happens to the air when something vibrates? (PIT: Puts Information Together)

   No answer

– Q: What do you know about the phrase "sound wave"? (CAR: Connects Author and Reader)
The story is in this book but when the air blows, it goes together and then it makes like a big air coming out and then every makes—well something like the bell or the choo choo trains like those are those things.

What does the phrase "sound wave" have to do with this text?

vibrations

+ Q: How can a bell make a sound wave? (PIT: Puts Information Together)
If the wind blows it or if somebody is in a church and there's a string pulled down they can just (mimes the moving back and forth of the string).

– Q: Why do you think ears can hear different kinds of sounds?
Like if somebody's talking . . . no it's your eardrums. If your old and you're hard of hearing . . . cause we have an old person in our house. We had to take care of him cause his family kicked him out of the house. Cause if you don't hear nothing then you don't know what nobody's saying.

Case Recap:

1. Review the case and the notes you have taken in response to the guiding questions one final time, and add or revise any information you may have missed.

2. Make a list of additional questions you have about the case. What further information do you need that might be explored in the case discussion?

3. Think about the elements, beyond comprehension, discussed in other chapters. Might any of these also be problem areas for Selena? Might any be areas of strength?

CASE 2: ASSESSMENT REPORT FOR KARI I.

Background Information

Child's name: Kari I.
Current age: 12
Current grade level: End of Grade 6

Referral

Both Kari's parents and her teacher requested that she be assessed.

Family and Medical History

Kari is 12 years old and lives with her father, stepmother, half-sister, and half-brother in a small town about 25 miles south of a small midwestern city. She sees her mother on weekends and special occasions. The primary language spoken in the home is English. She wears corrective lenses and is generally in good physical health.

Kari's stepmother completed a survey about her child as a learner. She noted that Kari has multiple interests and especially enjoys arts and crafts activities. She also stated that Kari is easily distracted and benefits from small group or one-on-one instruction. Kari's literacy interests at home include writing in a journal or diary, making cards for others, and reading books about animals, her favorite TV shows, and books by Jerry Spinelli. (See Figure 6.7 for the complete survey.)

Figure 6.7 Parent Survey for Kari I.: Child as Learner

1. What are your child's free-time interests?

   Scrapbooking (any type of arts & crafts activities), swimming, basketball, dancing, Disney TV shows, music, and board games

2. What types of books does your child enjoy?

   Jerry Spinelli books, books about animals, books from favorite TV shows

3. What types of writing does your child do at home?

   Journal, diary, sometimes writes to her friend or grandpa, enjoys making cards for family members

4. What are your observations about how your child learns?

   Kari learns more in small groups or one-on-one.

   She needs a lot of positive reinforcement.

   She is easily distracted or will try to change the subject if she doesn't want to discuss or do what she is asked to do. If you make the activity fun, she'll work much harder for you.

5. What are some other things you would like us to know about your child?

   Kari is the oldest child. She lived with her mom for the first 10 years of her life and has lived with us for about 2 years.

6. In what ways do you think we can best help your child?

   You can help Kari by being a positive role model and providing her with numerous opportunities to read and write.

Source: Form adapted from *Practical Aspects of Authentic Assessment: Putting the Pieces Together* (pp. 205–207), by B. Hill and C. Ruptic, 1994, Norwood, MA: Christopher-Gordon.

School History

Kari has just completed sixth grade at Central Elementary School. Her classroom teacher, Ms. Silsbury, reported that Kari is generally a happy person who wants to do well. During sixth grade, Kari received alternate small group reading instruction in a resource room setting as per her IEP. According to Ms. Silsbury, the program incorporates phonics, word recognition, spelling, vocabulary, morphology, grammar, listening, reading, speaking, and writing. She further noted that comprehension is difficult for Kari, along with understanding vocabulary words and concepts. She believes that Kari benefits most from repetition and frequent review.

Kari's mother gave permission for the examiner to review the IEP that was in place during her daughter's sixth grade year. In the report, the case manager noted, "Kari has more difficulties with comprehension than with word recognition but is able to locate information in the text if stated in the same way as in the question asked. She has difficulty integrating ideas in order to answer questions and putting answers into her own words." The case manager also stated, "Kari does well with weekly spelling lessons. She can write about familiar topics, but it is difficult for her to organize her ideas, use description, and vary her sentences."

Detailed Assessment Information

Session 1

Interest Survey. The examiner asked Kari to complete the interest survey independently. She enjoys playing basketball and volleyball and sports in general. She loves to do "outdoor things." At home, she writes stories and reads from all kinds of materials but especially likes to read mysteries. Spelling is her favorite school subject, while social studies, science, and penmanship are her least favorite because "they are boring."

Reading and Writing Surveys. After completing the interest survey, the examiner gave Kari two forms, *What I Think About Reading* and *What I Think About Writing* (Strickland, 2005), to finish independently. Kari began writing immediately but seemed to rush through her responses, eager to be finished. She noted that she had many books at home and was able to list a favorite author. She believed herself to be a good reader but defined a good reader as one who gets extra credit. She wrote that her mom was a good writer because she spelled "everything right." Kari views her own writing as "perfect." (See Figure 6.8 for complete survey results.)

Figure 6.8 Reading and Writing Survey Results for Kari I.

What I Think About Reading (Strickland, 2005, p. 22)	*What I Think About Writing* (Strickland, 2005, p. 23)
When did you learn to read? Who taught you? *Age 4. My mom*	When did you learn to write? Who taught you? *Age 5. My Kindergarden teacher.*
How often do you read? *every other day.*	What do you like to write at home? *about My little crazy brother.*
What do you enjoy reading in school or at home? *at home.*	What do you like to write about at school? *My friends*
Do you have books of your own? If so, what are the titles of some of them? *Yes, I have a lot of book I don't remember how many I have.*	What makes a person a good writer? *they get better at it. get extra credit*
Who is your favorite author? Your favorite book? *Dan Gutman. The Million Dollar Shot*	Who do you think is a good writer? Why is she good? *My Mom. She spells everything right.*
Do you like people to read aloud to you? *My parents.*	What are some topics you like to write about? *My pets, My favorite food and stuff like that.*
Do you like to read aloud or silently? Why? *Both, Because it is fun.*	Do you like to share your writing with other people? Why or why not? *No, because it is personal.*
Do you go to the library? *Yes.*	Do you like to read the writing of other people in your class? Why or why not? *Yes, because it is fun to read to other classmates.*
What do you think a good reader is? What do good readers do? *they get extra credit. They get good grades in school.*	What do you think about your writing? *It is perfect.*
Do you think you are a good reader? Why or Why not? *Yes, cause I'm a good reader*	Do you think writing is important? Why or why not? *Yes, so you do good in it.*
Do you think it's important to read? Why or why not? *Yes, Because It helps me.*	
What do you want to learn about reading? *how many Pages are in the book.*	

DRA Student Reading Survey (Beaver & Carter, 2006). As part of the Developmental Reading Assessment, the examiner asked Kari to complete the DRA Grades 6 through 8 Survey. She wrote quickly and wrote short responses. In the area of Wide Reading, she listed only one book that she had completed over the last couple of months, *Because of Winn Dixie* (DeCamillo, 2001), but she did indicate that she had read "a lot more." She also wrote that she used the number of pages and pictures as criteria for selecting books. In the area of Self-Assessment/Goal Setting, she listed pronouncing the words as her strength as a reader. She listed comprehension, vocabulary, and writing as her goals, and she wrote that in order to achieve her goals she needed to "do it and try your hardest." Kari's reading engagement score based on her responses was 2 out of a possible 8, putting her at the Intervention level. There was no clear evidence that she read multiple grade level texts across genres, and although she listed one area of strength as a reader (pronouncing the words), her goals and plans for achieving them were vague.

Session 2

Developmental Reading Assessment (DRA). Based on the initial information gathered from surveys and Kari's current grade level, the examiner chose the Level 50 set of texts to assess oral reading and comprehension. The text Kari chose to read was *Cry Foul* (Siburt, 2003), a fifth grade fiction piece that was the equivalent of Guided Reading Levels U through W (Fountas & Pinnell, 1996). In this nine-page story, Ramon and the other boys in the neighborhood meet regularly to play basketball. Ramon is angry with his cousin, Joseph, because he will not call fouls against the opposing team, resulting in Ramon's team losing games. Ramon finally learns that Joseph is not calling fouls because he believes he is protecting his family, who are undocumented aliens, by not making waves. The misunderstanding is cleared up and Ramon's team wins the next game.

For the first step in this assessment, the examiner asked Kari to complete an oral reading of the first page of text. Her rate of reading at 97 words per minute was moderate. She read with little expression and often did not pause between sentences. She made seven miscues, five of which altered meaning. Four of the seven miscues involved the omission of a single phrase. She made three substitutions, one insertion, and four self-corrections. Her oral reading accuracy was 97%.

Because her oral fluency score was within the instructional range, the examiner continued the assessment. She asked Kari to complete the prediction section and then provided her with the story and student booklet. Kari read the story silently and responded to the questions in the booklet independently.

Her written responses yielded a score of 10 in the area of comprehension, putting this text at the Intervention level. Her predictions were limited, and instead of writing questions she had about the first part of the story, she listed three facts from the first page. Her summary and responses to the Literal Comprehension section included the names of the main characters and a series of events in chronological order; however, not all events were correct. She was unable to provide a correct response to the Interpretation section. She did not seem to understand how to compare and contrast the two main characters. Her reflection statement was vague and without support. Finally, she checked the strategy labeled *I understood the character's feelings* in the Metacognitive Awareness section, but her explanation related more to the strategy labeled *I thought about similar experiences and stories*. See Figure 6.9 for a summary of her responses to the questions in the booklet.

Figure 6.9   After Reading Student Booklet Response for Kari I.

Text: *Cry Foul* (Siburt, 2003): *Level 50* (Grade Level Equivalent 5, Guided Reading Levels U–W)

Prediction: Scored 2 of 4 possible points: Provided one or two reasonable predictions related to the text. Written responses included below:
   In response to a request to list three questions she had while reading the first part of the story Kari wrote:*

1. *Joseph doesn't know how to play Basketball.*
2. *Joseph doesn't know how to count change so no one cheats him.*
3. *Joseph doesn't know how to read signs.*

*These are three facts from the first page of the story.

In response to a request to list three things she thought might happen in the story, Kari wrote the following:

1. *Joseph would like America.*
2. *Joseph would like his Nana.*
3. *Joseph would like to play with his cousin more often.*

Summary: Scored 2 of 4 possible points: Provided partial summary generally in own language with some important characters/events, included misinterpretations. Kari's written response is included below:

Ramon's mom said that he should bring his cousin to the playground. Joseph came from Cuba. Joseph got hurt cause he was guarding someone. Ramon was being mean to his cousin. Then Ramon got hurt from his friend Marco. (In the story, Marco hurt Joseph.) *Marco hit Ramon in the face in the B-ball game against the Stars.* (In the story, Marco hit Joseph in the face.) *Then the Stars lost the game the score was 21 to 17.*

Literal Comprehension: Scored 1 of 4 possible points: Included incorrect information. Questions and student responses are included below:

In response to the request to list three things she had learned about Ramon, Kari wrote the following:

1. *Ramon went to his cousins house.* (This did not happen in the story.)

2. *Ramon was losing his cool.*

3. *Ramon had run to Joseph and his friend Marco was yelling foul.* (In the story, Ramon ran to Joseph yelling at him to call the foul.)

Interpretation: Scored 1 of 4 possible points: Little or no understanding of important text implications. Student response included below:

In response to the request to tell how Ramon and Joseph were similar and different, Kari wrote the following:

Ramon and Joseph are cousins. They knew each other since they were babies. (No such information was provided in the story.) *They are different because they sometimes hate each other for no reason.* (While it may be inferred that Ramon was upset with Joseph, there is no evidence that the cousins hated each other.)

Reflection: Scored 2 of 4 possible points: Vaguely related or less significant message or information; general statement with no support. The question and Kari's response is included below:

Q: What do you admire the most about Joseph?

A: *Joseph was a good little kid.*

Q: Tell why.

A: *Because Joseph was always calling his fouls.* (The key problem in the story was that Joseph was *not* calling his fouls.)

(Continued)

Figure 6.9 (Continued)

Metacognition: Scored 2 of 4 possible points: Brief explanation of the use of one or more strategies; vague or general statements.

Strategy Used: Kari checked, "I understood the character's feelings."

In response to the request to give at least two specific examples from this story that show how she used this comprehension strategy Kari wrote the following:

I understood how they both felt because I was like that to with my friends. the thing is that I was playing Basketball and I got hit cause my friends are mean to me.

Source: Adapted from *DRA Teacher Observation Guide: Cry Foul, Level 50,* by J. Beaver and M. Carter, 2003, Parsippany, NJ: Celebration Press.

Case Recap:

1. Review the case and the notes you have taken in response to the guiding questions one final time, and add or revise any information you may have missed.

2. Make a list of additional questions you have about the case. What further information do you need that might be explored in the case discussion?

3. Think about the elements, beyond comprehension, discussed in other chapters. Might any of these also be problem areas for Kari? Might any be areas of strength?

CHAPTER SUMMARY

The act of comprehending is complex and requires interweaving prior knowledge, decoding ability, vocabulary knowledge, and reading comprehension strategies to meet the demands of varied texts. Helping struggling readers, including Selena and Kari, use all of the strategies good readers use effortlessly requires patience and a long-term commitment. For this population of learners, reading is difficult, confusing, and frustrating. Modeling and providing multiple opportunities for guided practice over time will help ease the frustration, erase the confusion, and make reading a more enjoyable activity in which children will want to engage. The final chapter in this book, "Focus on Engagement," discusses this sixth element necessary for reading success and its importance in helping children to persevere and develop into motivated, joyful readers.

Terms highlighted in this chapter

expressive language skills 182	receptive language skills 182
content load 183	retelling 186
think aloud 186	informal reading inventories 188
cloze 189	Comprehension Strategy Instruction (CSI) 189
Reciprocal Teaching 189	Gradual Release of Responsibility Model 192

FINAL QUESTIONS FOR REFLECTION AND RESPONSE

1. You may have concluded that both Selena and Kari have fair to adequate print skills and may have some weaknesses in the area of vocabulary knowledge. What evidence is there that either of the girls lacks comprehension skills or strategies that limit their ability to understand grade-level texts? It may help to revisit Table 6.1.

2. Consider the interventions that were described in this chapter or those you have learned of elsewhere. Which might be most effective to use with Selena? With Kari?

3. Using the information provided in this chapter, prepare a statement that describes how you will assess for and teach comprehension in your classroom.

Journals Online

Visit the student study site at www.sagepub.com/combsstudy to access recent, relevant, full-text journal articles from SAGE's leading research journals.

REFERENCES

Afflerbach, P., Pearson, D., & Paris, S. (2008). Clarifying differences between reading skills and reading strategies. *The Reading Teacher, 61*(5), 364–373.

Barone, D., Hardman, D., & Taylor, J. (2006). *Reading first in the classroom.* Boston: Allyn & Bacon.

Barr, R., Blachowicz, C., Bates, A., Katz, C., & Kaufman, B. (2007). *Reading diagnosis for teachers: An instructional approach* (5th ed.). Boston: Allyn & Bacon.

Barton, J., & Sawyer, D. (2003). Our students are ready for this: Comprehension instruction in the elementary school. *The reading teacher, 57*(4), 334–347.

Beaver J., & Carter, M. (2003). *DRA Teacher Observation Guide: Cry foul, Level 50.* Parsipanny, NJ: Celebration Press.

Beaver, J., & Carter, M. (2006). *Developmental reading assessment: 4–8* (2nd ed.). Parsippany, NJ: Celebration Press.

Block, C. (1999). Comprehension: Crafting understanding. In L. Gambrell, L. Morrow, S. Neuman, & M. Pressley (Eds.), *Best practices in literacy instruction* (pp. 98–118). New York: Guilford Press.

DeCamillo, K. (2001). *Because of Winn Dixie.* MA: Candlewick.

Dole, J., Duffy, G., Roehler, L., & Pearson, D. P. (1991). Moving from the old to the new: Research on reading comprehension instruction. *Review of Educational Research, 61*(2), 239–264.

Duke, N., & Pearson, D. (2002). Effective practices for developing reading comprehension. In A. Farstrup & S. J. Samuels (Eds.), *What research has to say about reading instruction* (3rd ed., pp. 206–242). Newark, DE: International Reading Association.

Ellery, V. (2009). *Creating strategic readers: Teachniques for developing competency in phonemic awareness, phonics, fluency, vocabulary, and comprehension.* Newark, DE: International Reading Association.

Fisher, D., Frey, N., & Lapp, D. (2009). *In a reading state of mind: Brain research, teacher modeling, and comprehension instruction.* Newark, DE: International Reading Association.

Fordham, N. (2006). Crafting questions that address comprehension stratgies in content reading. *Journal of Adolescent and Adult Literacy, 49*(5), 390–396.

Fountas, I., & Pinnell, G. (1996). *Guided reading: Good first teaching for all children.* Portsmouth, NH: Heinemann.

Gambrell, L., Block, C., & Pressley, M. (2002). Improving comprehension instruction: An urgent priority. In C. Block, L. Gambrell, & M. Pressley (Eds.), *Improving comprehension instruction: Rethinking research, theory, and classroom practice* (pp. 3–16). Newark, DE: International Reading Association.

Hacker, D. (2004). Self-regulated comprehension during normal reading. In R. Ruddell & N. Unrau (Eds.), *Theoretical models and processes of reading* (5th ed., pp. 755–779). Newark, DE: International Reading Association.

Harris, T., & Hodges, R. (1995). *The literacy dictionary: The vocabulary of reading and writing.* Newark, DE: International Reading Association.

Hill, B., & Ruptic, C. (1994). *Practical aspects of authentic assessment: Putting the pieces together.* Norwood, MA: Christopher-Gordon.

Hoyt, L. (2002). *Make it real: Strategies for success with informational texts.* Portsmouth, NH: Heinemann.

Hoyt, L. (2008). *Revisit, reflect, retell: Time tested strategies for teaching reading comprehension.* Portsmouth, NH: Heinemann.

Kear, D. J., Coffman, G. A., McKenna, M. C., & Ambrosio, A. L. (2000). Measuring attitude toward writing: A new tool for teachers. *The Reading Teacher, 54*(1), 14–24.

Keene, E. (2002). From good to memorable: Characteristics of highly effective comprehension teaching. In C. Block, L. Gambrell, & M. Pressley (Eds.), *Improving comprehension instruction: Rethinking research, theory, and classroom practice* (pp. 80–105). Newark, DE: International Reading Association.

Keene, E., & Zimmermann, S. (2007). *Mosaic of thought: The power of comprehension strategy instruction* (2nd ed.). Portsmouth, NH: Heinnemann.

Ketch, A. (2005). Conversation: The comprehension connection. *The Reading Teacher, 59*(1), 8–13.

Leslie, L., & Caldwell, J. (2000). *Qualitative reading inventory–3* (3rd ed.). Boston: Allyn & Bacon.

Lipson, M., & Wixson, K. (2003). *Assessment & instruction of reading and writing difficulty: An interactive approach* (3rd ed.). Boston: Allyn & Bacon.

May, F. (2001). *Unraveling the seven myths of reading: Assessment and intervention practices for counteracting thier effects.* Boston: Allyn & Bacon.

McKenna, M., & Dougherty Stahl, K. (2009). *Assessment for reading instruction.* New York: Guilford Press.

McKenna, M., & Kear, D. J. (1990). Measuring attitude toward reading: A new tool for teachers. *The Reading Teacher, 43,* 626–639.

McKeown, M., Beck, I., & Blake, R. (2009). Rethinking reading comprehension instruction: A comparison of instruction for strategies and content approaches. *Reading Research Quarterly, 44*(3), 218–253.

National Assessment of Educational Progress. (1998). *Reading framework for the national assessment of educational progress: 1992–1998.* Washington, DC: U.S. Department of Education, Office of Educational Research and Improvement.

National Reading Panel. (2000). *Teaching children to read: An evidenced-based assessment of the scientific research literature on reading and its implications for reading instruction.* Washington, DC: National Institute of Child Health and Human Development.

Northeast and the Islands Regional Technology in Education Consortium. (2004). *Technology and teaching children to read.* Retrieved August 2, 2010, from http://www.neirtec.org/reading_report

Pardo, L. (2004). What every teacher needs to know about comprehension. *The Reading Teacher, 58*(3), 272–280.

Paris, S., & Hamilton, E. (2009). The development of children's reading comprehension. In S. Israel & G. Duffy (Eds.), *Handbook of reserach on reading comprehension* (pp. 32–53). New York: Routledge.

Pearson, P. D., & Gallagher, M. C. (1983). The instruction of reading comprehension. *Contemporary Educational Psychology, 8,* 317–344.

Pressley, M. (1999). Self-regulated comprehension processing and its development through instruction. In L. Gambrell, L. Morrow, S. Neuman, & M. Pressley (Eds.), *Best practices in literacy instruction* (pp. 90–97). New York: Guilford Press.

Pressley, M. (2000). What should comprehension instruction be the instruction of? In M. Kamil, P. Mosenthal, P. D. Pearson, & R. Barr (Eds.), *Handbook of reading research* (Vol. 3, pp. 545–561). Mahwah, NJ: Lawrence Erlbaum.

Rand Reading Study Group. (2004). A research agenda for improving reading comprehension. In R. Ruddell & N. Unrau (Eds.), *Throetical models and processes of reading* (5th ed., pp. 720–754). Newark, DE: International Reading Association.

Rasinski, T., & Padak, N. (2008). *Evidence-based instruction in reading: A professional development guide to comprehension.* Boston: Pearson Education.

Reutzel, R., Camperell, K., & Smith, J. (2002). Hitting the wall: Helping struggling readers comprehend. In C. Block, L. Gambrell, & M. Pressley (Eds.), *Improving comprehension instruction: Rethinking research, theory, and classroom practice* (pp. 321–353). Newark, DE: International Reading Association.

Schmitt, C., & Sha, S. (2009). The developmental nature of meta-cognition and the relationship between knowledge and control over time. *Journal of Research in Reading, 32*(2), 254–271.

Siburt, R. (2003). *Cry foul.* Parsippany, NJ: Celebration Press.

Snow, C., Griffin, P., & Burns, M. (2005). *Knowledge to support the teaching of reading: Preparing teachers for a changing world.* San Francisco: Jossey-Bass.

Strickland, K. (2005). *What's after assessment? Follow-up instruction for phonics, fluency and comprehension.* Portsmouth, NH: Heinemann.

Sweet, A. P., & Snow, C. (1998). Reconceptualizing reading comprehension. In C. Block, L. Gambrell, & M. Pressley (Eds.), *Improving comprehension instruction: Rethinking research, theory, and classroom practice* (pp. 17–53). Newark, DE: International Reading Association.

Wilhelm, J. (2001). *Improving comprehension with think-aloud strategies.* New York: Scholastic.

Wilhelm, J. (2002). *Action strategies for deepening comprehension.* New York: Scholastic.

Woods, M., & Moe, A. (1999). *Analytical reading inventory* (6th ed.). Upper Saddle River, NJ: Simon & Schuster.

Zimmermann, S., & Hutchins, C. (2003). *7 keys to comprehension: How to help your kids read it and get it!* New York: Three Rivers Press.

CHAPTER 7
FOCUS ON ENGAGEMENT

Alice was beginning to get very tired of sitting by her sister on the bank, and of having nothing to do: once or twice she had peeped into the book her sister was reading, but it had no pictures or conversations in it, "and what is the use of a book," thought Alice "without pictures or conversation?"

—Lewis Carroll

Guiding Questions

Sections I through III of this chapter will help build your knowledge related to engagement and will prepare you to read and discuss the cases. As you read the sections, consider the following questions:

- What do we mean by engagement?
- Why is it important?
- What factors influence engagement?
- What are the characteristics of engaged and disengaged readers?
- How do we assess engagement?
- What are the overarching features of positive interventions?
- What interventions might help disengaged readers?

INTRODUCTION

Chapters 1 through 6 dealt with five of the essential elements of reading. Each was addressed separately, but in reality, they operate in concert to ensure the skill we need to identify, understand, and learn from what we read. This final chapter addresses a sixth essential element that undergirds all the others: **engagement**. As noted by Watkins and Coffey (2004), effective, strategic readers must possess both the *skill* and the *will* to read, and even the most skilled reader will remember little if she or he does not engage with the text. For those who struggle, the willingness to read and persist through difficulties wanes significantly over time. Children increasingly resist participating in activities that too frequently result in failure. Such disengagement can undermine even the best instruction in phonemic awareness, phonics, vocabulary, fluency, and comprehension and makes it very difficult to help children become independent lifelong readers (Malloy, Gambrell, & Smith-Williams, 2006).

In this chapter, you will meet Eddie and Lance. Both are disengaged readers, but their reasons for being so differ. Your challenge, as you prepare to discuss the cases, will be to discover the factors you believe to be the cause of their disengagement and to consider the ways you might help them become more engaged readers. The information provided in Sections I and II and the interventions discussed in Section III should help you make sense of the cases and guide you toward meeting this challenge.

SECTION I: WHAT DO WE KNOW ABOUT ENGAGEMENT?

What Do We Mean by Engagement and Why Is It Important?

In *The Literacy Dictionary,* Harris and Hodges (1995) defined *engagement* as "the emotional involvement of the reader in the process of responding to the content or reading as occurs in the total absorption in a story or play" (p. 73). Many of you reading this text can easily recall a time when you were swept up in a book and the present disappeared as you engaged fully with an unfolding narrative. Your investment with text involved not only emotional engagement, as described by Harris and Hodges (1995), but also behavioral engagement— performing the physical tasks necessary for reading to occur—and cognitive engagement—using strategies to self-monitor comprehension as well as question and learn from the text (Kelley & Clausen-Grace, 2009; Wigfield et al., 2008). Indeed, engagement is critical for comprehension and overall reading success (Guthrie & Wigfield, 2000; Wigfield et al., 2008).

Engagement is a powerful mediator for learning and reading achievement. Engaged readers read a lot, and in doing so, they practice strategies that lead to ever higher levels of skill. The more they read, the better they get at reading and the more they learn about the world. Increasing knowledge and competence motivates them to read more, which results in still higher levels of skill and understanding (Guthrie & Wigfield, 2000). Sadly, this relationship can work in reverse. Students who lack skill, who do not view themselves as readers, avoid or resist engaging with texts or do so in ineffective ways. Constant failure and disappointment increases their resistance, decreases competence, and undermines achievement. The disengaged reader is less likely to try to learn and more likely to give up when he or she encounters difficulty (Cunningham & Cunningham, 2002).

What Factors Influence Engagement?

Reading engagement is dependent on multiple interrelated factors. Whether or not a student chooses to engage in the act of reading, and at what level, is dependent on motivation, **self-efficacy**, ability, and prior experiences. In addition, factors such as perceived value and interest in the text and task, the amount of choice provided, the level of social interaction, and cultural expectations and values will have an impact on her or his willingness to engage. Each of these factors will be discussed in the following sections.

Motivation

Motivation and *engagement* are not synonymous terms, though they are sometimes presented as such in the literature. As defined previously, reading engagement involves action—an investing of emotional, physical, and cognitive energies in the act of reading (Kelley & Clausen-Grace, 2009; Wigfield et al., 2008). This does not happen unless motivation is in play because motivation is the force that drives engagement (Guthrie & Wigfield, 2000).

Motivation—the enthusiasm, interest, or commitment for doing something, in this case engaged reading—is dependent on the learner's goals (Guthrie, Wigfield, Metsala, & Cox, 2004) and is associated with his or her beliefs about competence, as well as interests and expectations (Huei-Yu Wang & Guthrie, 2004). The reader's goal, or purpose for reading, will determine what is learned (Cambourne, 2002). In general, there are three goal orientations, any of which a learner may bring to the reading task:

- **Mastery orientation:** The focus is on learning or mastering the content or attempting to improve one's abilities (Gaskins, 2008; Guthrie et al., 2004).
- **Performance orientation:** The focus is on receiving rewards or recognition and demonstrating that one is capable or can outperform others (Gaskins, 2008; Guthrie et al., 2004).
- **Work-avoidant orientation:** The focus is on avoiding the task and the work and energy involved in accomplishing it (Gaskins, 2008).

A mastery orientation is associated with **intrinsic motivation;** whereas, a performance orientation is associated with **extrinsic motivation.** Intrinsic motivation refers to the interest and enjoyment that readers bring to an activity, along with a desire to learn and a belief that mastering the task is its own reward. The intrinsically motivated are curious, self-confident, and willingly accept and, indeed, expect a challenge (Asselin, 2004; Guthrie & Wigfield, 2000). Extrinsic motivation refers to a response to external controls (such as being told to read) and the desire to receive rewards or external recognition or incentives for completing the task. Extrinsically motivated learners rely on competition, grades, prizes, and celebrations and expect public acknowledgment for their achievements (Asselin, 2004; Guthrie & Wigfield, 2000; Guthrie et al., 2004).

Learners may employ multiple goal orientations and read for both intrinsic and extrinsic reasons. A mastery orientation and intrinsic motivation, however, is more likely to result in the development of engaged, independent readers. Intrinsic motivation has a long-lasting positive effect on reading outcomes (Fink, 2008).

In addition, children who are intrinsically motivated to read tend to increase the amount and variety of their reading over time (Guthrie et al., 2004). They persist when challenged with difficult texts and comprehend text better than their more extrinsically motivated peers (Huei-Yu Wang & Guthrie, 2004). Those who read because they wish to meet teachers' or parents' expectations, avoid punishment, win prizes, or gain recognition tend to score lower on comprehension tasks. They use inefficient, surface-level strategies like guessing or memorization, resulting in the inefficient processing of text (Huei-Yu Wang & Guthrie, 2004). Furthermore, they may become dependent on extrinsic rewards, and once these cease, they may engage in work-avoidant or reading-avoidant behaviors since the task holds no intrinsic value (Snow, Griffin, & Burns, 2005).

Is all extrinsic motivation bad? Even though intrinsic rewards and a mastery orientation toward learning is the ultimate goal, it may not be possible when dealing with students who are strongly disengaged and resistant. Those who have a long and unhappy relationship with reading, who see no value in the activity, and who believe they cannot improve will be highly resistant and unlikely to read on their own, and the older they are, the worse their attitudes toward reading are likely to be (McKenna & Dougherty Stahl, 2009). Teachers may find that using extrinsic motivators initially, while helping students set goals and monitor their progress, is a necessary first step to help them believe in and see themselves as readers.

Self-Efficacy

Self-efficacy involves the beliefs, judgments, and perceptions we have about our capacity to successfully complete the tasks before us (Reutzel, Camperell, & Smith, 2002; Taboada, Guthrie, & McRae, 2008). Bandura (1997) provided the following characteristics of people with high and low self-efficacy:

- People with high self-efficacy are more likely to have high aspirations, take long views, think soundly, set themselves difficult challenges, and commit themselves firmly to meeting those challenges. They guide their actions by visualizing successful outcomes instead of dwelling on personal deficiencies or ways in which things might go wrong. (Bandura, 1997, para. 9)
- People with low self-efficacy avoid difficult tasks. They have low aspirations and weak commitment to their goals. They turn inward on their self-doubts instead of thinking about how to perform successfully. When faced with difficult tasks they dwell on obstacles, the consequence of failure and their personal deficiencies. Failure makes them lose faith in

themselves because they blame their own inadequacies. They slacken or give up in the face of difficulty, recover slowly from setbacks and easily fall victim to depression. (Bandura, 1997, para 10)

It is not difficult to make a connection between the characteristics of people with low self-efficacy and those we see in struggling readers. The negative beliefs they hold about themselves have a profound influence on their ability to engage in tasks, persist when things become difficult, and rebound quickly when they have been unsuccessful (Bempechat, 2008; Miller & Faircloth, 2009). It is a constant challenge for struggling readers to maintain positive self-efficacy when, time after time, they face words they do not recognize or understand and see texts as rolling waves of information that make little sense (Bempechat, 2008; Taboada et al., 2008). Over time, and as they compare themselves to other more successful read-

Engaged reading requires both skill and will. Without these, the act of reading is a dull, difficult, impossible task.

ers, they come to view themselves as stupid and incapable (Bempechat, 2008; Gambrell, Block, & Pressley, 2002). They definitely do not see themselves as readers and resist any activities requiring them to do literacy-related tasks (Casey, 2008; Gambrell et al., 2002).

Not only do they hold highly negative beliefs about their abilities; they adhere to the notion that competent readers never have trouble, always comprehend, read fast, know all the words, and never need to ask questions (Gaskins, 2008). One of the first tasks we face with struggling learners who have built such a belief system is to help them understand that they are capable and can be successful. If learners can see that success is possible because of their efforts, the probability of persistence increases (Gambrell et al., 2002). In addition, if we help them see that the ability to perform a given task well can fluctuate and that even competent learners struggle some of the time, the willingness of struggling learners to engage will improve (Cunningham & Cunningham, 2002). It is important to add, however, that guiding children toward high self-efficacy takes time, persistence, and a great deal of patience.

Ability

Reading engagement is linked inextricably to reading ability. If the process of learning to read, regardless the reason (language delay, learning disability, lack of early literacy experiences, etc.), becomes impossibly difficult and frustrating, there is nothing that will sustain the child's desire to engage in the reading process (Bempechat, 2008; Malloy et al., 2006). Struggling readers, as noted earlier, come to view themselves as unable to learn. The pleasure and enjoyment experienced by skilled readers is elusive; instead, reading feels like an unending punishment (Atkinson, 2006). Thus, resistance and avoidance become the tools for protection and success in the classroom. Lenters (2006) noted that "unsuccessful readers hide out in secondary classrooms, engaging in lengthy repertoires of coping strategies, none of which involves participating in the kinds of literate activities that will develop their facility with reading" (p. 142).

The relationship between context, ability, and engagement is important. Readers' abilities are context dependent. If the topics or genres are within readers' areas of interest or expertise, ability may be less of an issue because they will bring background knowledge (vocabulary, information, and experiences) about the topic or text to the act of reading. In addition, if interest is high, willingness to engage increases (Lenters, 2006). Finally, if the reader feels safe and supported, the willingness to tackle a difficult text is usually greater (Miller & Faircloth, 2009).

Prior Experiences

Children who have had early positive experiences with books and with learning about print are more likely to be engaged readers (Gambrell et al., 2002). These children have listened and joined in with parents, caregivers, and teachers during read alouds and interactive reading activities. They see the activity of reading as pleasurable and interesting, and the emotions they feel are associated with joy, excitement, and peacefulness. In contrast, learners who have had few or negative literacy experiences feel anxiety, self-disgust, and frustration (May, 2001). In addition, children who have been read to a lot and have explored their world through songs, rhymes, texts, or trips build rich prior knowledge that can help them connect with and more easily understand the variety of texts they encounter in school.

Other Factors

At least four other factors relate to whether or not a learner will choose to engage: perceived value or meaningfulness of the task; availability of choice in the text to be read or task to be completed; reader interest; and the level of social interaction surrounding the task. Students want to be convinced that what they are being asked to do will benefit them (Gaskins, 2008). This is especially true for learners who struggle with academic tasks. If they believe that learning to do whatever is being asked of them has value and meaning (it has the potential to help them gain a needed skill or understand more about an interesting topic or idea), they will be much more likely to engage (Cambourne, 2002).

Taboada and colleagues (2008) noted that "the desire to feel autonomous and in control is a natural human need" (p. 154). When learners are given a degree of choice, they feel in control and more capable. Teachers may offer different choices depending on the skill and interests of the learner. Readers may be able select the topic they wish to read about, the length or level of the text, the amount of time given to complete the task, or how they might go about demonstrating their learning. Regardless, when choice enters the picture, their willingness to participate will be enhanced (Gambrell et al., 2002).

It is a given that when we have interest in something we will spend more time pursuing activities related to it. When students are given access to appropriate texts that they find interesting, they will persist in reading. The result will be an increase in knowledge about the topic and, because of the extended time spent in practice with texts, an increase in reading skill (Fischer & Fusaro, 2008). Taboada and colleagues (2008) described two types of interest: situational and personal. **Situational interest** is tied to a particular event that arouses interest in a topic or domain; it is transitory in nature. **Personal interest** is related to the child's preexisting internal predisposition toward a particular topic or domain; it is enduring (Asselin, 2004). Teachers can create experiences that help situational interests evolve into personal interests, thereby increasing the likelihood that the child will seek out texts and materials to learn more about the topic.

In this context, *social interaction* refers to student-to-student or student-to-teacher dialogues designed intentionally to support engagement with text (Taboada et al., 2008). Teachers work to create interactive settings where learners feel accepted, important, and noticed by their teachers, classmates, and friends (Taboada et al., 2008). Collaboration with others in a respectful environment that promotes a sense of belonging and offers struggling learners comfort and reassurance increases students' engagement (Miller & Faircloth, 2009).

What Are the Characteristics of Engaged and Disengaged Readers?

Engaged readers are avid readers. They use reading as a means to an end and that end is new or deeper learning. Disengaged readers, on the other hand, are resistant readers. They bring a history of failure to the reading act. Too frequently, they are directed to complete reading and writing activities that are beyond their abilities. As a result, they respond with frustration and actively avoid literacy-related tasks (Miller & Faircloth, 2009). Table 7.1 lists several descriptors of engaged and disengaged readers.

Disengaged readers are likely to be passive readers who view reading as a boring activity. According to Mueller (2001), there are several reasons a student may view reading as dull and pointless:

- They see reading as decoding rather than understanding.
- They are not interested in the content.
- They have failed repeatedly to comprehend texts assigned to them.
- They view reading as an inactive task and cannot sustain attention to it.

Kelley and Clausen-Grace (2009) pointed out that reading engagement is not an all or nothing activity; rather, readers' willingness to engage with texts

Table 7.1 Descriptors of Engaged and Disengaged Readers

Engaged Readers	Disengaged Readers
Focus on text meaning and avoid distractions.	Get up from their seats several times during free reading time to get another book.
Are strategic and use multiple approaches to comprehend texts.	Do not seem willing to read a book from start to finish and do not appear to read outside of school.
Are intrinsically motivated to read to fulfill personal goals and desires.	Wander around the library and often select books they do not really want to read.
Are socially interactive in their approach; that is, they ask questions, evaluate learning, and share information within a literacy community (Guthrie & Wigfield, 2000, pp. 403–404).	Show a pattern of apathy to reading that is often part of a larger pattern of indifference to school (Au, 2002, p. 395).

can be described along a continuum. In their article, "Facilitating Engagement by Differentiating Independent Reading," they provided descriptors for a variety of readers, from "fake readers" to "bookworms." The information is synthesized in Table 7.2.

In addition to the assessment-related suggestions in the next section, consider using this table as a checklist to determine students' levels of engagement and design targeted instruction to meet each of their unique needs.

Table 7.2   Continuum of Reading Engagement

Type of Reader	Descriptors
Fake readers	• Appear to be reading but are really pretending • Avoiders who shuffle from bookcase to desk to pencil sharpener • Apathetic toward reading • Have rarely enjoyed a book
Challenged readers	• May have cognitive limitations, SES challenges, physical difficulties, or be English language learners • Common trait is that reading is difficult for them
Unrealistic/ wannabe readers	• Choose inappropriate texts • Seldom complete a book • Have comprehension issues because they select texts that are too difficult • View reading as finishing the book but rarely enjoy it
Compliant readers	• Read because they are told to • Rarely read for pleasure • Choose books randomly • Don't read outside of class • Don't think much about reading
Does nonfiction count readers	• Crave information • Thirst for knowledge and are curious about the world
I can but I don't want to readers	• Lack zeal for reading • Take a long time to complete a book • Usually read only when told to • When given a choice do not choose to read
Stuck in a genre or series readers	• Read willingly but within a specific genre or series (This is not a bad thing in itself, but it is important to help them add to their reading choices.)
Bookworms	• Book fanatics • Are models for engaged reading (Kelley & Clausen-Grace, 2009)

SECTION II: HOW DO WE ASSESS ENGAGEMENT?

Clearly, engagement has major implications—especially when dealing with students who are struggling readers. It is important to assess how these learners feel about reading, whether they see themselves as readers, whether they see reading as an important and useful activity, and how they use it in their lives. Such information is critical in order to plan and implement effective instruction (Snow et al., 2005). Several tools and processes are available, including teacher observations, questionnaires, inventories, and surveys.

Observations. Teacher observations of students' reading habits and activities can yield a good deal of anecdotal information about learners' engagement levels. Teachers should make note of how often students bring in books from home, whether or not they spontaneously seem excited about reading, how often they choose to read when there is down time in the classroom, and their level of participation as well as the content of their talk during book discussions (Snow et al., 2005). Use focused anecdotal notes to pinpoint patterns of behavior. As you observe children, write down what they say and do as they engage in reading and writing activities (formal and informal). Include descriptions of what students say and do. The more detailed the description, the easier it will be to develop effective instructional approaches. Write and review notes daily, and organize them in a systematic way (set up individual folders or pages in a notebook) so that the information is easily accessed and useful.

Questionnaires, Inventories, and Surveys. Interest and attitude questionnaires, inventories, and surveys are readily available and provide useful information. These may exist as separate assessments or be included in assessment packages such as the Analytical Reading Inventory (Woods & Moe, 1999) or the Developmental Reading Assessment Kit (Beaver & Carter, 2006). Interest inventories and questionnaires can prove invaluable when trying to entice a struggling reader to engage with text. For many of these readers, unless there is some match to a deep abiding interest, there is little hope of helping them to see reading as an enjoyable activity. As noted before, inventories are readily available in assessment books (e.g., Hill & Ruptic, 1994; McKenna & Dougherty Stahl, 2009) or online (by entering "reading interest inventories" as a search term). It is possible to develop an interest inventory using a survey tool such as *Survey Monkey* (www.surveymonkey.com), which may be more entertaining for students to complete than paper-and-pencil surveys.

The *Burke Reading Interview* (Goodman, Watson, & Burke, 1987), also referred to as the *Burke Reading Inventory,* consists of a series of questions designed to discover how learners feel about themselves as readers. During the

10-question interview, readers are asked to consider what they (or someone they think is a good reader) would do when encountering challenging texts. They are asked about how they learned to read and whether or not they consider themselves good readers. The readers are also asked a question designed to help them set goals to improve as readers.

Two popular surveys, sometimes called the *Garfield surveys*, were discussed in earlier chapters. The Elementary Reading Attitude Survey, developed by McKenna and Kear (1990), and the Writing Attitude Survey, developed by Kear, Coffman, McKenna, and Ambrosio (2000), target students' perceptions about reading and writing. More recently, McKenna, Simkin, Conradi, and Lawrence (2008) developed a survey aimed at middle and secondary students. Students are asked to respond to a 6-point Likert scale for each of 41 items that address the following categories: recreational reading in print settings, academic reading in print settings, recreational reading in digital settings, and academic reading in digital settings.

It is important to observe learners as they complete the attitude survey tools because they may circle items for a host of reasons, not all of which may relate to their attitude about literacy activities. For example, some children with whom I have worked have circled the Garfield face they like the best, or one they thought I would want them to choose. Clear instructions, observation, and redirection will help to improve results.

SECTION III: WHAT INTERVENTIONS MIGHT PROMOTE READING ENGAGEMENT?

What Are the Overarching Features of Positive Interventions?

It is no surprise that children who struggle to read become increasingly negative about reading. Helping them develop a desire for reading is not accomplished easily; there is no quick fix (Guthrie & Cox, 2001). Still, there are things that we can do to help them. Effective interventions that increase the likelihood of engagement include one or more of these features: demystifying learning, supporting self-efficacy, incorporating students' interests, supporting choice and control, encouraging social interaction, and scaffolding learning.

Demystifying Learning. Too often, struggling readers come to believe that they simply do not have the capacity to learn. They believe that others, whom they perceive to be effective readers, learn easily and well and never make mistakes.

While it is not always easy to change children's negative views about themselves, it is critical that we help them understand how learning works so they can begin to see themselves as learners and persevere when tasks become difficult. As a first step, Gaskins (2008) suggested teaching and modeling the following principles about learning:

- What people learn is based on what they already know.
- Strategies for monitoring and controlling learning will help you know when you do or do not understand and then you can take action.
- New information is easier to understand, remember, and use if it is attached to prior knowledge.
- Organized knowledge is easier to recall than random information.
- Information that is thoughtfully and deeply processed is more likely to be understood and used.
- Concepts and strategies that are repeatedly practiced and applied are not likely to be forgotten. (p. 106)

When children are part of an environment that embraces the principles of learning, mistakes that *all* readers make are recognized as a typical and recurring part of daily learning (Bempechat, 2008). In addition to teaching and modeling principles of learning, teachers who continually communicate the following expectations will support struggling students who may otherwise remain disengaged:

- Becoming an effective reader is an extremely worthwhile enterprise that will greatly enhance the quality of your life.
- All members of this learning community are capable—no one can fail to become an effective reader.
- The best way to become an effective reader is to share and discuss the processes and understandings you are developing with others; take risks both as a member of a group and individually and reflect on the feedback you receive.
- When you discuss your understanding of texts, justify your statements, comments, and opinions using believable and sensible arguments and examples.
- It is safe for you to take a risk in this setting.
- You have full understanding when you have transformed the meaning and skills that someone else demonstrated into a set of meaning and skills uniquely your own. (Cambourne, 2002, p. 31)

Cambourne (2002) further suggested that teachers who routinely use the following activities to communicate the expectations listed previously will help children understand them and make them their own:

- Comment about texts and books during read alouds.
- Respond to learner's approximations offering immediate and appropriate feedback.
- Comment about effective reading strategies and skills during share time, think alouds, and demonstrations.
- Draw students' attention to the features of texts and writing processes authors use. (Cambourne, 2002, pp. 31–32)

Teachers serve as the primary role models and must consistently demonstrate approaches to learning that they want their students to emulate (Au, 2002). In addition, they should bring in other adult models who reflect the cultural backgrounds represented in the classroom. They can share their stories about learning to read and the way that reading is important in their lives. All of these efforts, routinely and consistently enacted, will help struggling learners better understand that learning to read, although difficult and complex, is worthwhile and not beyond them.

Support Self-Efficacy. In order to become effective readers, children need to believe in themselves and their ability to learn to read. This foundational belief will lead them to engage with texts in independent and effective ways that will ensure deep and sustained learning. Teachers can support students' development of self-efficacy in several ways. First, they can help students set achievable goals that focus on mastering either the content itself or the skills needed to learn the content (Bempechat, 2008). As noted earlier in this chapter, students who adopt a mastery orientation to goal setting are intrinsically motivated to learn and see reading as a means to understanding more about their world (Taboada et al., 2008). Second, teachers can provide clear and appropriate feedback that helps students see their progress toward meeting the goals (Guthrie & Wigfield, 2000). This will help them become aware of their growing competence, and that will positively affect their self-efficacy.

As noted by Taboada et al. (2008), once personal goals have been set, teachers can further support the development of self-efficacy in the following ways:

- Provide short manageable assignments that offer students the opportunity to meet their goals.
- Offer multiple opportunities to help students develop expertise on a topic of interest to them.

- Provide students with texts matched to their reading levels and multiple opportunities to read them for the express purpose of building fluency.
- Provide explicit instruction to help them become competent users of the strategies and skills needed to comprehend a variety of texts.
- Offer specific and timely feedback focused on the task or behavior needed to complete the given assignment.

Struggling readers have had more than their share of failure. They are vulnerable and too easily lose hope and faith in themselves. They need carefully structured and scaffolded opportunities, often over a long time period, in order to hold onto a vision of themselves as successful and able readers.

Incorporate Students' Interests. All children are interested in something, and many children are interested in many things. Capitalizing on those interests is a key means of getting children connected to texts since they are more likely to engage in reading activities that relate to their interests (Malloy et al., 2006). Other consequences of using topics that are of interest to students include the following:

- Natural connections to prior knowledge to aid in their comprehension of texts
- The likelihood of employing the comprehension strategies they are aware of to help them uncover meaning
- An increase in their time on task, which is needed for strategic processing of texts (Snow et al., 2005)

Once interests are known, instructional conditions can be designed that nurture those interests and build the learner's enthusiasm and excitement for reading (Taboada et al., 2008). These conditions are as follows:

- Provide real-world experiences that help connect students' experiences with related texts (Taboada et al., 2008).
- Create opportunities for students to ask their own questions and pursue answers within supportive learning environments (Taboada et al., 2008).
- Encourage students to use different modes of self-expression to share what they are learning from texts (Taboada et al., 2008).
- Read aloud from high-interest, challenging, and thought-provoking texts (Au, 2002).
- Connect students to texts that they will enjoy and can read independently (Au, 2002).
- Invite students to read series books (such as Junie B. Jones, Arthur, Artemis Fowl) to foster interest and build skill by reading familiar

content, structure, characters, and vocabulary across the texts in a series (Meyer & Rose, 1999).

- Organize book clubs or literature circles to build on students' interests and desires to work with peers (Au, 2002).
- Provide a variety of narrative and expository texts that address students' interests (Edmunds & Bauserman, 2006).

Support Choice and Control. We all like to have choice when being asked (or told) to do something. Being given choices allows us to build or maintain our need for autonomy, that feeling that we are in control rather than being controlled (Asselin, 2004; Gaskins, 2008). Children are no different; choice and control are motivating factors for them. Taboada and colleagues (2008) recommended the following actions to address students' needs for choice and control:

- Give students choices that are academically relevant *and* personally meaningful, so they can become "experts" on a topic.
- Scaffold choices for students—some students will need more highly structured tasks than others; some students will need to learn how to select books that are a good match for their skill levels.
- Give students many opportunities and different ways to share the knowledge they have built from their reading.
- Provide students with a voice in the ways they will be evaluated. (pp. 155–156)

In addition to these ideas, Guthrie and Wigfield (2000) suggested that teachers let students decide the sequence of activities during an exploration of a topic or theme, which books they will read, and how they will read them (aloud or silently, in pairs, chorally, or independently). Edmunds and Bauserman (2006) further advised that teachers should provide ample time during the school day for students to read books they have themselves selected. Whether they are struggling or effective readers, children seek to be in control of their environment, and the appropriate use of choices during literacy activities affords an opportunity for teachers to meet students' needs while promoting reading engagement.

Encouraging Social Interaction. Social interaction increases children's motivation and engagement (Asselin, 2004). Guthrie and Wigfield (2000) noted that students who feel a sense of belonging in the classroom and believe they are recognized and affirmed as individuals are more motivated to engage in literacy activities. In addition, building a social structure that supports a team and partnership approach toward learning increases the likelihood of success for struggling readers. This creates a win-win situation. Success leads to greater levels of engagement and investment, and higher levels of engagement and investment result in greater achievement (Snow et al., 2005).

There are several ways to support social interactions in the classroom. Teachers can promote open discussions and model ways students can help and learn from each other. Collaborative learning approaches such as think-pair-share (e.g., pairs of students respond to teacher questions or a problem-solving challenge after talking with each other for a short period of time), literature circles, and paired or partner reading require students to work together to solve problems and to come to a mutual understanding of text or content. Teachers can also assign teams of students to learn about content as they study a topic and work on short- or long-term projects (Guthrie & Cox, 2001; Taboada et al., 2008). As students work together, teachers are free to assess children's progress in skill development, content learning and collaborative efforts, and engagement.

Teams of students working to learn content can support and engage struggling readers.

Scaffolding Learning. Children who struggle with reading lack both the skill and will to engage with texts. Can we blame them? Very few of us would continue to take on tasks that we had failed at repeatedly. Even if we convince these wary and doubting readers to take a risk, they will likely approach the task with little confidence that they will succeed. Thus, it is important to have scaffolds in place to encourage perseverance and ensure success, at least early on. Teachers can do many things to help struggling readers become more competent and confident, but the following three are essential. First, a teacher can provide materials and tasks that are "just right"—that are within the range of the learner's current abilities but allow for an appropriate level of challenge, so his or her skill level can increase (Gaskins, 2008). Second, a teacher can provide explicit strategy instruction. This involves a three-step process: (1) explain the strategy, why it is useful, and when and where to use it; (2) model using the strategy through a think aloud; and (3) work with the learner in a one-on-one conference setting and provide just-in-time support as the learner attempts to apply the strategy (Guthrie & Cox, 2001; Taboada et al., 2008). Third, a teacher can provide targeted and immediate feedback that helps the learner know whether or not her or his attempts are correct and what should be done next. Scaffolding students' attempts in these ways provides the critical support necessary to build skill and self-confidence.

What Specific Interventions Might Promote Engagement?

Each of the specific instructional interventions described in this section includes many or all of the features discussed previously and has a positive effect on student engagement. The four interventions presented here are Voluntary Reading as Social Practice (VRSP), Readers Theatre, Concept Oriented Reading Instruction (CORI), and Dictated Stories.

VRSP. Voluntary Reading as Social Practice, described by Rosalie Fink (2008), is an approach similar to Sustained Silent Reading (SSR). In both approaches, children are afforded daily opportunities to read silently for an extended period of time. Each child selects the book she or he wants to read, but may receive some coaching from the teacher to be sure it is not beyond her or his current ability—although it may provide some challenge. The difference between the two approaches is that VRSP has an added component that highlights social interaction. After the daily silent reading time, children discuss their books with a peer, parent, tutor, or teacher. The goal of the discussion is not strategy instruction; rather, it is a relaxed discussion meant to increase enthusiasm about reading that will encourage children to read even more books.

Readers Theatre. This instructional activity has long been used as a tool to increase reading fluency (see Chapter 4). It is also highly motivating and leads to increasing levels of literacy engagement among struggling and resistant readers (Fink, 2008; Worthy & Prater, 2002). The activity involves students in the rehearsal and performance of an unmemorized script. The use of props is minimal. In addition, there is little physical action; rather, the goal is for the learner to deliver a fluent reading of the script that conveys its meaning. The following general procedures, described by Worthy and Prater (2002), are typically employed when using this approach:

1. Select or write a text for the performance.
   - Texts may be poems, short scenes from quality literature, famous speeches, teacher or student drafts, commercially available scripts, or those easily found on literacy-related websites.
   - Scripts should not be above the readers' instructional levels.

2. Prepare for the performance.
   - The teacher begins by modeling a fluent reading of the script.
   - The teacher then provides guided practice as students read and reread the script.
   - Students work as partners or small groups, practicing the scripts until they reach a performance level. The teacher moves among groups, monitoring and providing feedback.

3. Performance day.
   - No special staging is necessary. Students may find it more comfortable to use a music stand or podium to place their script as they read.
   - Provide an authentic, enthusiastic, accepting audience for the performers.

Students who struggle may not want to perform in front of a group initially, but as their fluency develops through practice, their fears subside.

CORI. Concept Oriented Reading Instruction was developed by Guthrie and Wigfield (Guthrie & Cox, 2001) as a reading comprehension program designed to improve students' learning of science and social studies content while improving strategic reading and engagement. This approach targets nonfiction texts, a genre that is often used to draw in reluctant readers. After the teacher selects a theme or topic of study to explore over a number of weeks and develops learning goals, the CORI framework unfolds in four phases:

1. Students observe or take part in a real-world activity and discuss what they observe and ask questions. The teacher facilitates the discussion and documents the questions.

2. Students search for information to answer their questions. The teacher provides multiple texts and materials that are interesting and within the ability range of the students.

3. As students read and learn about their topic, the teacher provides explicit instruction in the comprehension strategies needed to help them understand what they read. Students generally work in teams while learning about the topic of study.

4. After several weeks of study, students present what they have learned to others.

This approach is intended to be used at the school or classroom level; however, its elements—real-world experiences, student choice, interesting texts, strategy instruction, collaboration, and assessment—make it a valuable approach for small groups and individual learners as well.

Dictated Stories. The Dictated Story, also known as the *Language Experience Approach,* has a long history as an approach to beginning reading instruction (Lipson & Wixson, 2003). In general, students dictate and read stories that are related to their interests and their experiences. Because students use their own language to produce the story, there is a greater likelihood that they will be successful in reading and understanding the text. In addition, because the stories are created by the students themselves, they are inherently interested in reading what they have written. The five steps in implementing this approach are listed here:

1. Explain the approach to the students, indicating that they will be sharing a story or experience and you will be writing it. It may be helpful to brainstorm ideas for a story or event before actually asking the child to launch into the dictation.

2. Ask the child to dictate the story, and as she or he does so, wait until each thought is complete before recording it.

3. Record exactly what the child says, repeating each word aloud as you write it and making sure that the child is watching you.

4. Read the story aloud to the child and encourage him or her to join in.

5. Ask the child to read the story to you.

The dictated stories should be short enough to read back the story in one setting. If the student likes to draw, it may be more interesting to him or her to build a story so that he or she can insert pictures or draw pictures to add to the story. It is also valuable to include instruction in sight word recognition, phonics, and vocabulary as the student rereads the stories she or he created.

Intervening With Technology. Technology is a powerful means of engaging 21st-century learners. Many, if not all, of the tools described in Chapters 2 through 6 will be of interest to learners, including those who struggle. E-books, games, and activities, provided they are within the learner's instructional range, will provide the practice and support necessary to help struggling readers move forward. In addition, producing and posting podcasts and vodcasts that either respond to texts or transform them will engage learners while deepening their understanding. Two additional resources not yet mentioned are listed here:

- *Text to Speech Software.* There are a number of commercial and free software packages available that convert webpages, e-mails, and documents to speech. Some, like NaturalReader (www.naturalreaders.com/), can convert written text into MP3 files that can be uploaded into an iPod or saved on a CD. Versions of this software that reads text as you type it by the letter, word, or sentence are available for a modest cost. The quality varies, so it is a good idea to preview the software before downloading or purchasing it.
- *iPod and iPad Applications.* The *Story Kit* application allows students to substitute their own text in four classic children's stories, thus creating their own books while leaving the illustrations intact.

SECTION IV: THE CASES

The two assessment case reports that follow will help you explore the issues related to engagement that were discussed in this chapter. As you read, consider the factors that seem to be impacting Eddie's and Lance's engagement. Think, too, about the elements of effective interventions described previously as well as the instructional approaches you might employ to help these learners.

Guiding Questions

Section IV of this chapter will help you reflect on what you have learned about engagement and apply your understandings to two particular cases. Read each case quickly to get the gist of what it is about and to identify the issues. Read each case a second time, and when you come to a stop sign in the case, jot down your answers to the following questions:

- What important facts have been revealed at this point in the case?

- Based on what you know so far, what do you think might be going on? It may help to respond to the following prompt: Could it be that . . . ?

- What are the learner's strengths and needs?

- What further assessments or interventions might you try to confirm your ideas?

CASE 1: ASSESSMENT REPORT FOR EDDIE J.

Background Information

Child's name: Eddie J.
Current age: 9
Current grade level: End of Grade 3

Referral

Eddie's teacher and parents requested that he be assessed.

Family and Medical History

Eddie is nine years old and lives with his father and mother in a small city in the upper Midwest. He has an older sister who lives outside of the home.

He is in good health overall. Recently, he was diagnosed with **ADD/ADHD** and is taking a stimulant medication to control its effects.

Eddie's mother completed the survey *My Child as a Learner*. She described Eddie as an active boy who loves all kinds of sports. He also enjoys drawing. She indicated that he has very low self-confidence when it comes to reading and writing, but he does well in math. She noted that he is on medication for ADHD and will soon be reevaluated by a specialist. (See Figure 7.1 for the complete survey.)

Figure 7.1 Parent Survey for Eddie J.: Child as Learner

1. What are your child's free-time interests?

   Art—loves to draw things/color marker them—cutting

   Sports—loves hockey. He is a squirt hockey player. He has played hockey for 5 years. Loves it!

   Hobbies—basketball, biking, rollerblading, skateboarding, scooter

   TV shows—the Disney Channel

   Playstation games

2. What types of books does your child enjoy?

   Chapter books but he struggles.

3. What types of writing does your child do at home?

   Not a whole lot unless copying something. He has it set in his mind that it is too hard and he can't do it so we fight with him to do it usually at school is better than with his parents.

4. What are your observations about how your child learns?

   Very smart in Math. Very intelligent in outside things. Listens when he shouldn't but not when told to. He learns when he shouldn't but not when he should. He is better one on one like at school.

5. What are some other things you would like us to know about your child?

   He wants to learn but has to be pushed to do it because he has it set in his mind he can't. He is on a stimulant medication. Somewhat not working right now. He will see the doctor next month to be thoroughly evaluated on ADHD or something that might be wrong with his brain thinking.

6. In what ways do you think we can best help your child?

   One on one, motivating him that he can do it. Alot of praise for his achievements.

Source: Form adapted from *Practical Aspects of Authentic Assessment: Putting the Pieces Together* (pp. 205–207), by B. Hill and C. Ruptic, 1994, Norwood, MA: Christopher-Gordon.

School History

Eddie attends a small neighborhood school of about 450 students. Ms. Ironberg, his teacher, reported that he has been involved in a variety of individualized and small group reading programs in the classroom and resource room. She noted that he is currently reading at Guided Reading Level E (Fountas & Pinnell, 1996), and although he made gains during the year, he still struggles. She stated, "Eddie does not get too enthusiastic about any-thing. . . . He works best on a one-to-one basis. I have found that Eddie will sometimes shut down if he is in a group. I feel he is afraid to take a risk and possibly make a mistake in front of his peers." Figure 7.2 presents Ms. Ironberg's full response to the questionnaire.

Figure 7.2 Classroom Teacher Referral Form for Eddie J.

1. Please describe the nature of the child's reading and writing. What does this child do well and in what areas do you perceive weakness?

   Eddie is now reading at a Level "E." He has made some gains this year, but still struggles. He tends to just look at the beginning letter of some words and blurt out any word that comes to mind that begins with that sound. His writing has also improved. It is still often difficult to read because of spelling issues. He has beautiful cursive writing.

2. Instructional strategies, activities, etc., used with this child.

   Eddie used the Academy of Reading program for a short time this year. He has been in Reading Recovery. He has worked with "Fast Track Action Reading." He used the Milestones Reading (EdMark) for his individualized reading program in the classroom as well as guided reading books. Focused Reading Series in the resource room as well as guided reading books.

3. What is the child's attitude toward reading?

   Eddie is just beginning to see himself as a reader. He does not get too enthusiastic about <u>anything</u>. He will not ask for assistance when he needs it, but will write down anything. He tries to "fake read" difficult books during silent reading to seem like everyone else. His main interest in life is hockey.

4. What special services does this child receive?

   Eddie goes to speech for help with understanding words in content areas. He goes to the LD teacher for math at the present time and earlier receive assistance with reading (before he began Reading Recovery).

5. What approach(es) do you think this child will benefit from?

   Eddie works best on a one-to-one basis. I have found that he will sometimes shut down if he is in a group. I feel he is afraid to take a risk and possibly make a mistake in front of his peers.

Detailed Assessment Information

Session 1

Interest Survey. Eddie dictated his response to the "About Me" survey. He told the examiner that he would rather "sleep in" than go to school. He added that math was easy for him to learn because he loved it. His interests included hockey, car racing, baseball, and golf. He said he wants to be a race car driver when he grows up.

Attitudes About Reading and Writing. Eddie completed the Garfield Reading and Writing Attitude Surveys (Kear et al., 2000) independently while the examiner observed. His percentile rank on the Reading Attitude Survey was 57, with a preference in recreational reading (57th percentile) over academic reading (47th percentile). On the Writing Survey, his full-scale percentile rank was 27. There seemed to be weak alignment with the results of the reading survey and the information provided by his mother and teacher: that is, Eddie's self-reported attitudes toward reading and writing were more positive than those reported by his mother and teacher.

Burke Reading Interview (Goodman et al., 1987, pp. 219–220). The examiner recorded Eddie's answers to the 10 questions on the interview (see Figure 7.3). It was clear that Eddie felt that he had only one strategy as a reader and that it was guessing. He was unable to list any strategies that others might use to unlock words. Interestingly, however, he rated himself as a good reader.

Figure 7.3   Burke Reading Interview Results for Eddie J.

1. When you are reading and come to something you don't know, what do you do?
   Leave it. Say it however it sounds good.

2. Do you ever do anything else?
   No

3. Who do you know who is a good reader?
   Dad

4. What makes him/her a good reader?
   They just read

(Continued)

Figure 7.3 (Continued)

5. Do you think she/he ever comes to a word she/he doesn't know when reading?
   Yes

6. If your answer is yes, what do you think she/he does about it?
   I don't know

7. What do you think is the best way to help someone who doesn't read well?
   Find out on their own.

8. How did you learn to read? What do you remember? What helped you to learn?
   At school

9. What would you like to do better as a reader?
   Bigger words—not first grade words.

10. Describe yourself as a reader.
    No response

11. Using a scale of 5 to 1, with 5 being a terrific reader, what overall rating would you give yourself as a reader?
    4

Source: Form in *Reading Miscue Inventory: Alternative Procedures* (pp. 219–220), by Y. Goodman, D. Watson, and C. Burke, 1987, Katonah, NY: Richard C. Owens.

Session 2

Developmental Reading Assessment (DRA; Beaver, 2001). Based on the information provided by Ms. Ironberg, Eddie's mother, and Eddie himself, the examiner selected a Level 6 DRA text (Guided Reading Level D, Fountas & Pinnell, 1996; *Time to Play,* Beaver & Richards, 2002) to begin the assessment. In keeping with the directions, Eddie looked through the pictures in the story and responded to the following prompt: "Tell me what Pam and Lee did after school." His answers indicated that he accurately predicted what would happen in the story. Even though his fluency was lacking during the oral reading portion of the assessment, his accuracy rate was 97%, with two substitutions and three self-corrections. He was able to recall all events but responded with a literal interpretation only. When asked what his favorite part of the story was, he said, "It is not a kind of book I would read." (See Figure 7.4 for detailed results.)

Figure 7.4 Summary DRA Assessment for Eddie J.

Text: *Time to Play: Level 6* (Grade Level Equivalent 1, Guided Reading Level D)

Previewing and Predicting Response (after completing a picture walk):
Eddie gathered enough information to make several appropriate predictions.

Oral Reading Miscues			
Page/Line	Text Words	Words Said	Error Type
2/1	friends	frinds	Substitution
2/2	liked	looked	Self-correction
3/3 (reread)	No	On	Substitution
4/3	No	On	Self-correction
4/3	she	said	Self-correction

Total Errors: 2
Accuracy: 97%
Total Self-Corrections: 3

Fluency

Eddie read word by word with a few short phrases. He read with little intonation.

At Difficulty

Eddie used picture clues heavily and initial sound cues. He reread one line of text and self-corrected his error (*on* for *no*)

Comprehension (Score of 19: Adequate Comprehension)

Eddie was able to retell most of the events in order, although he did not state the names of the characters, referring to them only as "he" and "she." He required no additional prompts or questions when asked to retell. When asked to tell his favorite part of the story he said, "It's not a kind of book I would read."

Source: Adapted from *DRA Observation Guide*, by J. Beaver, 2002, Parsippany, NJ: Celebration Press.

Because this text appeared to be an easy one for Eddie, the examiner went on to a Level 8 (Guided Reading Level E, Fountas & Pinnell, 1996; *Duke,* 1997). He looked at the pictures and gave some limited information about each. He read the text orally with little intonation and usually in short phrases. When he came to words he did not know, he studied the picture and then seemed to guess at the word. He had difficulty with words that should have been part of his sight word vocabulary (*big, could, was, keep*). His accuracy rate was 91%, with six substitutions, two omissions, and four self-corrections. He recalled some of the events in the story but needed prompting. When asked what the story made him think of, he responded, "Nothing." He seemed much more frustrated and unsure with this text. (See Figure 7.5 for detailed results.)

Figure 7.5   Summary DRA Assessment for Eddie J.

Text: *Duke: Level 8* (Grade Level Equivalent 1, Guided Reading Level E)

Previewing and Predicting Response (after completing a picture walk):
Eddie gathered limited information and commented briefly about the action in each picture.

Oral Reading Miscues			
Page/Line	Text Words	Words Said	Error Type
3/1	big	dig	Self-correction
4/1	liked	looked	Self-correction
4/2	could*	shaked	Substitution
4/2	do	did	Substitution
4/2	tricks	thing	Substitution
Page 4 line 2 read: He could do lots of tricks. Eddie said: *He shaked did lots of thing.*			
4/3	sit	shake	Substitution
5/1	arm	hand	Substitution
6/1	a	the	Substitution
6/1	Duke	——	Omission (examiner said the word)
7/1	Duke	Dake	Self-correction

Source: Adapted from *DRA Observation Guide,* by J. Beaver, 2002, Parsippany, NJ: Celebration Press.

| 7/1 | clean | —— | Omission |
| 7/2 | was | has | Self-correction |

Eddie said, "I forgot that word." He became very frustrated with the line of text, and the examiner told him the word was could. He then continued.

Total Errors: 8

Accuracy: 91%

Total Self-Corrections: 4

Fluency

Eddie read in short phrases with little intonation.

At Difficulty

Eddie used picture clues heavily and initial sound cues (on page 7, he sounded out the word *keep*). He paused several times. He self-corrected four miscues, three of which would have resulted in altering the meaning of the text.

Comprehension (Score of 15: Some Comprehension)

Eddie was able to recall some of the events. He responded with only a literal interpretation. He required two prompts when asked to retell and responded adequately. He recalled the boy's name, Jim, but referred to Duke as "the dog." When asked to tell his favorite part of the story he said, "The end. I just liked it." He made no connections to the text.

Session 3

Writing Assessment. In this final session, the examiner provided Eddie with a pencil and lined paper and asked him to write about something in which he was interested. He quickly selected racing as his topic and wrote a short five-line story. The examiner prompted him to add details, but he was neither enthusiastic nor willing to do so. The examiner then offered to write for him if he would consider building on his story. He agreed and added much more detail that demonstrated his knowledge about and interest in racing (see Figure 7.6).

Figure 7.6 Writing Sample for Eddie J.

On Sat-day was the world of the Oatlaws, it was Qaalifying I Qaaifiyg5 it was taim Por the het I win the het. It was the A Main race. I was in the front row. *start* The green flag was out and a guy hit me in the wall and I flipped. I was shaky and nervous but okay. Then I took out my yellow back up car with flames. I had to start in the back row. I was flying fast to 1st place. There were three more laps to go and I was nervous. Then there were two more laps to go. The white flag was out, last lap. Then I came around the turn I ran out of fuel but I still won. I won $2,000.00 and I was a champion.

Additional Information

Examiner Anecdotal Notes

- *Gets frustrated easily with unknown words.*
- *Is aware of strategies but may not feel safe to use them.*
- *When he encountered difficulty, he began to shut down almost immediately, rarely persevering beyond the first sign of struggle.*
- *He believes he is incapable of reading well and is not motivated to take risks.*

Case Recap:

1. Review the case and the notes you have taken in response to the guiding questions one final time, and add or revise any information you may have missed.

2. Make a list of additional questions you have about the case. What further information do you need that might be explored in the case discussion?

3. Think about the elements, beyond engagement, discussed in other chapters. Might any of these also be problem areas for Eddie? Might any be areas of strength?

CASE 2: ASSESSMENT REPORT FOR LANCE K.

Background Information

Child's name: Lance K.
Current age: 11
Current grade level: End of Grade 5

Referral

Lance's teacher requested that he be assessed. Parental permission was given.

Family and Medical History

Lance is 11 years old and lives with his father and mother in a small city in the upper Midwest. He is an only child. According to his **IEP,** he is in good health overall but is slightly color-blind. He wears glasses to correct for near-sightedness. In third grade, he was tested for and found to have a **Central Processing Disorder.** As a result, he has difficulties understanding speech when there is background noise and when information is presented rapidly. Also, Lance takes a non-stimulant medication daily to control the effects of ADD.

Neither of his parents returned the parent survey, and so information relayed by his mother was drawn from Lance's IEP. She expressed concern that he does not pass through all of the sleep cycles and believes he may have a sleep disorder. Also, she noted that Lance has a "very soft heart" and is afraid of being hurt or hurting someone else's feelings. He tends to be quite emotional but has been less so in fifth grade than in past years.

School History

Lance attends a small neighborhood school of about 300 students. Ms. West, his teacher, reported that he appears to read at Guided Reading Level R (Fountas & Pinnell, 1996). He routinely uses two strategies, rereading and attending to visual cues, when he loses meaning, but he tends to skip words. Ms. West believes that Lance has a good vocabulary, which helps him identify words.

Lance receives instruction in the regular classroom setting and in the resource room. Partner and group reading and book discussions are regular classroom procedures. The special education teacher has used the **Neurological Impress Method (NIM)** as well as a number of Reading Recovery procedures with Lance. All of his teachers enjoy his humor and believe that he is a "great kid." (See Figure 7.7 for compete details.)

Figure 7.7 Classroom Teacher Referral Form for Lance K.

1. Please describe the nature of the child's reading and writing. What does this child do well and in what areas do you perceive weakness?

   Lance appears to read at Level R (Fountas and Pinnell Guided Reading Levels). This is below his peers. He reads relatively slowly although this has improved this year. He does use strategies such as rereading when it does not make sense. He does seem to tend to use more visual cues to read words. He often skips words and then goes back to reread. He has a good vocabulary and this helps him figure out words too. It is harder for him to retell the story or summarize. Lance has great ideas for writing. He needs reminders to use beginning capital letters and ending punctuation.

2. Instructional strategies, activities, etc., used with this child.

   Lance has been included in the regular classroom reading instruction during 5th grade. This has included partner reading and group reading. He writes reflections and takes part in discussions. In the resource room, he has had some instruction using neurological impress (choral reading with the teacher to increase reading speed). The resource teacher is trained in Reading Recovery, so some of these methods are used with him also. We work on him being a "problem-solver" in his reading. In the classroom he uses the computer for many writing projects.

3. What is the child's attitude toward reading?

   He has a great sense of humor and greatly enjoys funny books. He will laugh out loud! Also, he enjoys "Harry Potter-like" books which include magic. He is a great kid.

4. What special services does this child receive?

   Lance receives ½ hour of Special Education services daily for reading. He also receives support in his classroom from his teacher and para-educator. He has been found to have Central Auditory Processing difficulties and needs directions repeated NOT rephrased.

Detailed Assessment Information

Session 1

Interest Survey. Lance completed the interest survey independently. He wrote that he plays computer games outside of school and only reads as a last resort, but does like the Bunnicula series books (Guided Reading Level Q, Fountas & Pinnell, 1996) and fantasy or scary books. His goal for the year was to learn to read "a little faster." His sense of humor shone through in response to Question 12: What else would you like me to know about you? Lance wrote, "My dog is cute but evil."(See Figure 7.8 for the complete survey.)

Figure 7.8 Interest Survey for Lance K.

1. What kinds of things do you like to do outside of school?
    Play burnout 3 for the PS2

2. What organized activities do you do outside of school?
    Ride bike home

3. What do you write about at home?
    No Response

4. What kinds of things do you like to read at home?
    As a last resort the buniccula seris

5. What do you like to read about?
    Fantasy/scarey P.S. buniccula!

6. What do you want to be when you grow up?
    I don't quite know what I want to do.

7. What are your parents' jobs? What kinds of things do they do at work?
    My mom work at the medical school.

8. What is your favorite subject at school? Why? Least favorite? Why?
    Lunch and science lunch gives you time to rest and eat. Science I can't remember eneything

9. What would you really like to learn about next year? Why?
    I want to learn to read a little faster.

10. What's something about you people at school might not know?
    I'm a very good actor

(Continued)

Figure 7.8 (Continued)

11. Have you ever travelled? Where?

    Pecin

    Mineapolis

12. What else would you like me to know about you?

    My dog is cute but evil.

Source: Original form can be found in *Practical Aspects of Authentic Assessment: Putting the Pieces Together* (pp. 174–175), by B. Hill and C. Ruptic, 1994, Norwood, MA: Christopher-Gordon.

Attitudes About Reading and Writing. Lance completed the Garfield Reading and Writing Attitude Surveys (Kear et al., 2000) independently. His percentile rank on the Reading Attitude Survey was 17, with a small preference in academic reading (26th percentile) over recreational reading (20th percentile). On the Writing Survey, his full-scale percentile rank was 61. There was alignment between the results of the reading survey and the information provided by Lance and his teacher.

Burke Reading Interview (Goodman et al., 1987, pp. 219–220). Lance completed the answers to the 10 questions on the interview (see Figure 7.9). He mentioned two strategies for working out unknown words: sound it out or skip it. His goal for reading was to read faster. This was consistent with his responses in the interest survey. He rated himself somewhere between a three and a two as a reader.

Figure 7.9 Burke Reading Interview Results for Lance K.

1. When you are reading and come to something you don't know, what do you do?

   I try to figure it out or scip it

2. Do you ever do anything else?

   usually no

3. Who do you know who is a good reader?

   Mom

4. What makes him/her a good reader?

   she reads very fast

5. Do you think she/he ever comes to a word she/he doesn't know when reading?

   no

6. What do you think is the best way to help someone who doesn't read well?

   No Response

7. How did you learn to read? What do you remember? What helped you to learn?

   by sounding out words.

8. What would you like to do better as a reader?

   I'd like to read faster

9. Describe yourself as a reader.

   I read sometime.s

10. Using a scale of 5 to 1, with 5 being a terrific reader, what overall rating would you give yourself as a reader?

    I'm some ware in between 3 and 2.

Source: Form in *Reading Miscue Inventory: Alternative Procedures* (pp. 219–220), by Y. Goodman, D. Watson, and C. Burke, 1987, Katonah, NY: Richard C. Owens.

Session 2

Developmental Reading Assessment (DRA; Beaver, 2001). DRA Student Reading Survey. In preparation for the DRA, the examiner asked Lance to complete the accompanying DRA Grades 6 through 8 Survey. The results mirrored those of the surveys he completed in the last session, but he stated that he visualizes as he reads, adding another strategy to his repertoire. Still, reading fast remained a key goal for Lance: "I'm starting to read vary fast. Sometimes I mix up words read. I'd still like to read faster." In addition, he noted that he was not reading anything right now, in school or at home. His engagement score for Wide Reading was two of four (*Titles generally below grade level; limited reading experiences*) and two of four for Self-Assessment and Goal Setting (*Vague strength(s) and goal(s) identified; vague or no plan*). The total score of four for this section was within the instructional range.

Based on his teacher's information, that he was reading at Guided Reading Level R (Fountas & Pinnell, 1996), the examiner chose a Level 40 text about wolves. *A Pack of Wolves* (Leon, 2003) is a nonfiction text of 10 pages. It provides general information about the gray wolf, including types of gray wolves, their daily lives as pack animals, how they hunt and parent, and why they need to be protected.

When the examiner handed the text to Lance, he turned the pages quickly and commented worriedly about how long it seemed. His cheeks became red and his eyes filled with tears. He did not want to read the text aloud, fearing that he would not be able to read it fast enough. The examiner encouraged him, noting that he would only read the first page aloud and then he could read the remainder silently. He responded, "OK, I guess."

Lance's overall oral reading rate at 68 words per minute was slow. He pushed through the first paragraph of the text, paying little or no attention to end punctuation and repeating several words. In the first six lines of text, he made 10 repetitions. In the remaining two paragraphs, he slowed down but continued to repeat many single words and short phrases. He also made many self-corrections. His overall accuracy rate was 97%. This was within the independent range for this text, so the examiner asked Lance to complete the prediction portion in the student booklet, read the remainder of the text, and respond to the questions in the booklet.

Lance's prereading predictions were vague indicating limited knowledge about or interest in the content of the text. As he read the remainder of the book, he appeared to move from page to page at a rapid pace. He did not pause to look at the pictures or read the captions. His written responses yielded a total score of 10 in the area of comprehension, putting this text at the *Intervention* level. His summary drew information from the page he had read aloud and the first paragraph of the silent reading portions. He did not mention any of the general categories listed in the text nor did he refer to any details beyond the first few pages. In the section labeled *Literal Comprehension*, Lance completed only one of the three columns, and this information came from the beginning pages of the text. He did not address the interpretation question, perhaps because the related information was located on the last two pages of the text. His reflection statement was a fact about wolves from page 1 and was not well supported. Although he did check three of the six strategies listed in the *Metacognitive Awareness* section, the examples he gave were merely repetitions of two of the strategies he had listed. See Figure 7.10 for a summary of his responses to the questions in the booklet.

Figure 7.10 After Reading Student Booklet Response for Lance K.

Text: *A Pack of Wolves* (Leon, 2003): *Level 40* (Grade Level Equivalent 4, Guided Reading Levels P–R)

Prediction: Scored 1 of 4 possible points: Provided illogical or unrelated prediction and or questions.

In response to request to list several things he might learn from the text:

Stuff about wolfs.

In response to request to list several questions that might be answered:

1. *How they can be.*

2. *How fast they are.*

Summary: Scored 2 of 4 possible points: Provided partial summary generally in the language of the text; with one misinterpretation. Lance's response was a listing of six facts taken from the first four paragraphs of text. He did not include any information on the remaining 5½ pages of book.

Written response included below:

A wolf weighs between 50 to 145. Also their tails are 2 feet long. The wolf can see a rabbit from 400 yards away. Also when the wind is right a wolf can smell prey a mile away. The gray wold lives in a pack of 6 to 15 and they stay in the same area and some are 500 squre miles. Also a being a loan wolf it has to hunt but together they can take down Moose Bear and Buffalo.*

**The line of text stated only that wolves can kill a moose. Neither bear nor buffalo were mentioned.

Literal Comprehension: Scored 2 of 4 possible points: Little information from the text.

Lance completed a table in the student booklet listing facts about gray wolves. For Column 1, he was able to list the types of gray wolves pictured on page 2 of the text. For Column 2, he wrote only that they ate meat even though the text provided much more detail about their diet on page 7. For Column 3 he recalled only that the lead wolf eats first, missing three other details noted on page 6.

(Continued)

Figure 7.10 (Continued)

Interpretation: Scored 0 of 4 possible points because his response to the question, "Why do you think wolves are protected in some places?" was "I don't know."

Reflection: Scored 2 of 4 possible points: Vaguely related or less significant message or information; general statement with no support. Questions and Lance's responses are included below:

Q: What do you think is the most important thing about gray wolves?

A: *It's the biggest member of the dog family*

Q: Tell why.

A: *There are a lot of facts in my head so I choose 1.*

Metacognition: Scored 2 of 4 possible points: Brief explanation of the use of 1 or more strategies; vague or general statements.

Strategies Used: Lance checked the following items:

- I recalled what I know about the topic.
- I decided what was important to remember.
- I pictured what was happening.

In response to the request to give examples from the text on what he did to help him understand it, Lance wrote the following:

I reamemberd what I alreaIy knew

I just pictured what was happening

Source: Questions taken from *DRA4–8 Teacher Observation Guide for Pack of Wolves,* by J. Beaver and M. Carter, 2003, Parsippany, NJ: Celebration Press.

Additional Information

Examiner Anecdotal Notes

- *Lance repeats words in the middle of sentences. He will add a word, go back, and omit the added word.*
- *Lance seemed overwhelmed by a lot of print on a page. He struggled with negative emotions when asked to read a whole page.*
- *When he finished the text, I complimented him on the reading. He didn't take the compliment very well. I am not sure why he has the idea that a good reader is a fast reader.*

Case Recap:

1. Review the case and the notes you have taken in response to the guiding questions one final time, and add or revise any information you may have missed.

2. Make a list of additional questions you have about the case. What further information do you need that might be explored in the case discussion?

3. Think about the elements, beyond engagement, discussed in other chapters. Might any of these be problem areas for Lance? Might any be areas of strength?

CHAPTER SUMMARY

This final chapter challenged you to consider the role that engagement plays in learning to read. This element has not always been given the same amount of attention and importance as the other elements discussed in this book. When considering the cases of Eddie and Lance, however, it is clear that unless attention is paid to their lack of engagement, helping them build the skill and will to read will be greatly compromised. They are not beginning readers. Their difficulties have built over a number of years, leading to poor self-efficacy and an entrenched fear of failure. Building their desire to engage, to "get lost in a book," will take sustained support as well as caring mentors who can model reading and responding to books as a joyful activity.

Terms highlighted in this chapter

engagement 222	self-efficacy 223
mastery orientation 224	performance orientation 224
work-avoidant orientation 224	instrinsic motivation 224
extrinsic motivation 224	situational interest 228
personal interest 228	ADD/ADHD 242
IEP 251	Central Processing Disorder 251
Neurological Impress Method (NIM) 251	

FINAL QUESTIONS FOR REFLECTION AND RESPONSE

1. After reading the information in this chapter and the cases of Eddie and Lance, what role do you believe engagement plays in learning to read?

2. What are the particular challenges a teacher faces when dealing with readers who are disengaged? How might you address those challenges?

3. Compare and contrast the cases of Eddie and Lance. Consider their levels of and reasons for disengaging. Will the same interventions work for both students?

4. How might you create a classroom environment that promotes engagement for readers like Eddie and Lance?

Journals Online

Visit the student study site at www.sagepub.com/combsstudy to access recent, relevant, full-text journal articles from SAGE's leading research journals.

REFERENCES

Asselin, M. (2004). Supporting sustained engagement with texts. *Teacher Librarian, 31*(3), 51–52.

Atkinson, C. (2006). Key stage 3 pupils' views about reading. *Educational Psychology in Practice, 22*(4), 321–336.

Au, K. (2002). Mulitcutural factors and the effective instruction of students of diverse backgrounds. In A. Farstrup & S. J. Samuels (Eds.), *What research has to say about reading instruction* (3rd ed., pp. 392–413). Newark, DE: International Reading Association.

Bandura, A. (1997). Self-efficacy. *Harvard Mental Health Letter, 13*(9), 4–5.

Beaver, J. (2001). *Developmental reading assessment: K–3 teacher resource guide: Revised.* Parsippany, NJ: Celebration Press.

Beaver, J., & Carter, M. (2006). *Developmental reading assessment: 4–8* (2nd ed.). Parsippany, NJ: Celebration Press.

Beaver, J., & Richards, K. (2002). *Time to play.* Parsippany, NJ: Celebration Press.

Bempechat, J. (2008). Reading success: A motivational perspective. In R. Fink & S. J. Samuels (Eds.), *Reading success: Interest and motivation in an age of high-stakes testing* (pp. 75–97). Newark, NJ: International Reading Association.

Cambourne, B. (2002). Holistic, integrated approaches to reading and language arts instruction: The constructivist framework of an instructional theory. In A. Farstrup & S. J. Samuels (Eds.), *What research has to say about reading instruction* (3rd ed., pp. 25–47). Newark, DE: International Reading Association.

Casey, H. (2008). Engaging the disengaged: Using learning clubs to motivate struggling adolescent readers and writers. *Journal of Adolescent and Adult Literacy, 52*(4), 284–294.

Cunningham, P., & Cunningham, J. (2002). What we know about how to teach phonics. In A. Farstrup & S. J. Samuels (Eds.), *What research has to say about reading instruction* (pp. 87–109). Newark, DE: International Reading Association.

Duke. (1997). Parsippany, NJ: Celebration Press.

Edmunds, K., & Bauserman, K. (2006). What teachers can learn about reading motivation through conversations with children. *The Reading Teacher, 59*(5), 414–424.

Fink, R. (2008). High-interest reading leaves no child behind. In R. Fink & S. J. Samuels (Eds.), *Inspiring reading success: Interest and motivation in an age of high-stakes testing* (pp. 19–61). Newark, DE: International Reading Association.

Fischer, K. W., & Fusaro, M. (2008). Using student interest to motivate learning. In R. Fink & S. J. Samuels (Eds.), *Inspiring reading success: Interest and motivation in an age of high-stakes testing* (pp. 62–74). Newark, DE: International Reading Association.

Fountas, I., & Pinnell, G. (1996). *Guided reading: Good first teaching for all children*. Portsmouth, NH: Heinemann.

Gambrell, L., Block, C., & Pressley, M. (2002). Improving comprehension instruction: An urgent priority. In C. Block, L. Gambrell, & M. Pressley (Eds.), *Improving comprehension instruction: Rethinking research, theory, and classroom practice* (pp. 3–16). Newark, DE: International Reading Association.

Gaskins, I. (2008). Ten tenets of motivation for teaching struggling readers and the rest of the class. In R. Fink & S. J. Samuels (Eds.), *Inspiring reading success: Interest and motivation in an age of high-stakes testing* (pp. 99–116). Newark, DE: International Reading Association.

Goodman, Y., Watson, D., & Burke, C. (1987). *Reading miscue inventory: Alternative procedures*. Katonah, NY: Richard C. Owens.

Guthrie, J., & Cox, K. (2001). Classroom conditions for motivation and engagement in reading. *Educational Psychology Review, 13*(3), 283–302.

Guthrie, J., & Wigfield, A. (2000). Engagement and motivation in reading. In M. Kamil, P. Mosenthal, P. D. Pearson, & R. Barr (Eds.), *Handbook of reading research* (pp. 403–422). Mahwah, NJ: Lawrence Erlbaum.

Guthrie, J., Wigfield, A., Metsala, J., & Cox, K. (2004). Motivational and cognitive predictors of text comprehension and reading amount. In R. Ruddell & N. Unrau (Eds.), *Theoretical models and processes of reading* (5th ed., pp. 929–953). Newark, DE: International Reading Association.

Harris, T., & Hodges, R. (1995). *The literacy dictionary: The vocabulary of reading and writing*. Newark, DE: International Reading Association.

Hill, B., & Ruptic, C. (1994). *Practical aspects of authentic assessment: Putting the pieces together*. Norwood, MA: Christopher-Gordon.

Huei-Yu Wang, J., & Guthrie, J. (2004). Modeling the effects of intrinsic motivation, extrinsic motivation, amount of reading, and past reading achievement on text comprehension between U.S. and Chinese students. *Reading Research Quarterly, 39*(2), 162–186.

Kear, D. J., Coffman, G. A., McKenna, M. C., & Ambrosio, A. L. (2000). Measuring attitude toward writing: A new tool for teachers. *The Reading Teacher, 54*(1), 14–24.

Kelley, M., & Clausen-Grace, N. (2009). Facilitating engagement by differentiating independent reading. *The Reading Teacher, 63*(4), 313–318.

Lenters, K. (2006). Resistance, struggle and the adolescent reader. *Journal of Adolescent & Adult Literacy, 50*(2), 136–146.

Leon, V. (2003). *A pack of wolves*. Parsippany, NJ: Celebration Press.

Lipson, M., & Wixson, K. (2003). *Assessment & instruction of reading and writing difficulty: An interactive approach* (3rd ed.). Boston: Allyn & Bacon.

Malloy, J. A., Gambrell, L., & Smith-Williams, G. (2006). Supporting students motivation to read. In C. Cummins (Ed.), *Understanding and implementing reading first intiatives: The changing role of administrators* (pp. 116–126). Newark, DE: International Reading Association.

May, F. (2001). *Unraveling the seven myths of reading: Assessment and intervention practices for counteracting their effects.* Boston: Allyn & Bacon.

McKenna, M., & Dougherty Stahl, K. (2009). *Assessment for reading instruction.* New York: Guilford Press.

McKenna, M., & Kear, D. J. (1990). Measuring attitude toward reading: A new tool for teachers. *The Reading Teacher, 43,* 626–639.

McKenna, M., Simkin, C., Conradi, K., & Lawrence, C. (2008). *Development of an adolescent reading attitude survey.* Paper presented at the annual meeting of the National Reading Conference, Orlando, FL.

Meyer, A., & Rose, D. (1999). *Learning to read in the computer age.* Wakefield, MA: Cast. Retrieved August 20, 2010, from http://www.cast.org/publications/books/ltr/index.html

Miller, S., & Faircloth, B. (2009). Motivation and reading comprehension. In S. Israel & G. Duffy (Eds.), *Handbook of research on reading comprehension* (pp. 307–322). NY: Routledge.

Mueller, P. (2001). *Lifers: Learning from at-risk adolescent readers.* Portsmouth, NH: Heinemann.

Reutzel, R., Camperell, K., & Smith, J. (2002). Hitting the wall: Helping struggling readers comprehend. In C. Block, L. Gambrell, & M. Pressley (Eds.), *Improving comprehension instruction: Rethinking research, theory, and classroom practice* (pp. 321–353). Newark, DE: International Reading Association.

Snow, C., Griffin, P., & Burns, M. (2005). *Knowledge to support the teaching of reading: Preparing teachers for a changing world.* San Francisco: Jossey-Bass.

Taboada, A., Guthrie, J., & McRae, A. (2008). Building engaging classrooms. In R. Fink & S. J. Samuels (Eds.), *Reading success: Interest and motivation in an age of high-stakes testing* (pp. 141–166). Newark, DE: International Reading Association.

Watkins, M. W., & Coffey, D. Y. (2004). Reading motivation: Multidimensional and indeterminate. *Journal of Educational Psychology, 96*(1), 110–118.

Wigfield, A., Guthrie, J., Perencevich, K., Taboada, A., Lutz Klauda, S., Mcrae, A., et al. (2008). Role of reading engagement in mediating effects of reading comprehension instruction on reading outcomes. *Psychology in Schools, 45*(5), 432–445.

Woods, M., & Moe, A. (1999). *Analytical reading inventory* (6th ed.). Upper Saddle River, NJ: Simon & Schuster.

Worthy, J., & Prater, K. (2002). "I thought about it all night": Readers theatre for reading fluency and motivation. *The Reading Teacher, 56*(3), 294–297.

Glossary

academic vocabulary Those terms and phrases that are especially important to understanding the concepts taught in mathematics, science, language arts, and social studies curriculums.

ADD/ADHD (Attention Deficit Disorder/ Attention Deficit Hyperactivity Disorder) ADD is a learning disorder characterized by student behaviors of distractibility, impulsivity, and a short attention span. ADHD includes these behaviors as well as a high degree of motor activity.

alphabetic principle The idea that there are systematic and predictable relationships between the spoken sounds of our language and the written letters or combinations of letters in our alphabet.

analogizing Using known words or word parts as an aid to identifying an unknown word—if I know the *b* sound in *bake* and I know the word *call,* I can identify a new word, *ball.*

analogy-based An instructional approach to word identification that engages students in a study of word families or word parts as well as ways to use what they already know to identify new words.

analytic phonics An instructional approach to word identification that teaches children a store of sight words and relevant

generalizations first and then asks them to apply these to indentify unknown words.

automatic-alphabetic phase The final phase of word learning, by which time the reader recognizes most words in text automatically by sight and is facile in applying various strategies to attack unfamiliar words.

automaticity model Cognitive model created by LaBerge and Samuels (1974) that suggests that individuals have limited amounts of attention or cognitive capacity available for complex tasks and, in order to deal successfully with all of the activities that make up a task, a certain number of them must become automatic.

Central Processing Disorder A deficiency in the brain's ability to process incoming auditory signals effectively.

closed sort A word-sorting activity in which the teacher selects the type of sorting the children will do. The children are told what word features to look for.

cloze An assessment procedure used to determine whether or not a student is likely to comprehend a given text. It involves deleting words from a prose selection, generally every fifth word, and asking students to replace them based on the surrounding context. The words replaced must be an exact match to those in the text.

Comprehension Strategy Instruction (CSI) An instructional intervention that explicitly teaches the comprehension strategies that effective readers use and supports readers as they learn to use the strategies independently.

Concepts About Print An assessment task originally designed by Marie Clay to reveal what a child knows about features of books and print. It can be found in M. Clay, (2002), *An observation of early literacy achievement* (2nd ed.), Portsmouth, NH: Heinemann.

consolidated-alphabetic phase A phase of word learning during which the child develops a solid working knowledge of recurring spelling patterns and commonly occurring suffixes.

content load The amount of content in a text. The amount of content and the complexity of the ideas presented can prove challenging to struggling readers.

contextual analysis The most common method of word identification, using the context within and surrounding the sentence to determine what the word is.

conventional spelling A stage in spelling development during which the child correctly spells common words.

Curriculum-Based Measurement (CBM) An assessment developed originally by Stan Deno in the late 1970s; used to monitor reading development over time. Generally, the child is asked to read for one minute and the teacher counts the number of errors. The assessment is repeated over time, and individual scores are charted to see whether the child's reading fluency is improving. In addition, the child's scores may be compared with those of typically developing readers at the same age or grade level.

decoding The ability to pronounce the words a reader encounters in text.

DIBELS (Dynamic Indicators of Basic Early Literacy Skills) A set of seven procedures and measures to assess early literacy skills including phonemic awareness, alphabetic principle, fluency, comprehension, and vocabulary. For more detail, go to http://www.dibels.org/dibels.html

emergent literacy A term used to describe children's growing awareness of print from birth to the period when conventional reading and writing has been established.

engagement The emotional, behavioral, and cognitive involvement of the reader in the process of responding to a text.

expressive language skills The ability to communicate a message that can be understood by others.

expressive vocabulary All the words that we can produce in speaking or writing.

extrinsic motivation A desire or determination to engage in an activity that originates outside the student; directed by others and may involve rewards or punishments.

fluency The ability to read accurately with expression and meaning while maintaining an appropriate speed.

frustration reading level The reading level of materials that are too challenging for students to read successfully, even with support.

full-alphabetic phase A phase of word learning during which the child develops a good working knowledge of the major sound-symbol correspondences and uses that knowledge to decode unfamiliar words.

Gradual Release of Responsibility Model An instructional model incorporating a three-phased process for scaffolding student learning. In Phase 1, the teacher is fully responsible for the lesson and provides explicit instruction in strategy use through modeling. During Phase 2, the teacher slowly gives the students responsibility through guided practice. In Phase 3, the students take full responsibility and independently practice the strategy to develop skill and fluency.

graphophonic cueing   Children use their knowledge about letters and their sounds to identify a word.

heterogeneity   In relation to vocabulary development, the notion that knowing a word is dependent on the word's function and structure (article *the* vs. noun *ladder.*

IEP   Individualized Education Plan designed to meet the needs of students with disabilities as identified through an in-depth evaluation.

incrementality   In relation to vocabulary development, the notion that word learning occurs in small steps over time and that each time a word is encountered, a bit more about it is understood.

independent reading level   The reading level of materials that are not challenging for students and can be read independently without support.

informal reading inventories   An assessment tool that includes the use of a series of graded word lists and passages to determine a reader's strengths and needs in word identification and comprehension.

instructional reading level   The reading level of material that is challenging but not frustrating for students to read when provided with instructional support.

Interactive Writing   Similar to language experience charts in that the teacher guides the students in the creation of a text that might be a classroom message, a story, or a shared experience. However, the children take turns writing as the text is built collectively, rather than the teacher doing all the writing.

intrinsic motivation   A desire or determination to engage in an activity that originates from within the student.

invented spelling   Children's own unique spellings of words that reveal their understandings of the conventions of English, including spelling, punctuation, and capitalization.

language experience chart   A chart that is built by the teacher as the children dictate a story or event.

lexicon   The entire set of words known by the child.

mastery orientation   The goal is to learn or master the content and/or to engage in a task in order to improve one's ability.

metacognition   Individuals' awareness of and control over their own learning.

miscue analysis   A term used to denote the assessment of the mistakes made when reading words, usually in extended text. The goal is to determine what the reader knows about mapping sounds to letters to form words.

morphemic analysis Breaking down the word into its smallest unit of meaning, a morpheme.

multidimensionality In relation to vocabulary development, this involves knowing a word's spoken form, written form, grammar, frequency in the language, denotative and connotative meanings, antonyms, synonyms, and appropriate affixes, as well as collocations (other words that occur frequently with it).

Neurological Impress Method (NIM) A form of paired reading where the teacher reads with the student. They sit side by side. The teacher reads slightly faster than the student, supporting the student while providing a model of fluent reading.

onset The initial consonant sound or sounds in a word.

open sort A word-sorting activity in which the children decide what word features they will use to sort the words.

partial-alphabetic phase A phase of word learning during which the child develops a rudimentary knowledge of the alphabetic principle and uses letters (usually initial letters) and context to guess unfamiliar words.

performance orientation The goal is receiving rewards or recognition and demonstrating that one is capable or can outperform others.

personal interest Interest in a topic of study that already exists within the student and is enduring.

phoneme The smallest unit of sound that distinguishes one word from another.

phonemic awareness A subset of phonological awareness. It is awareness that speech is made up of a sequence of sounds and involves the ability to focus on and manipulate spoken sounds in words.

phonetic spelling A stage in spelling development during which the child spells words as they sound; all phonemes are represented in a word, though the spelling may be unconventional.

phonic analysis Sounding out a word letter by letter, by spelling pattern, by letter clusters, or by syllables.

phonological awareness The ability to divide sentences into words and words into syllables and to identify common phonemes (smallest units of sound).

polysemy In relation to vocabulary development, this refers to knowing the multiple meanings of words.

pre-alphabetic phase A phase of word learning during which the child has little working knowledge of the alphabetic principle—that is, no understanding that letters in words map to sounds.

pre-communicative spelling A stage in spelling development during which the child uses letters for writing words by stringing them together randomly without corresponding to particular letter sounds.

predicting In the area of word recognition, this involves using letter clues, the surrounding context, and knowledge about rules that govern the structure of the language (syntax) to guess what a word might be. In the area of comprehension, this involves using prior knowledge, picture clues, and what has already been read to make a guess about what will happen next.

print referencing style   Using verbal and nonverbal techniques to engage children's attention to the print during read alouds. This includes asking questions about the print, making comments about the print, and tracking print with one's finger.

productive abilities   Language skills involving the ability to produce the phonemes in English, to combine phonemes into syllables, onsets and rimes, and words, and to create expressions that exhibit the prosodic characteristics of the language.

prosody   The phrasing, stress, and intonation in oral language that conveys meaning.

receptive abilities   Language skills involving the ability to note the difference between two phonemes, hear the number of syllables in words, recognize as words those words that are already in a child's oral vocabulary, recognize a word's onset and rime, and take notice of the prosody (rhythmic patterns, pitch, and intonation) of the language.

receptive language skills   The ability to attend to and understand what is communicated, including literal and figurative language.

receptive vocabulary   All the words that we understand when a person speaks or when we encounter them in text.

Reciprocal Teaching   An instructional intervention that engages students in learning

about and using four comprehension strategies at once: predicting, questioning, clarifying, and summarizing.

Response to Intervention   A three-tiered approach of assessment and instruction of learners that allows for the early identification of students who are struggling. At Tier 1, the teacher implements assessments to identify students achieving below the level of their peers. These students move into Tier II instruction involving additional assessments to identify specific problems and provide small-group instruction to address student needs. A student who still fails to respond moves into Tier III instruction, which is usually individualized.

retelling   An assessment and instructional strategy that requires students to recall what they have read immediately following the reading of a passage, aloud or silently.

rime   The remainder of the word chunk. In the word *tap, /t/* is the onset and */ap/* is the rime.

running record   An assessment task designed to reveal a child's reading behaviors when reading authentic texts.

scaffolded instruction   A form of instruction beginning with high support from a teacher or tutor; that support is gradually withdrawn as the student is able to demonstrate the behaviors sought on her own.

self-efficacy   The beliefs, judgments, and perceptions we have about our ability to successfully complete the tasks set before us.

semantic cue   Children use their knowledge about meanings of parts of words or the surrounding context to identify a word.

semantics   Relating to the meanings of words.

semiphonetic spelling stage   A stage in spelling development during which the child represents some of the sounds of a word with letters, often initial and/or final sounds.

sight word   Any word that the reader is able to recognize automatically—on sight.

situational interest   Interest in a topic of study that takes place around an event and is transitory in nature.

stanine   A stanine is a type of score used in many norm-referenced standardized tests. The term is short for *standard nine-point scale,* ranging from 9 to 1. A score of 1, 2, or 3 is considered to be below average. A score of 4, 5, or 6 is average, and a score of 7, 8, or 9 is considered above average.

syntactic cue   Children use their knowledge about the order of words in sentences to identify a word.

syntactics   Relating to the rules governing the structure of a phrase or sentence.

synthetic phonics   An instructional approach to word identification that first teaches children the individual sounds represented by letters and letter combinations and how to blend those sounds to pronounce words. Then, the relationships or phonics generalizations that apply are identified.

think aloud   The process of saying aloud what is being thought. In assessment, the reader is asked to stop at points during the reading and share what she or he is thinking or doing. In instruction, the teacher stops at points that demonstrate strategies and skills proficient readers use and describes what she or he is thinking or doing.

Tier 1 words   As described by Beck, McKeown, and Kucan (2002), words labeled as Tier 1 words are basic and so ubiquitous in the language that they rarely need instruction.

Tier 2 words   As described by Beck, McKeown, and Kucan (2002), words labeled as Tier 2 are encountered across texts and in everyday conversation and can be used across a variety of contexts. These contrast with Tier 1 words, which are basic and so ubiquitous in the language that they rarely need instruction, and Tier 3 words, which appear less often and have specific narrow meanings.

Tier 3 words   As described by Beck, McKeown, and Kucan (2002), words labeled as Tier 3 are words that appear less often than Tier 1 or 2 words and have specific, narrow meanings.

transitional spelling   A stage in spelling development during which the child begins to accurately represent the word, although the spelling might not yet be totally accurate.

word consciousness   An awareness of words, their meanings, and the ways meanings change and grow, as well as an interest in words and motivation to increase word knowledge.

word structure   The roots, prefixes, suffixes, and syllables in a word that allow one to be able to identify it.

work-avoidant orientation   The goal is avoiding the task and the work needed to accomplish it.

INDEX

ABOUT THE AUTHOR

Barbara Combs, PhD, is a professor in the Department of Teaching and Learning and is the Associate Dean for Teacher Education in the College of Education and Human Development at the University of North Dakota. She has more than 30 years of teaching experience as both a secondary English teacher and a teacher educator. Over the last 15 years, she has taught a variety of literacy-related courses, including those related to the diagnosis and instruction of struggling readers. Her research interests focus on reading assessment, reading comprehension, and the ongoing development of pre- and inservice teachers, especially in the area of classroom literacy instruction. Dr. Combs's articles have appeared in *Journal of Natural Inquiry and Reflective Practice,* the *College Reading Association Yearbook,* and the *Language and Literacy Spectrum.* She has also conducted more than 50 referred and invited presentations at conferences for the International Reading Association (IRA), the Association of Literacy Educators and Researchers, the Association of Teacher Educators (ATE), the American Association of Colleges of Teacher Education (AACTE), and the American Educational Research Association.

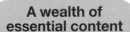